黄脅威

PISTOLWHIP

黄脅威

The Yellow Menace

Written by Jason Hall
Illustrated by Matt Kindt

認定

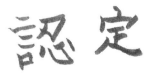

Sharlene Kindt: Color art (page 52)
Valerie Ford: Costume Design
M. Kindt: Cover Design, Art Direction, Additional Writing
J. Hall: Additional Layouts, Art Direction

Published by Top Shelf Productions,
P.O. Box 1282, Marietta, GA 30061-1282

For Top Shelf Productions:
Chris Staros—Editor Brett Warnock—Production
www.topshelfcomix.com

For Pistolwhip Comics:
Edna Whalenstein—Editor-in-Chief
Visit the Pistolwhip Comics Electronic Headquarters
www.pistolwhipcomics.com

Hall, Jason
Kindt, Matt
Pistolwhip: The Yellow Menace / Jason Hall & Matt Kindt
ISBN: 1-891830-35-X
Graphic Novels, Cartoons, Sequential Art
First Printing, Printed in Canada

目次

Table of Contents

Chapter One

無線

Radio

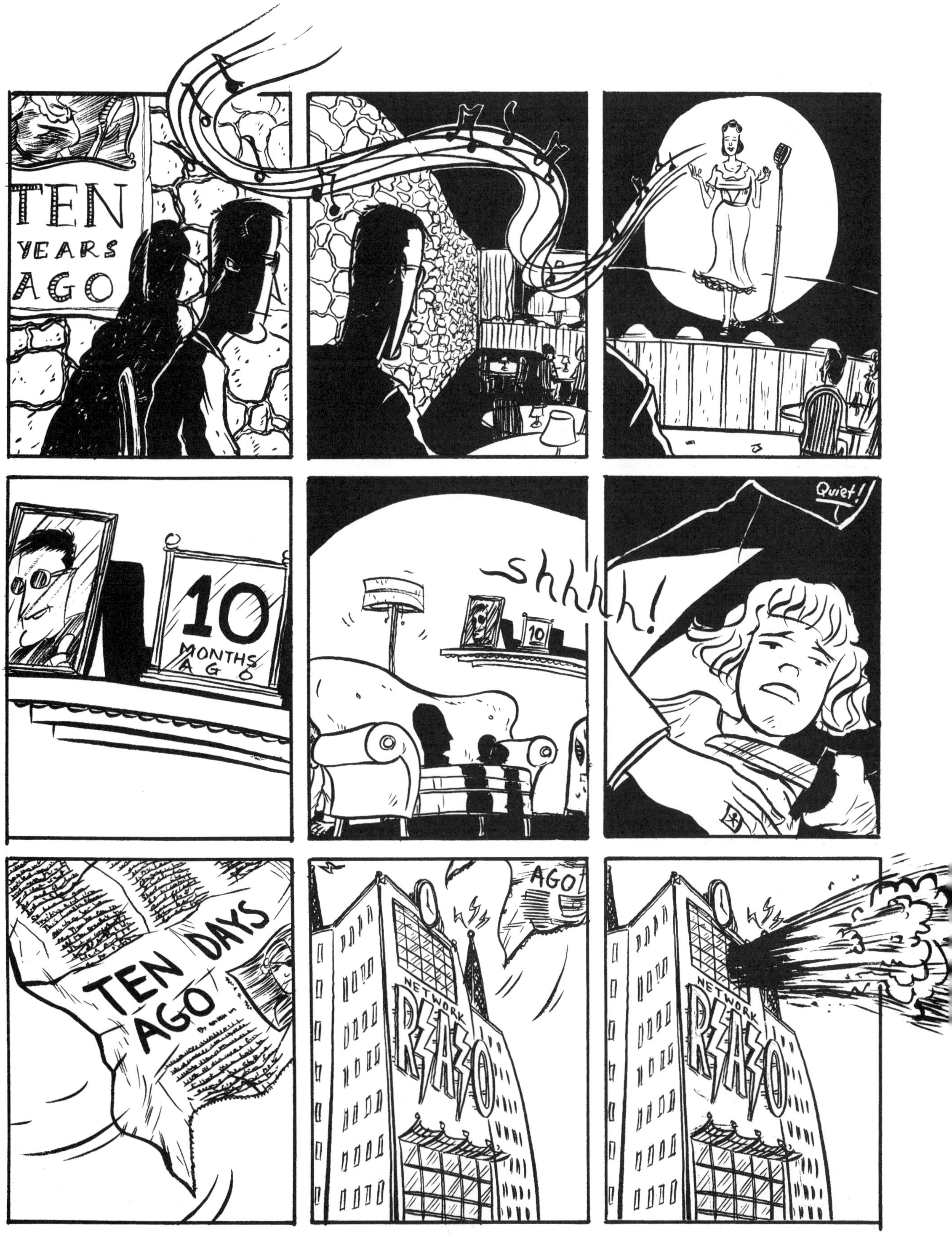
TEN
YEARS
AGO
10
MONTHS
AGO
shhhh!
Quiet!
TEN DAYS
AGO
AGO
NETWORK
REASO
NETWORK
REASO

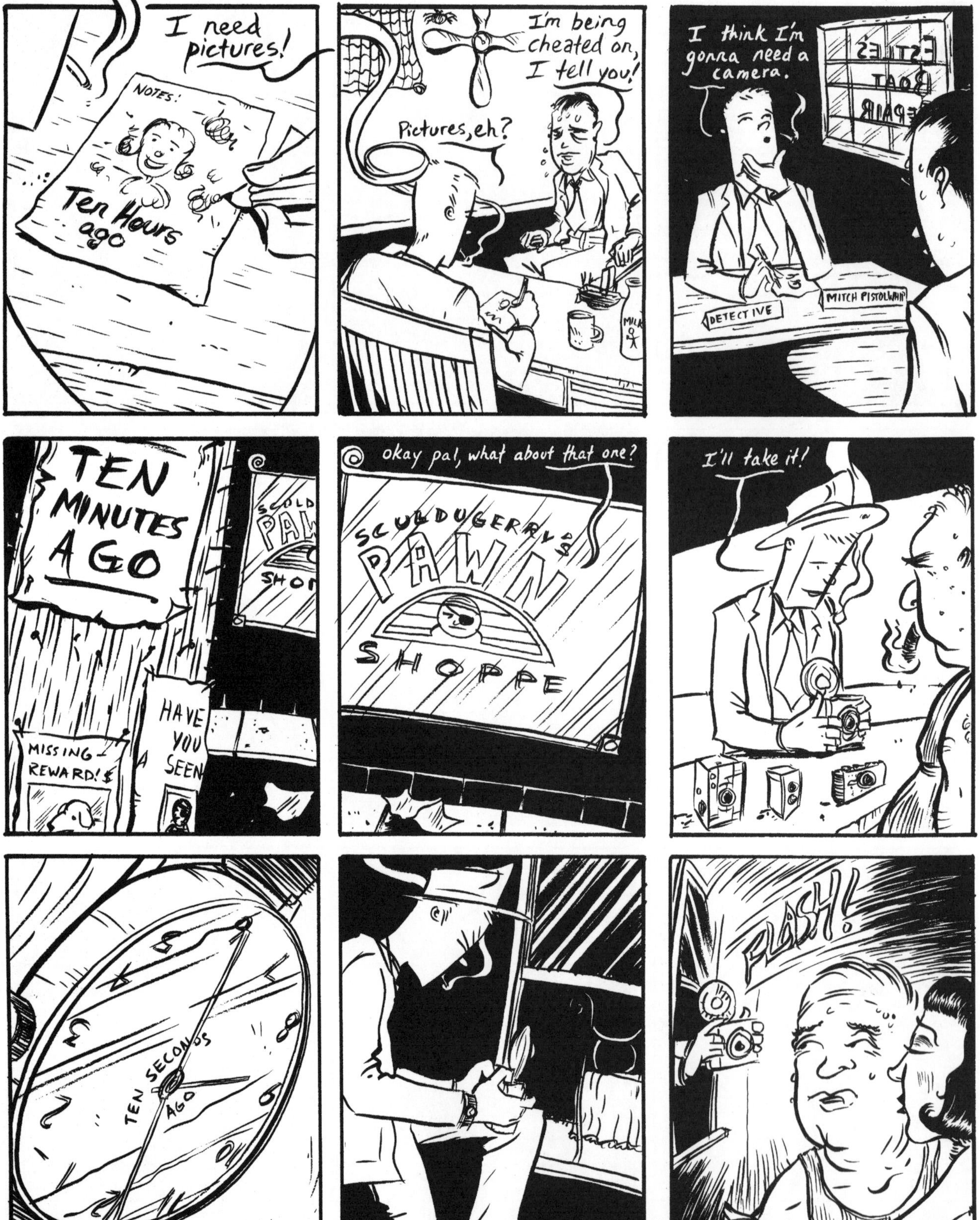

I need pictures!
NOTES:
Ten Hours ago
I'm being cheated on, I tell you!
Pictures, eh?
MILK
I think I'm gonna need a camera.
DETECTIVE
MITCH PISTOLWHIP
TEN MINUTES AGO
HAVE YOU SEEN
MISSING - REWARD! $
okay pal, what about that one?
SCULDUGERRY'S PAWN SHOPPE
I'll take it!
TEN SECONDS AGO
FLASH!

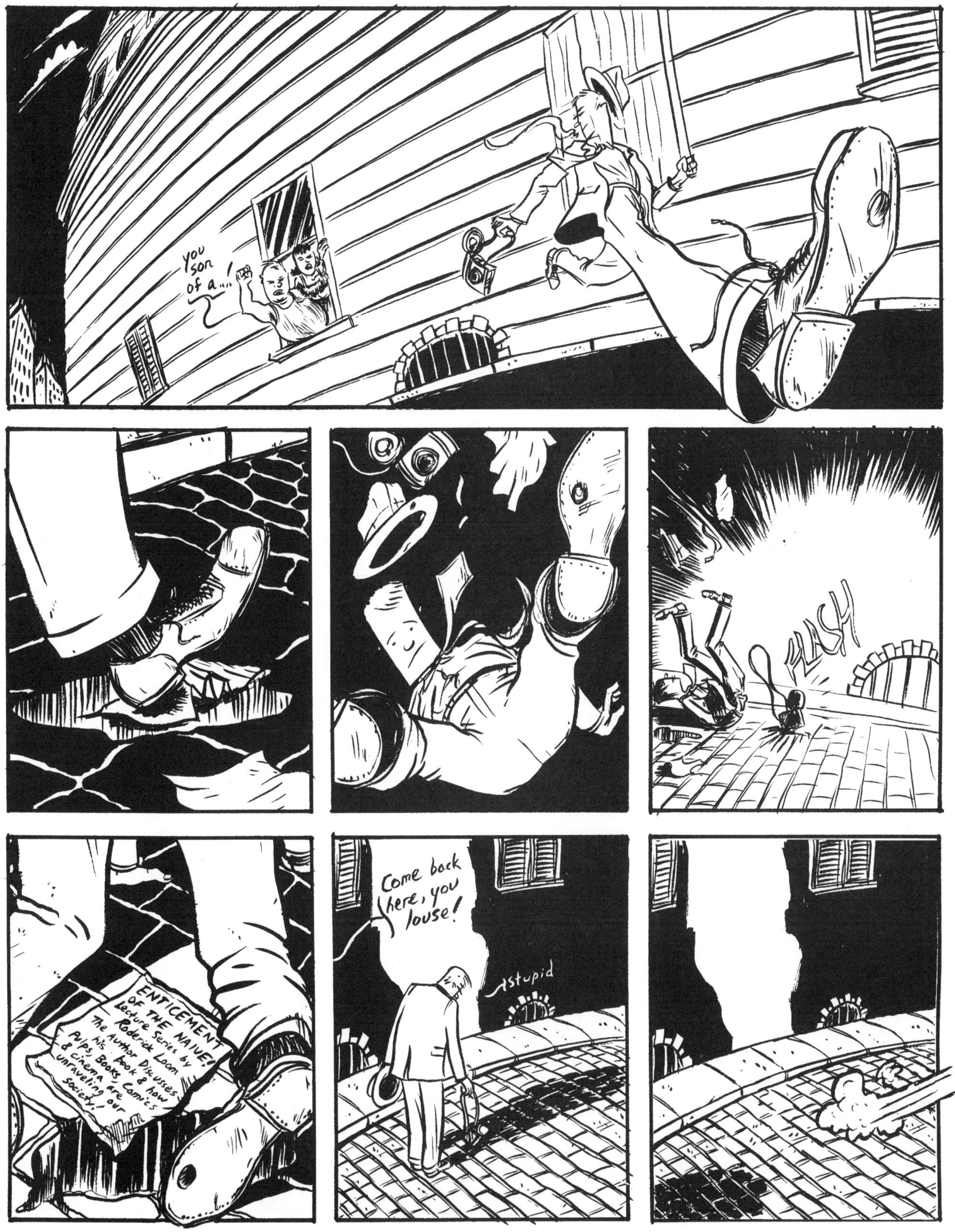
you son of a...!
FLASH
ENTICEMENT OF THE NAIVE!
Lecture Series by Roderick Loom
The Author Discusses his Book & how Pulps, Books, Comics & cinema are unraveling our society!
Come back here, you louse!
stupid

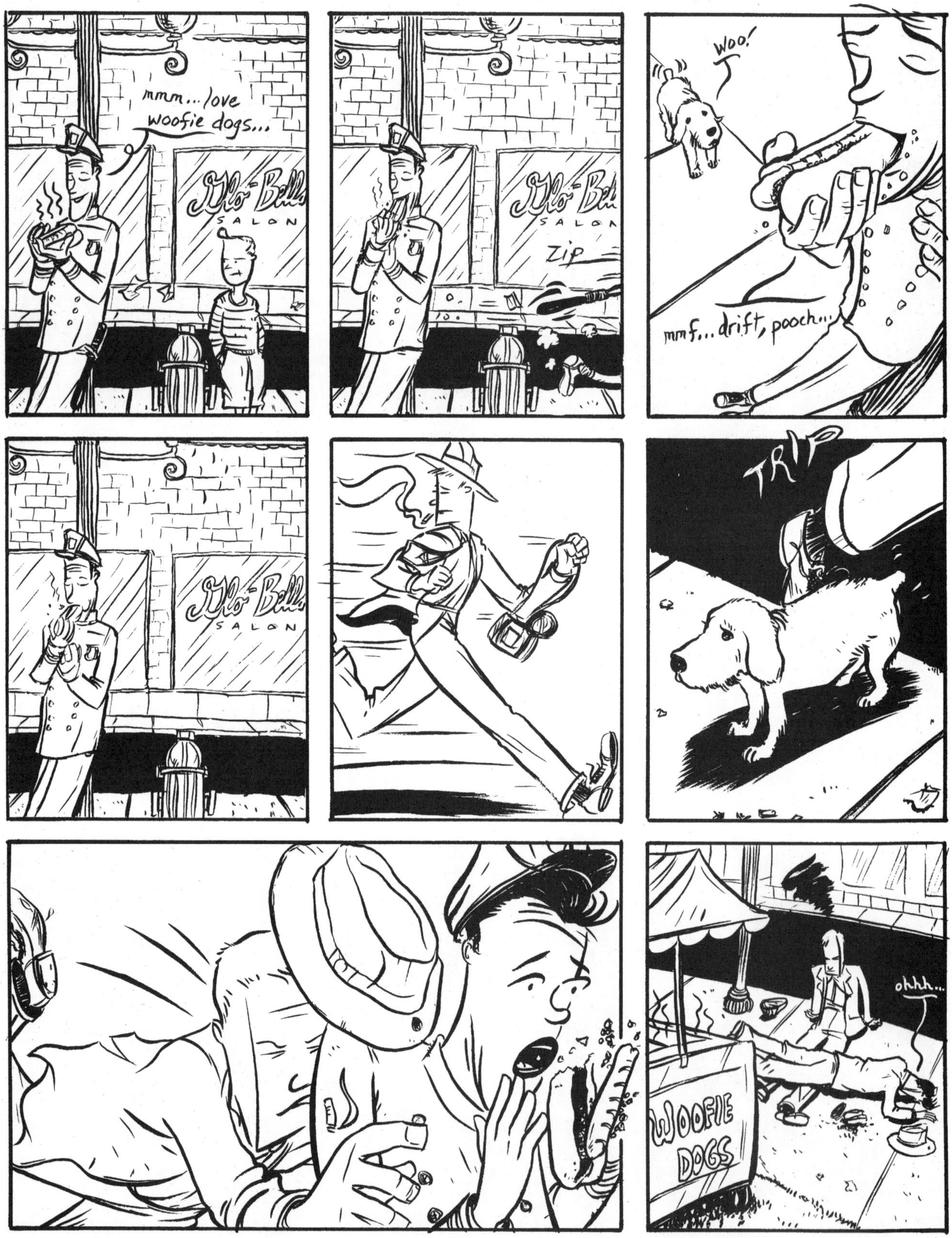
mmm... love woofie dogs...
Glo-Bell's SALON
Glo-Bell's SALON
zip
WOO!
mmf... drift, pooch...
Glo-Bell's SALON
TRIP
ohhh...
WOOFIE DOGS

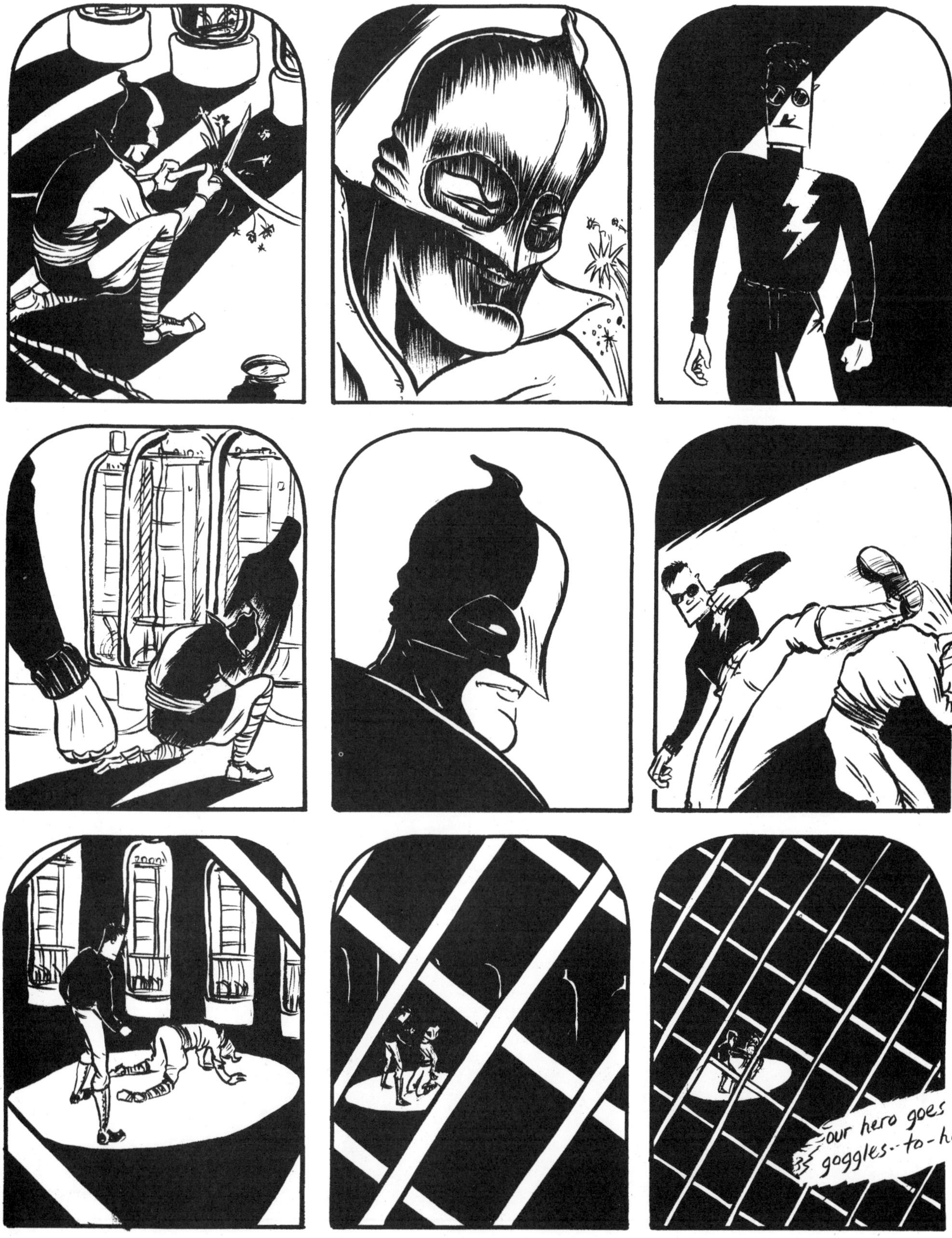
our hero goes
goggles-to-hood~

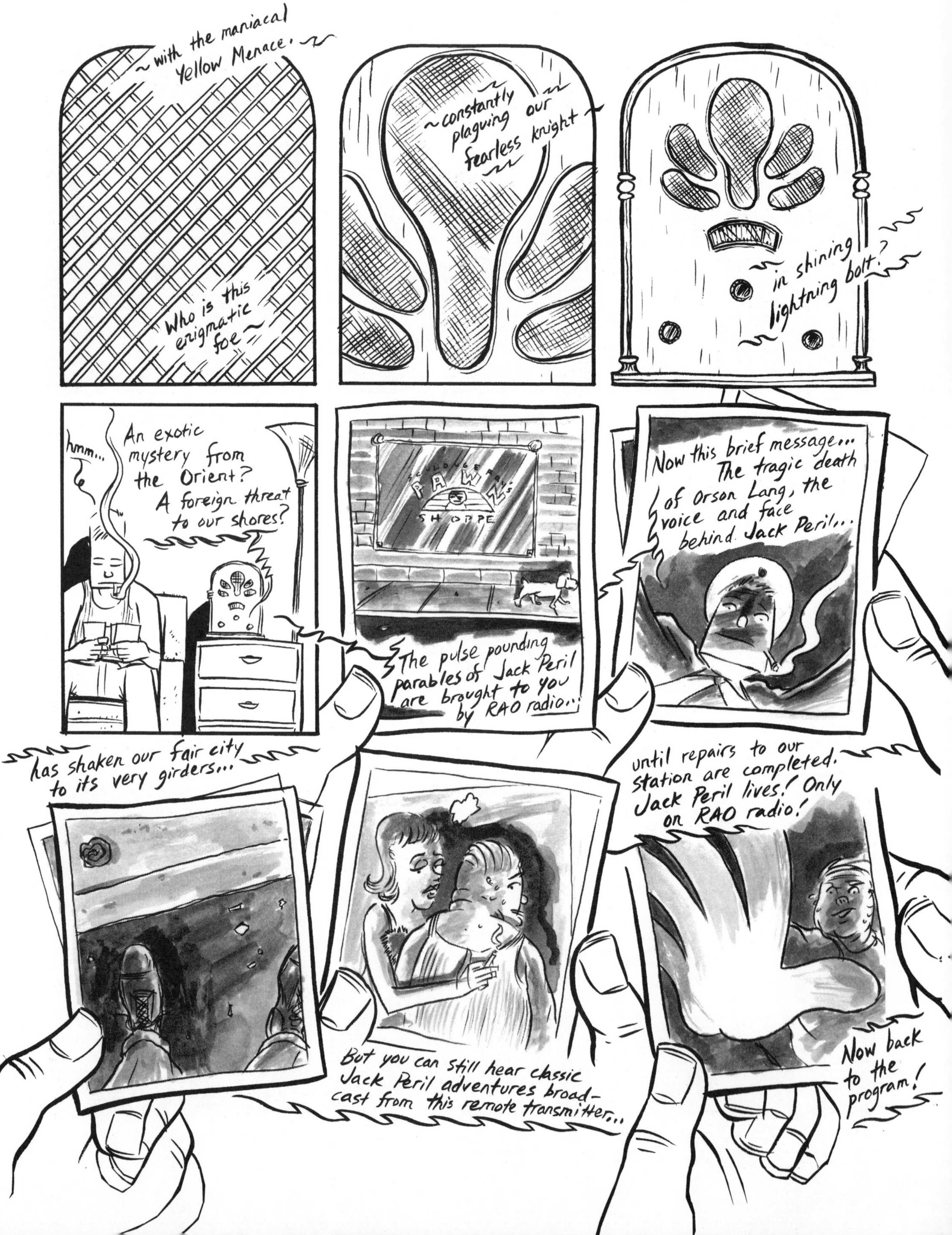
~with the maniacal Yellow Menace.~
Who is this enigmatic foe~
~constantly plaguing our fearless knight~
~in shining lightning bolt?~
hmm...
An exotic mystery from the Orient? A foreign threat to our shores?
The pulse pounding parables of Jack Peril are brought to you by RAO radio...
PAWN SHOPPE
Now this brief message... The tragic death of Orson Lang, the voice and face behind Jack Peril...
has shaken our fair city to its very girders...
But you can still hear classic Jack Peril adventures broad-cast from this remote transmitter...
until repairs to our station are completed. Jack Peril lives! Only on RAO radio!
Now back to the program!

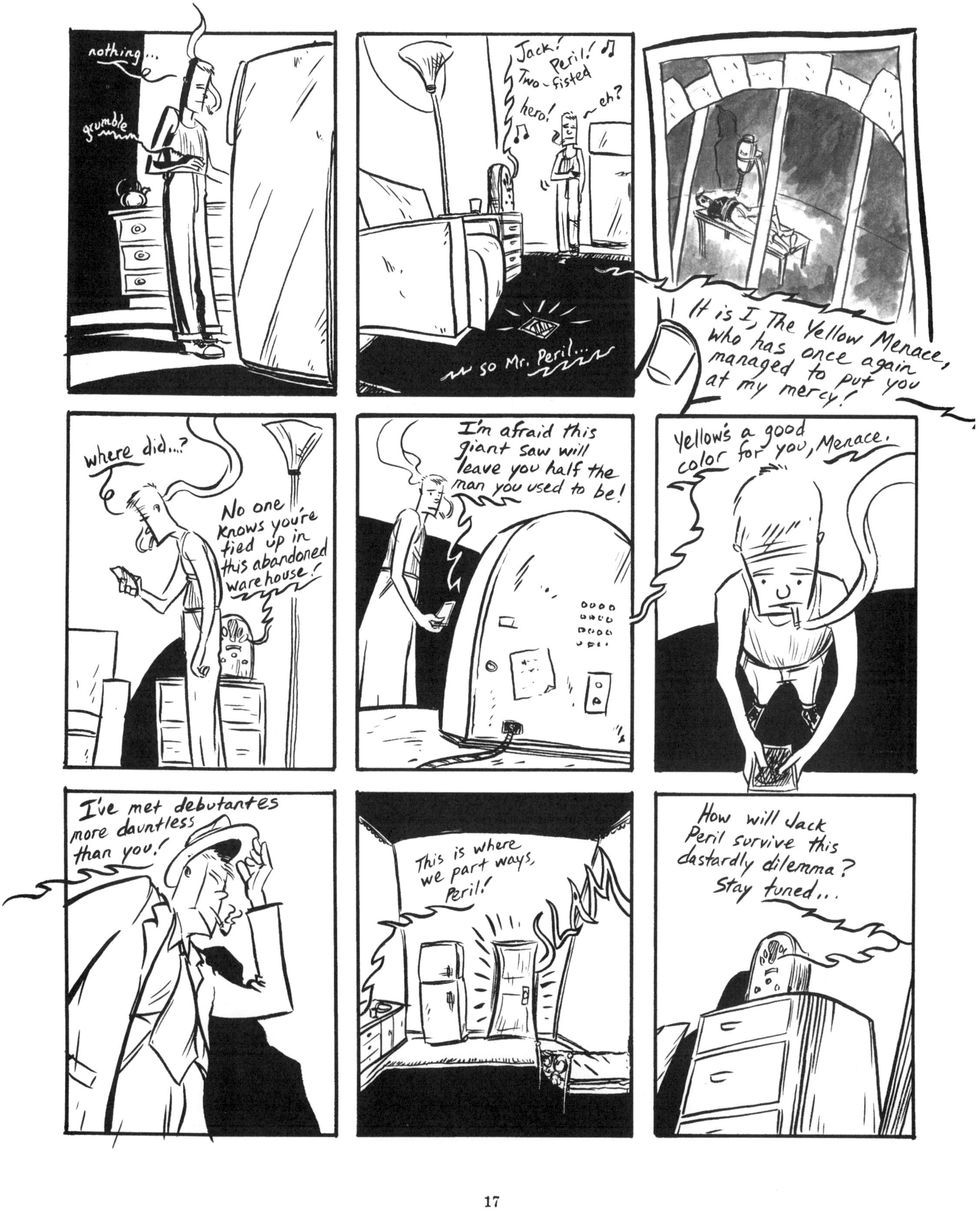

nothing...
grumble
Jack! Peril! Two-fisted hero!
eh?
so Mr. Peril...
It is I, The Yellow Menace, who has once again managed to put you at my mercy!
where did...?
No one knows you're tied up in this abandoned warehouse!
I'm afraid this giant saw will leave you half the man you used to be!
Yellow's a good color for you, Menace.
I've met debutantes more dauntless than you!
This is where we part ways, Peril!
SLAM
How will Jack Peril survive this dastardly dilemma? Stay tuned...

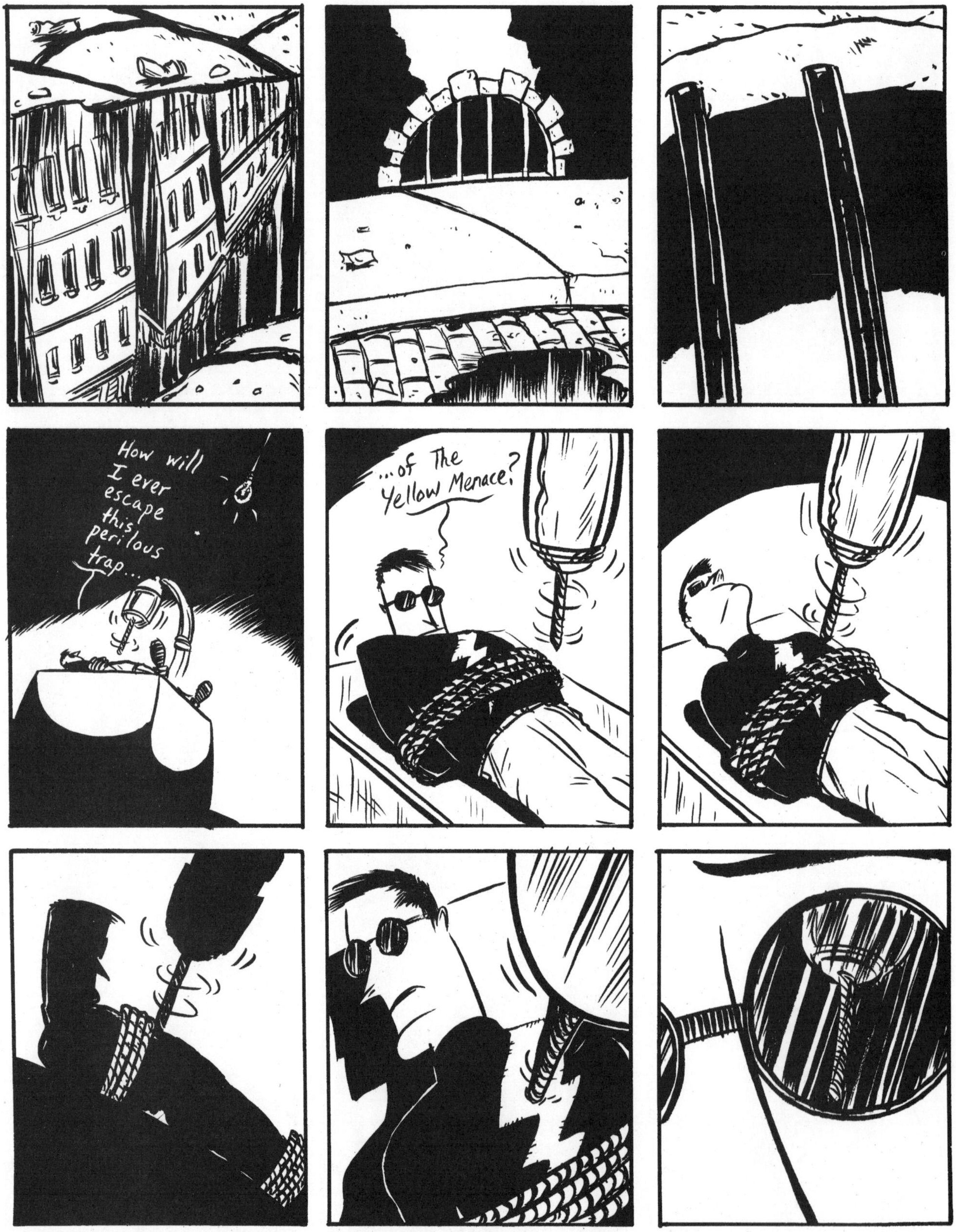
How will I ever escape this perilous trap...
...of The Yellow Menace?

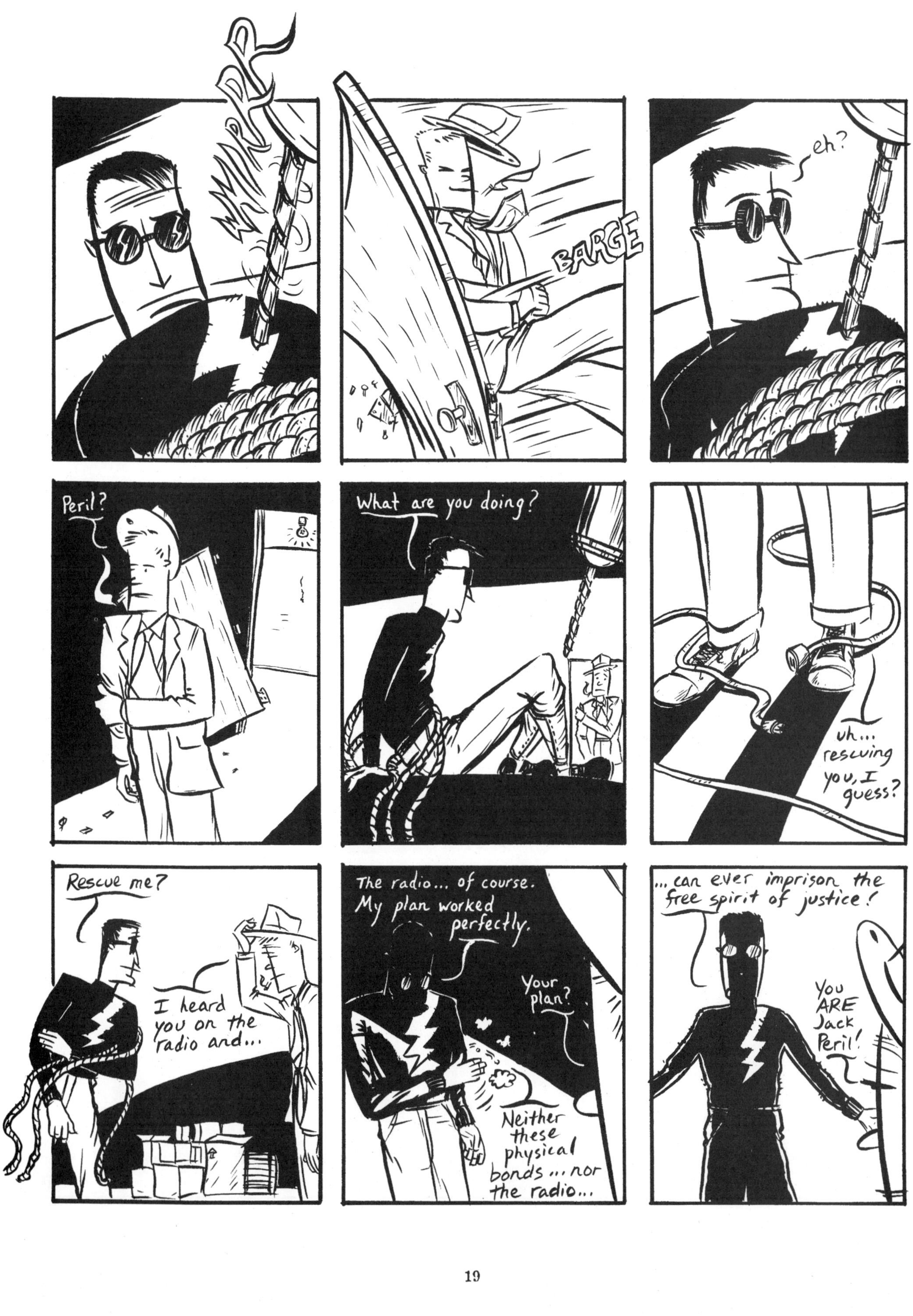

BARGE
eh?
Peril?
What are you doing?
uh... rescuing you, I guess?
Rescue me?
I heard you on the radio and...
The radio... of course. My plan worked perfectly.
Your plan?
Neither these physical bonds ... nor the radio...
... can ever imprison the free spirit of justice!
You ARE Jack Peril!

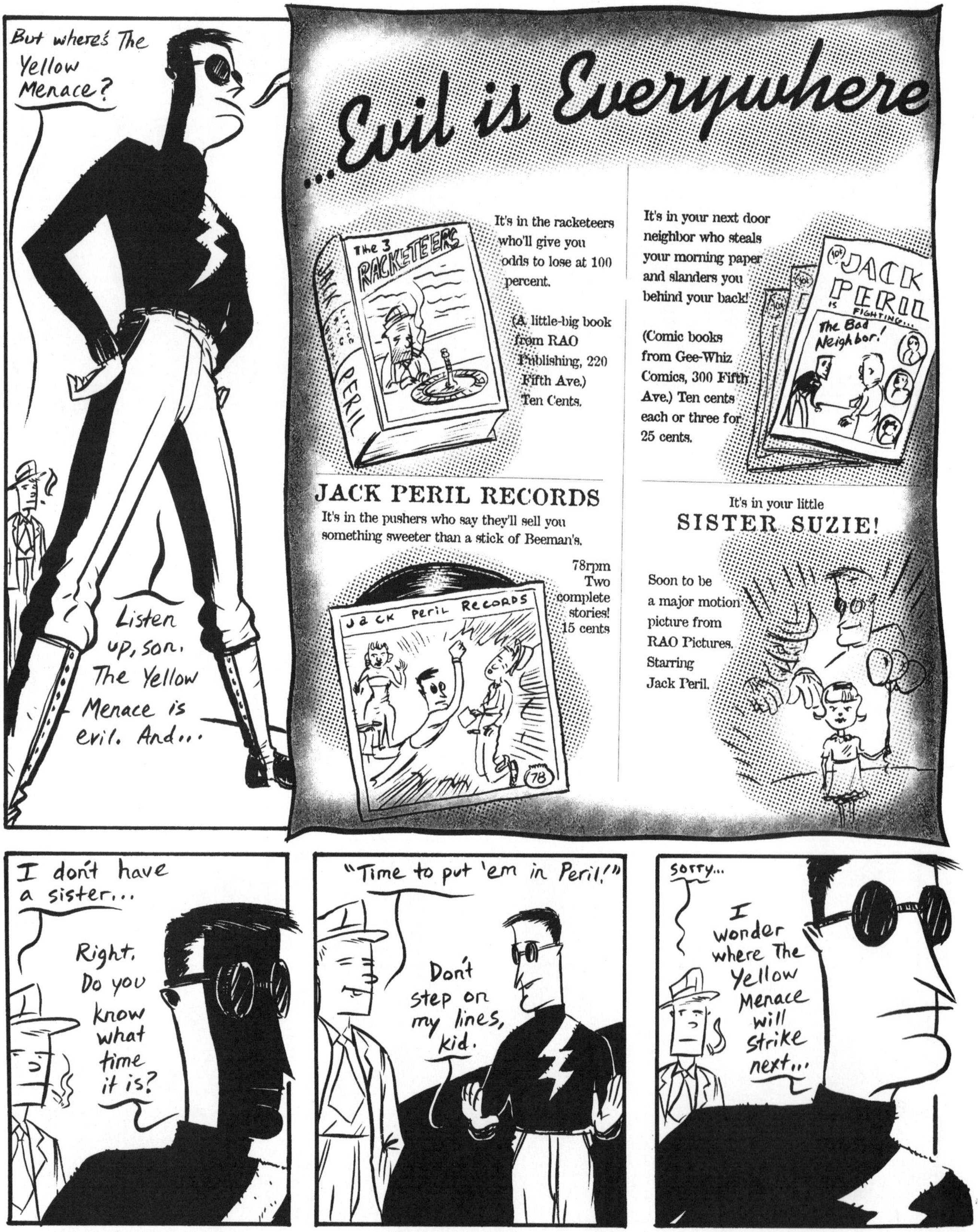
But where's The Yellow Menace?
...Evil is Everywhere
It's in the racketeers who'll give you odds to lose at 100 percent.
(A little-big book from RAO Publishing, 220 Fifth Ave.) Ten Cents.
The 3 RACKETEERS
JACK PERIL
It's in your next door neighbor who steals your morning paper and slanders you behind your back!
(Comic books from Gee-Whiz Comics, 300 Fifth Ave.) Ten cents each or three for 25 cents.
JACK PERIL IS FIGHTING... The Bad Neighbor!
JACK PERIL RECORDS
It's in the pushers who say they'll sell you something sweeter than a stick of Beeman's.
78rpm Two complete stories! 15 cents
JACK PERIL RECORDS
It's in your little SISTER SUZIE!
Soon to be a major motion picture from RAO Pictures. Starring Jack Peril.
Listen up, son. The Yellow Menace is evil. And...
I don't have a sister...
Right. Do you know what time it is?
"Time to put 'em in Peril!"
Don't step on my lines, kid.
Sorry...
I wonder where The Yellow Menace will strike next...

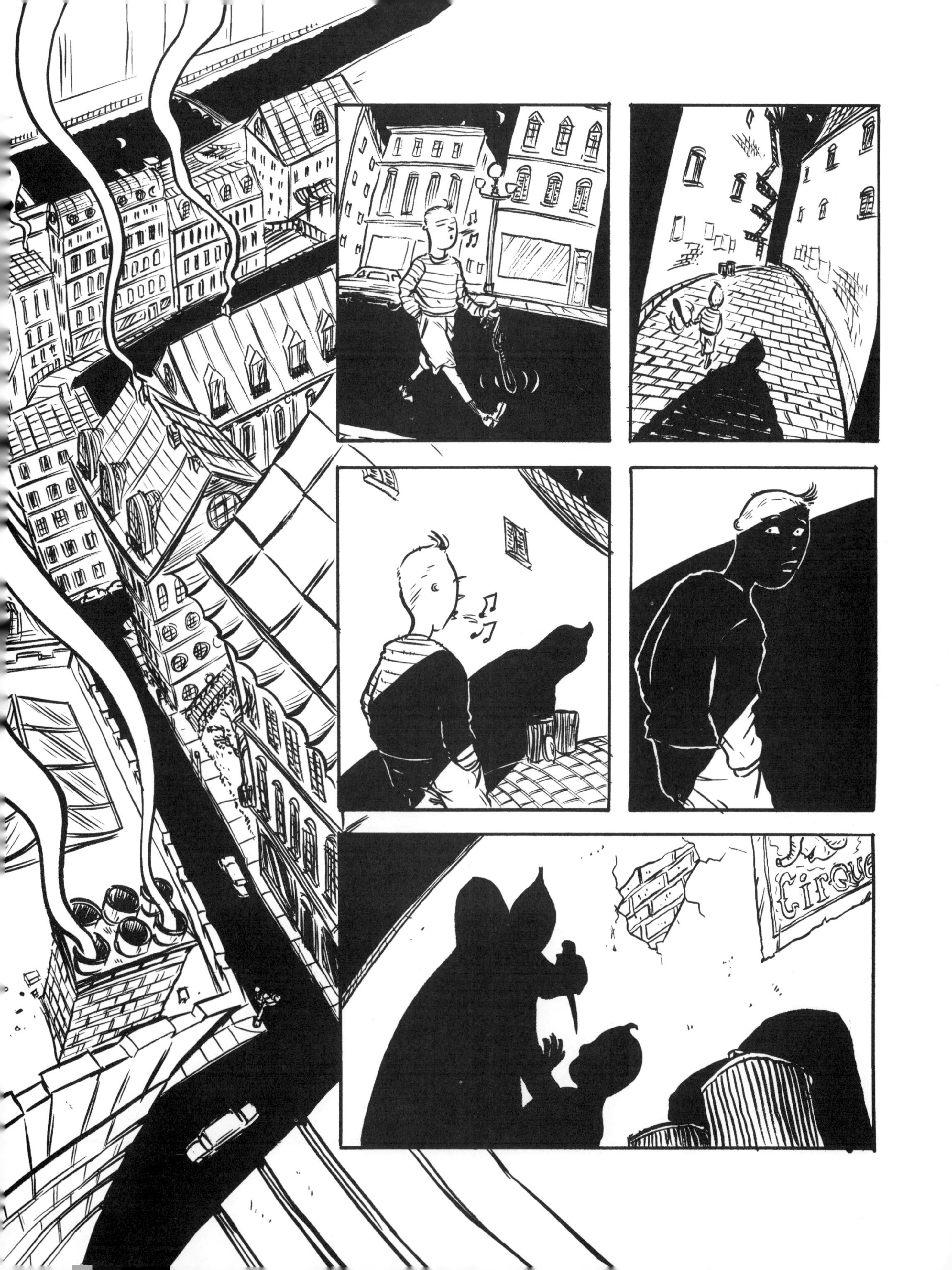
Cirque

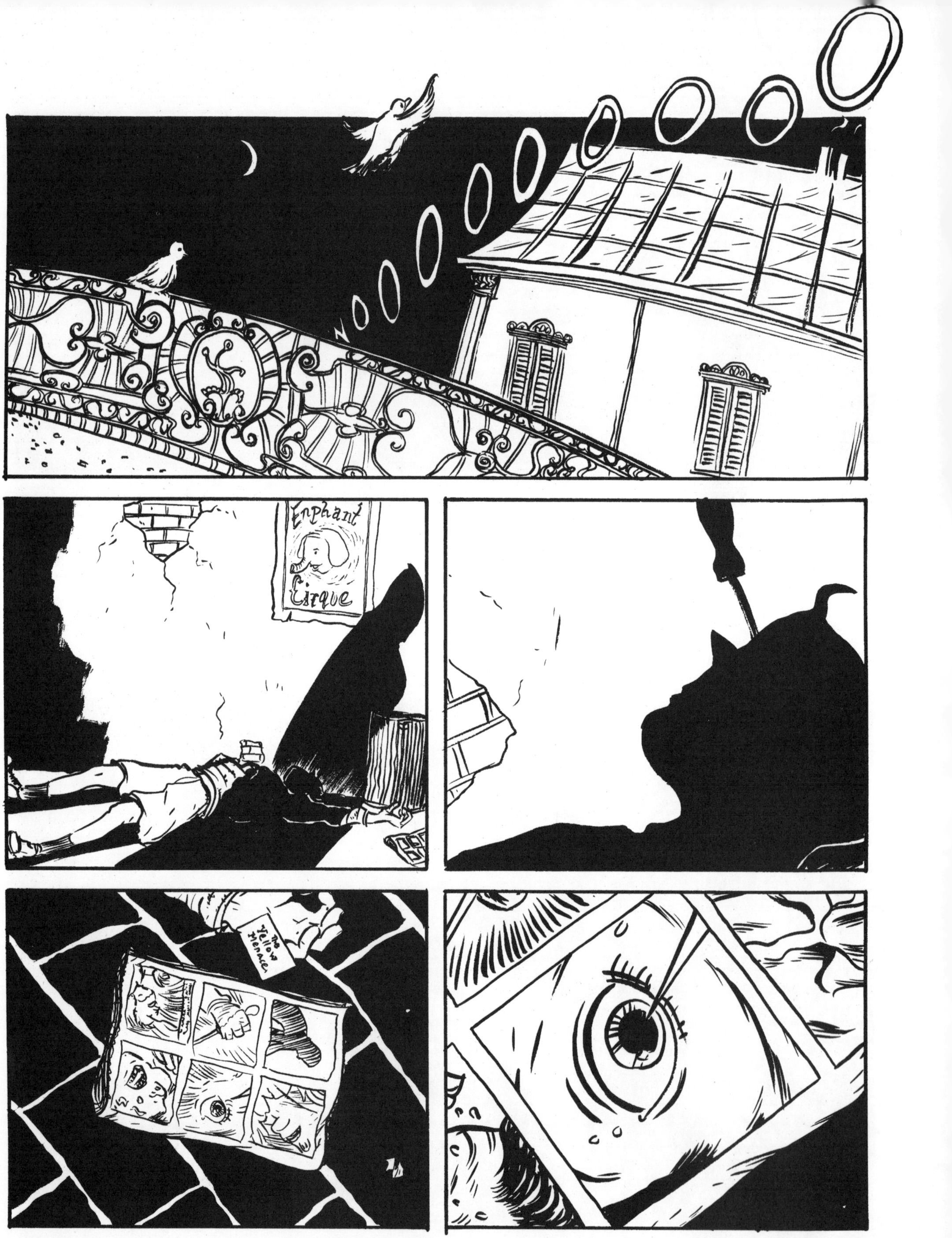
NOOOOOOOOO
Enphant Cirque
The Yellow Menace

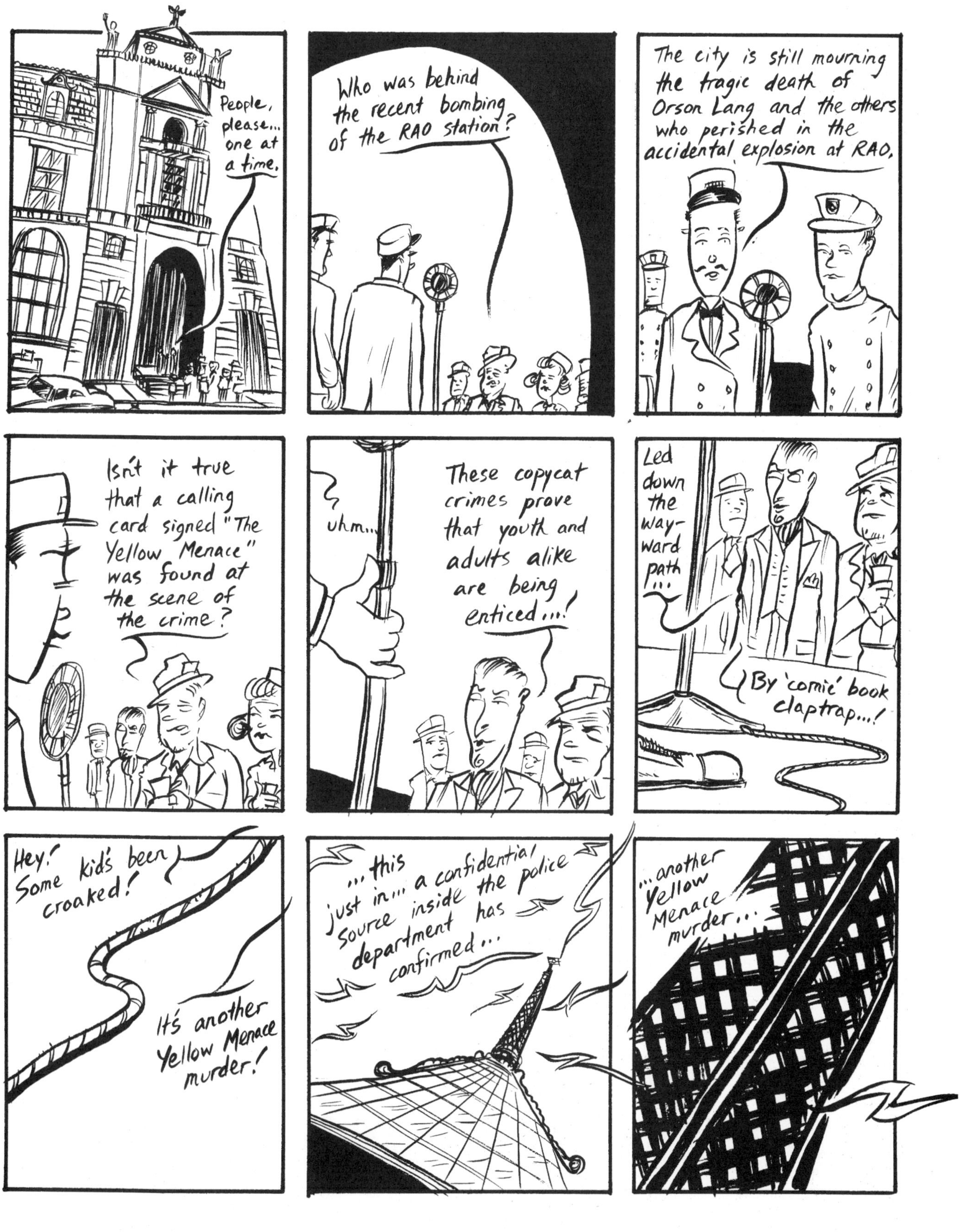
People, please... one at a time.
Who was behind the recent bombing of the RAO station?
The city is still mourning the tragic death of Orson Lang and the others who perished in the accidental explosion at RAO.
Isn't it true that a calling card signed "The Yellow Menace" was found at the scene of the crime?
uhm...
These copycat crimes prove that youth and adults alike are being enticed...!
Led down the way-ward path...
By 'comic' book claptrap...!
Hey! Some kid's been croaked!
It's another Yellow Menace murder!
...this just in... a confidential source inside the police department has confirmed...
...another Yellow Menace murder...

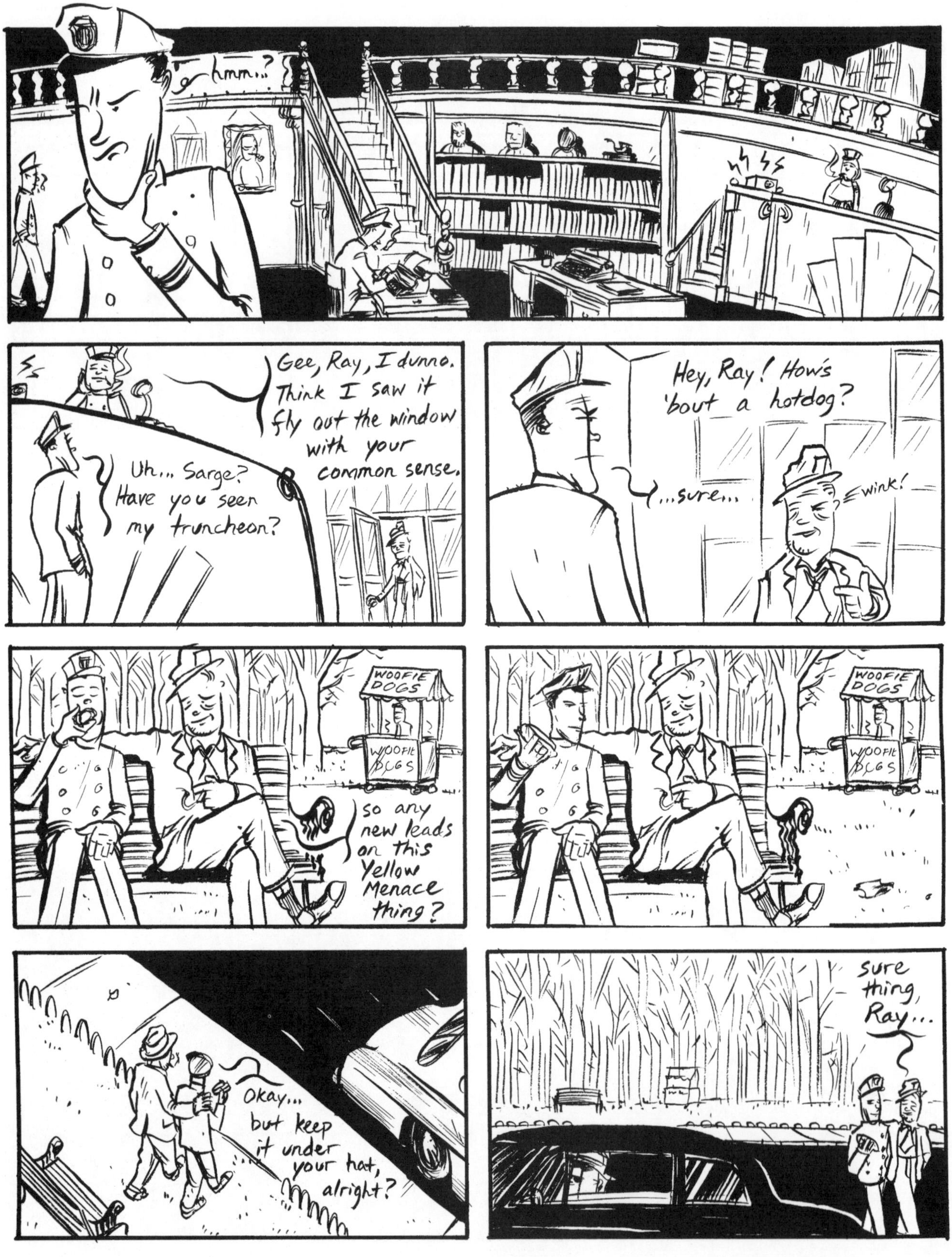
hmm...?
Uh... Sarge? Have you seen my truncheon?
Gee, Ray, I dunno. Think I saw it fly out the window with your common sense.
Hey, Ray! How's 'bout a hotdog?
...sure...
wink!
WOOFIE DOGS
WOOFIE DOGS
so any new leads on this Yellow Menace thing?
WOOFIE DOGS
WOOFIE DOGS
Okay... but keep it under your hat, alright?
Sure thing, Ray...

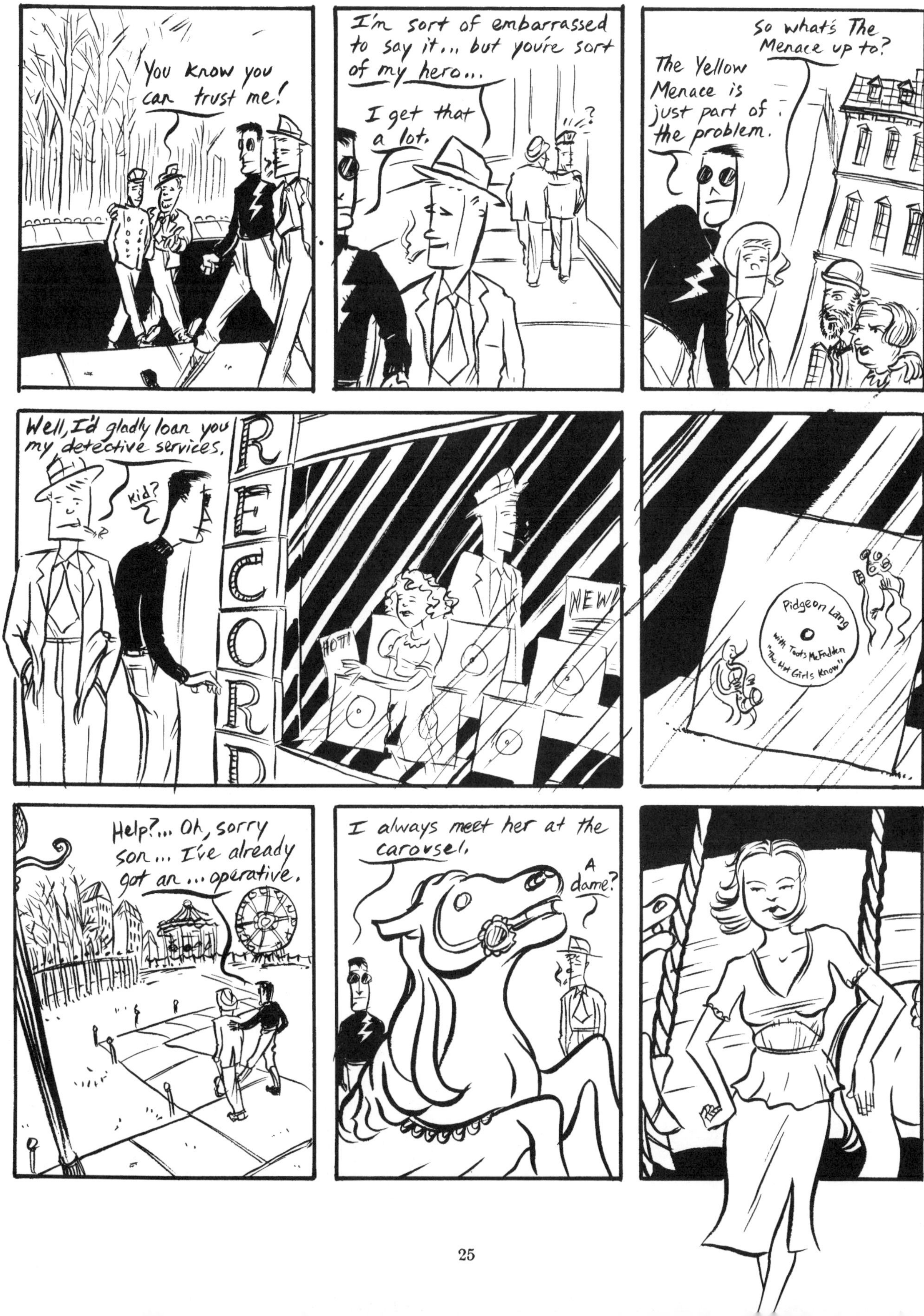
You know you can trust me!
I'm sort of embarrassed to say it... but you're sort of my hero...
I get that a lot.
?
So what's The Menace up to?
The Yellow Menace is just part of the problem.
Well, I'd gladly loan you my detective services,
kid?
RECORD
NEW!
HOT!
Pidgeon Lang
with Toots McFadden
"The Hot Girls Know"
Help?... Oh, sorry son... I've already got an... operative.
I always meet her at the carousel.
A dame?

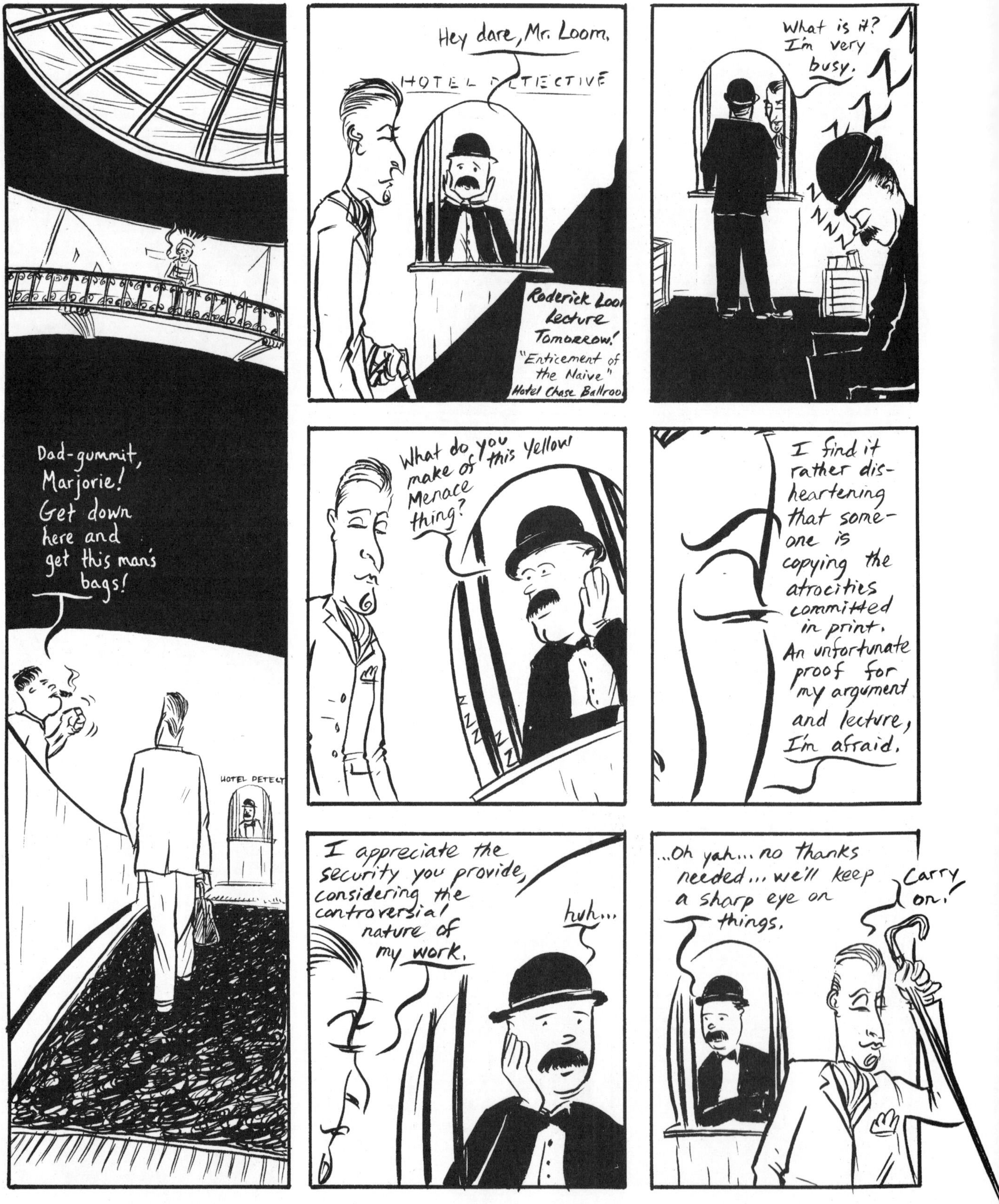
Dad-gummit, Marjorie! Get down here and get this man's bags!
HOTEL DETECT
Hey dare, Mr. Loom.
HOTEL DETECTIVE
Roderick Loom Lecture Tomorrow! "Enticement of the Naive" Hotel Chase Ballroom
What is it? I'm very busy.
What do you make of this Yellow Menace thing?
I find it rather disheartening that someone is copying the atrocities committed in print. An unfortunate proof for my argument and lecture, I'm afraid.
I appreciate the security you provide, considering the controversial nature of my work.
huh...
...Oh yah... no thanks needed... we'll keep a sharp eye on things.
Carry on!

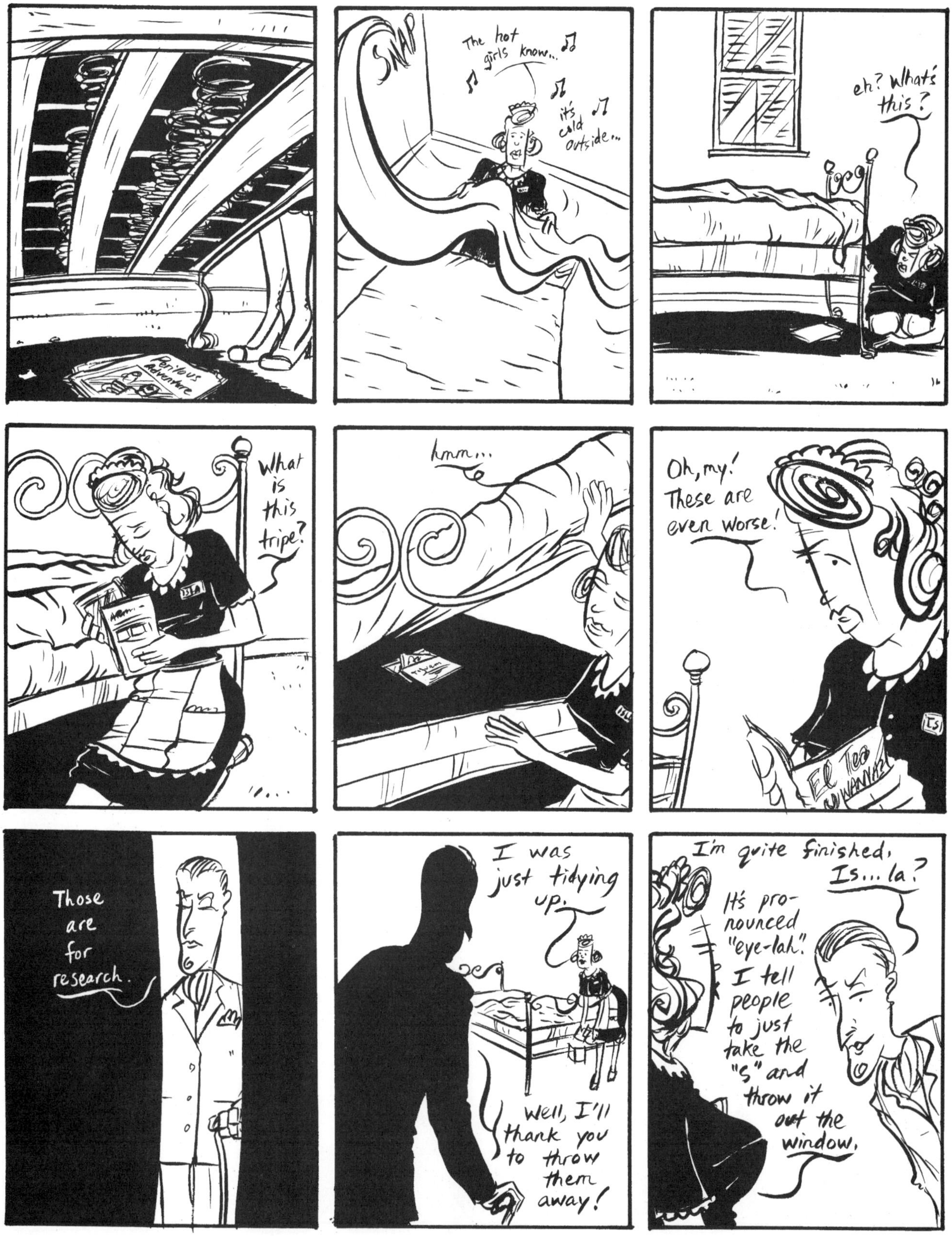
Perilous Adventure
SNAP
The hot girls know...
it's cold outside...
eh? What's this?
What is this tripe?
hmm...
Oh, my! These are even worse!
Those are for research.
I was just tidying up.
Well, I'll thank you to throw them away!
I'm quite finished, Is...la?
It's pronounced "eye-lah." I tell people to just take the "s" and throw it out the window.

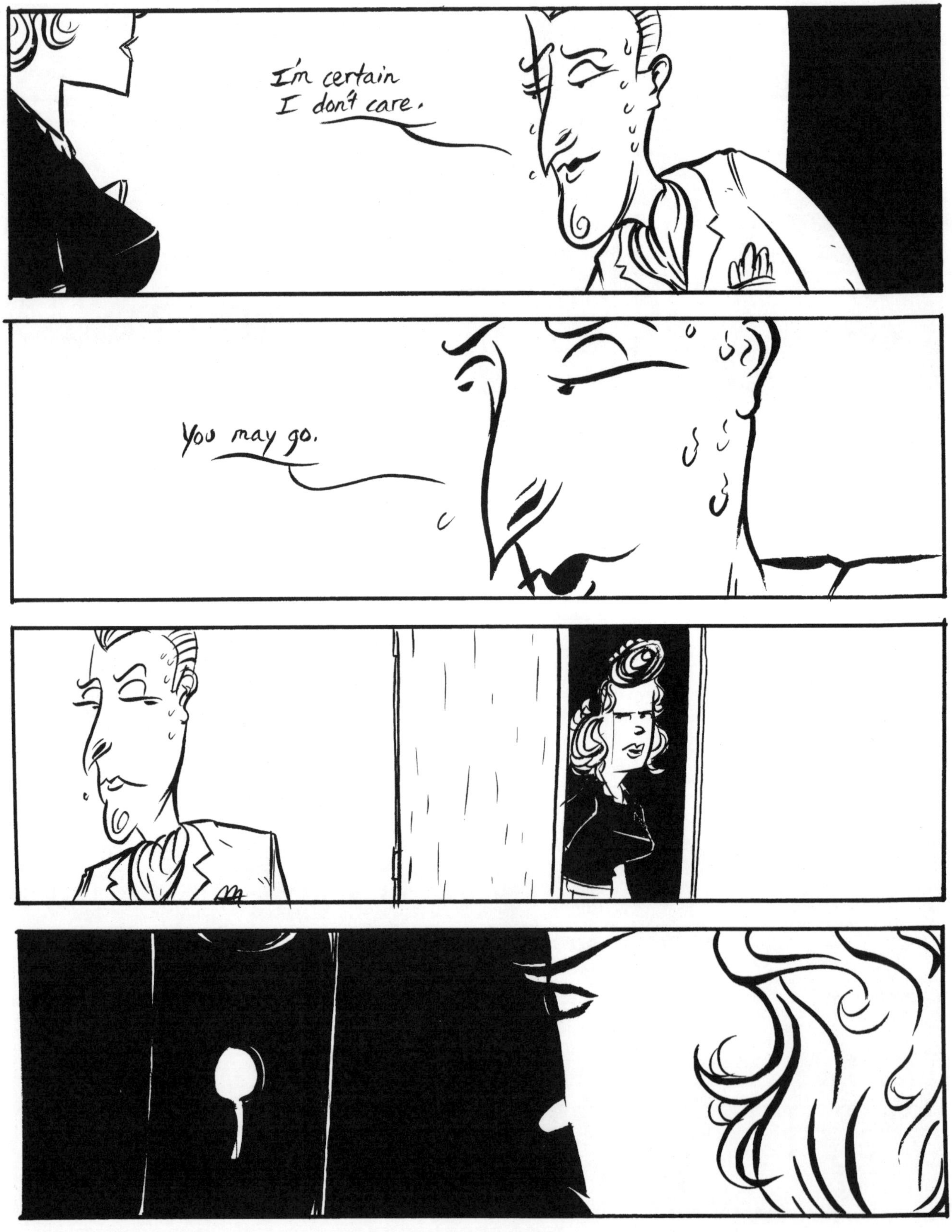
I'm certain I don't care.
You may go.

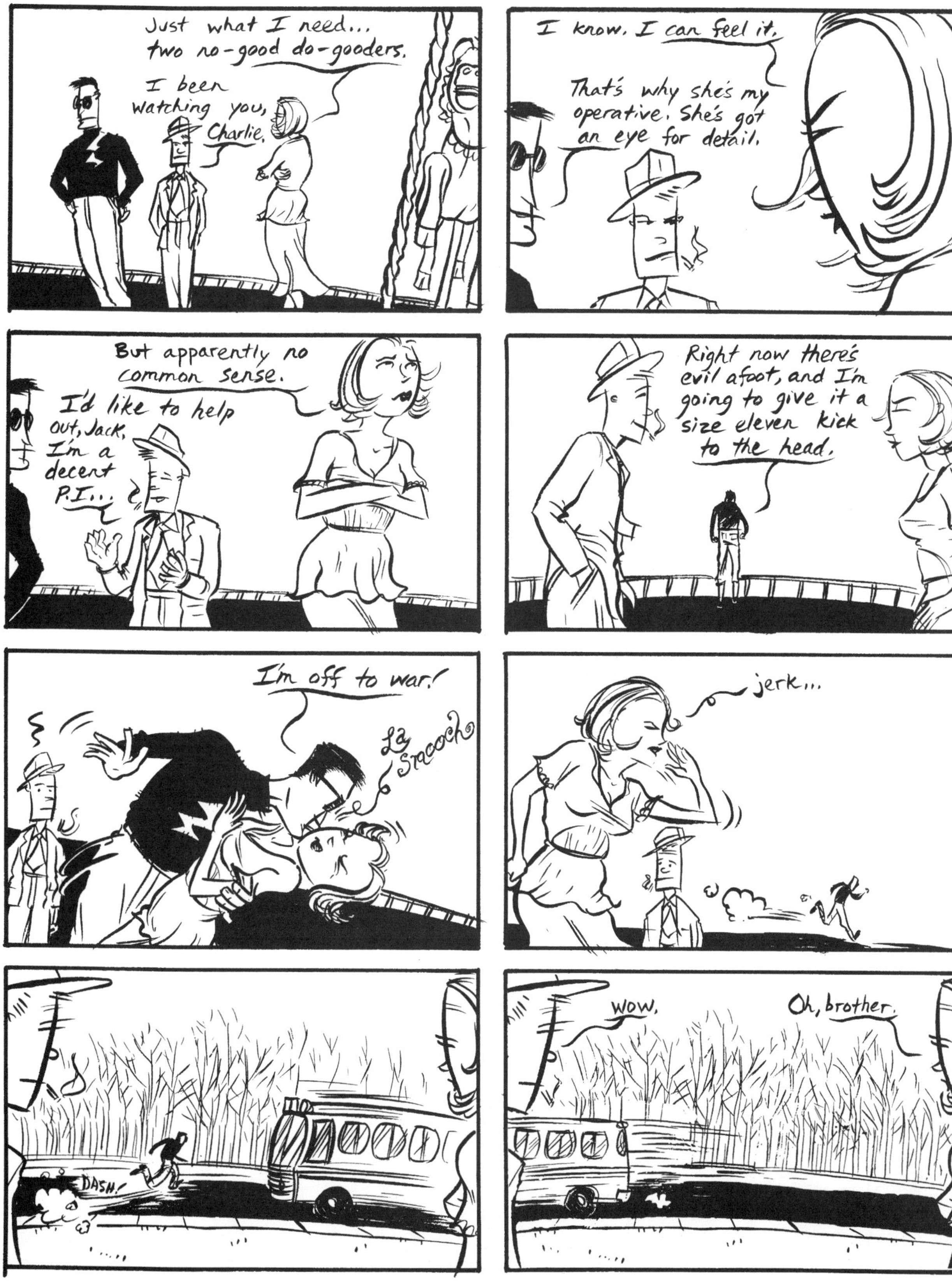

Just what I need... two no-good do-gooders.
I been watching you, Charlie.
I know. I can feel it.
That's why she's my operative. She's got an eye for detail.
But apparently no common sense.
I'd like to help out, Jack, I'm a decent P.I...
Right now there's evil afoot, and I'm going to give it a size eleven kick to the head.
I'm off to war!
La Smooch
jerk...
DASH!
WOW.
Oh, brother.

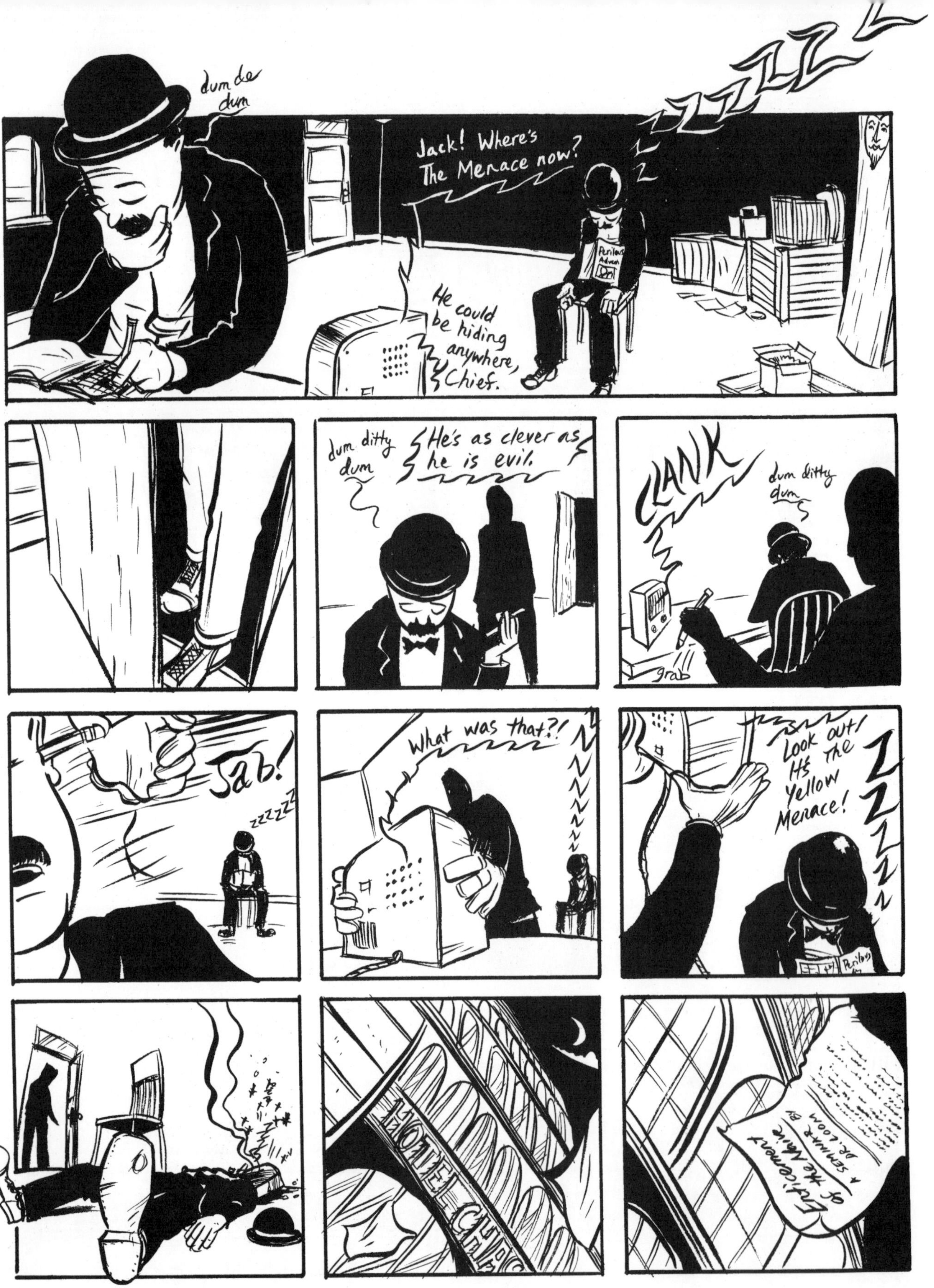

dum de dum
Jack! Where's The Menace now?
ZZZZZZZZZ
He could be hiding anywhere, Chief.
dum ditty dum
He's as clever as he is evil.
CLANK
dum ditty dum
grab
Jab!
zzzzz
What was that?!
Look out! Its the Yellow Menace!
ZZZZZ
Enticement
+ SEMINAR BY DR. LOOM

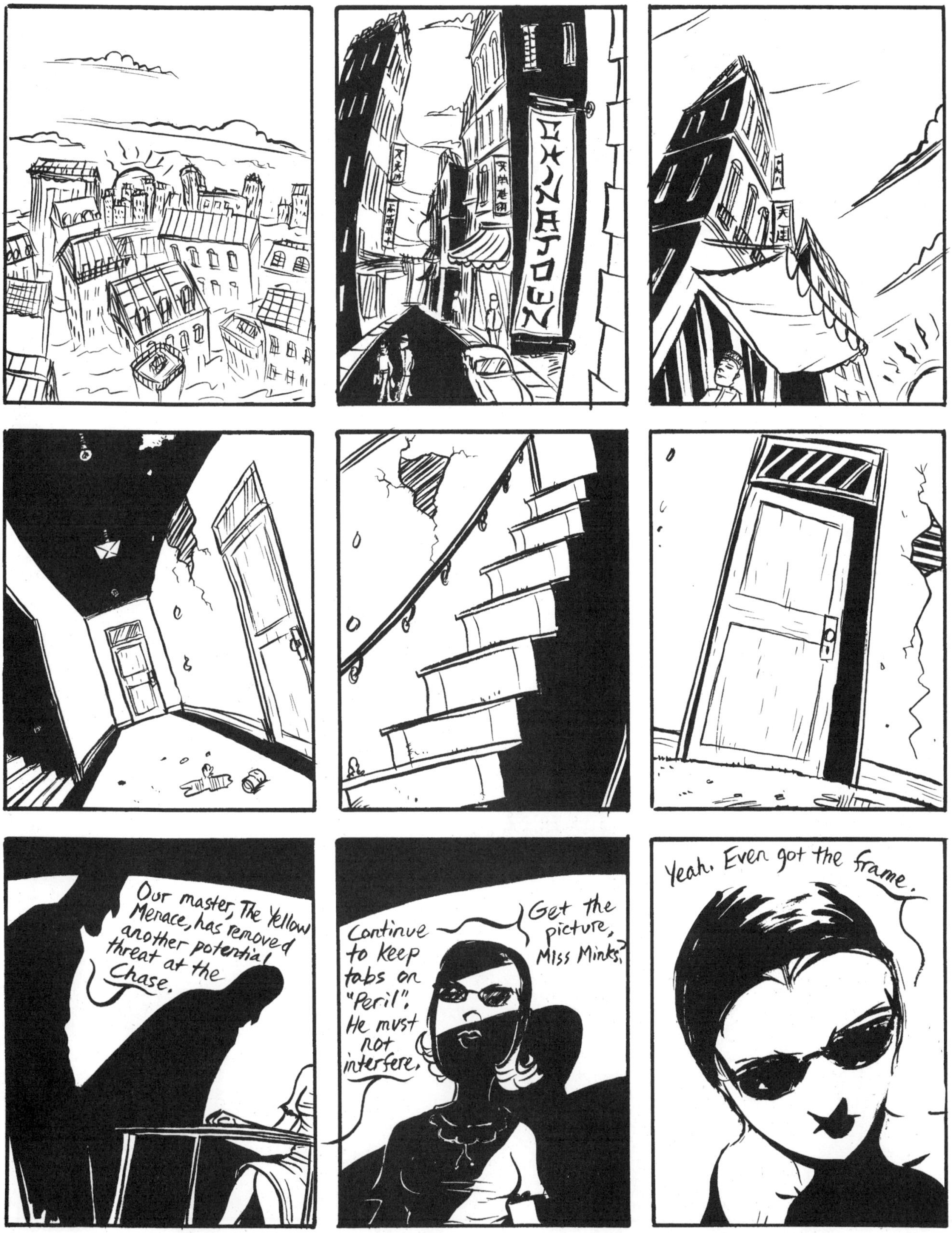
CHINATOWN
Our master, The Yellow Menace, has removed another potential threat at the Chase.
Continue to keep tabs on "Peril". He must not interfere.
Get the picture, Miss Minks?
Yeah. Even got the frame.

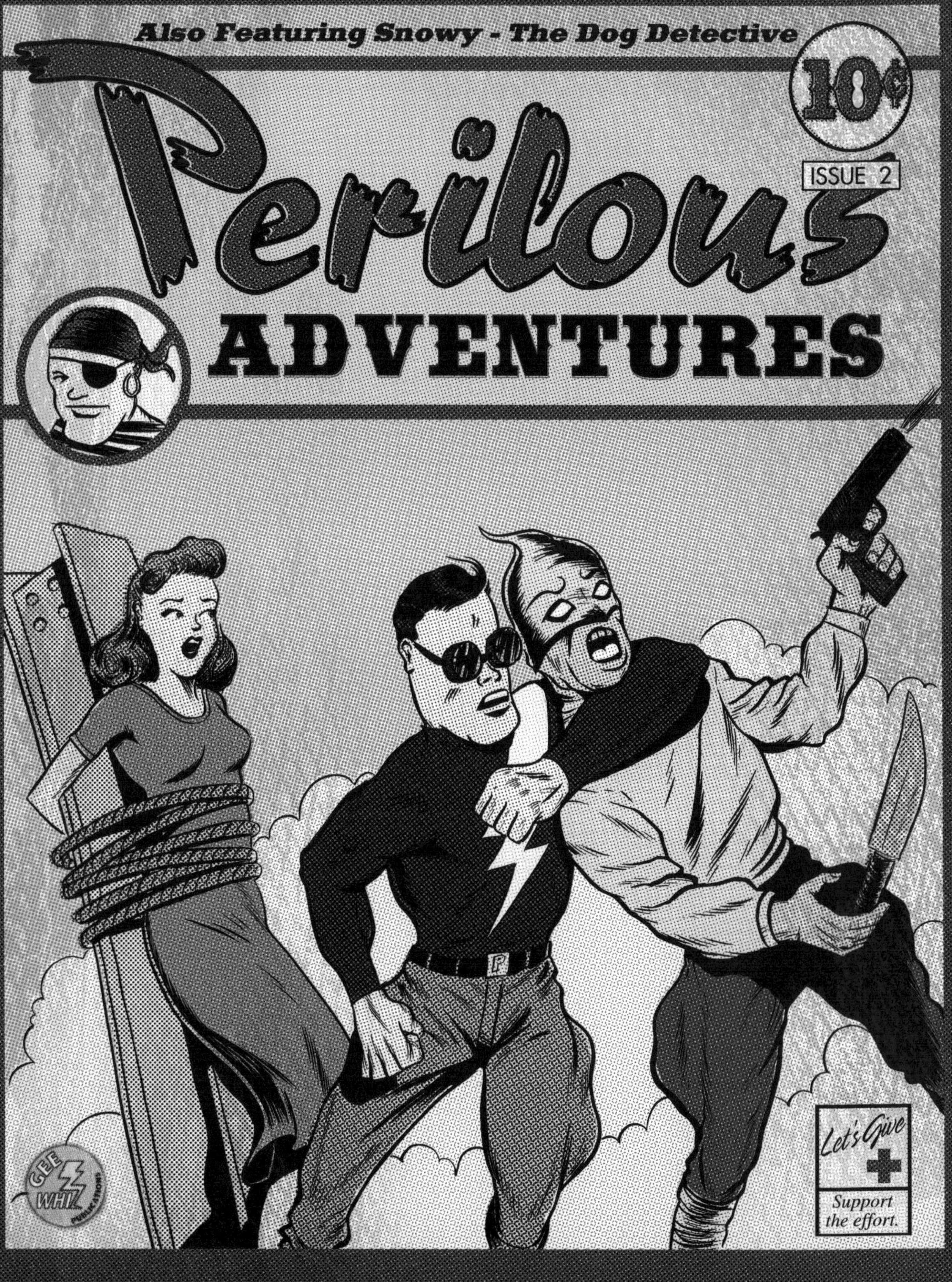
Also Featuring Snowy - The Dog Detective
10¢
ISSUE 2
Perilous
ADVENTURES
GEE WHIZ
Let's Give
Support the effort.

Chapter Two

漫画

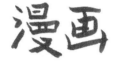

Comics

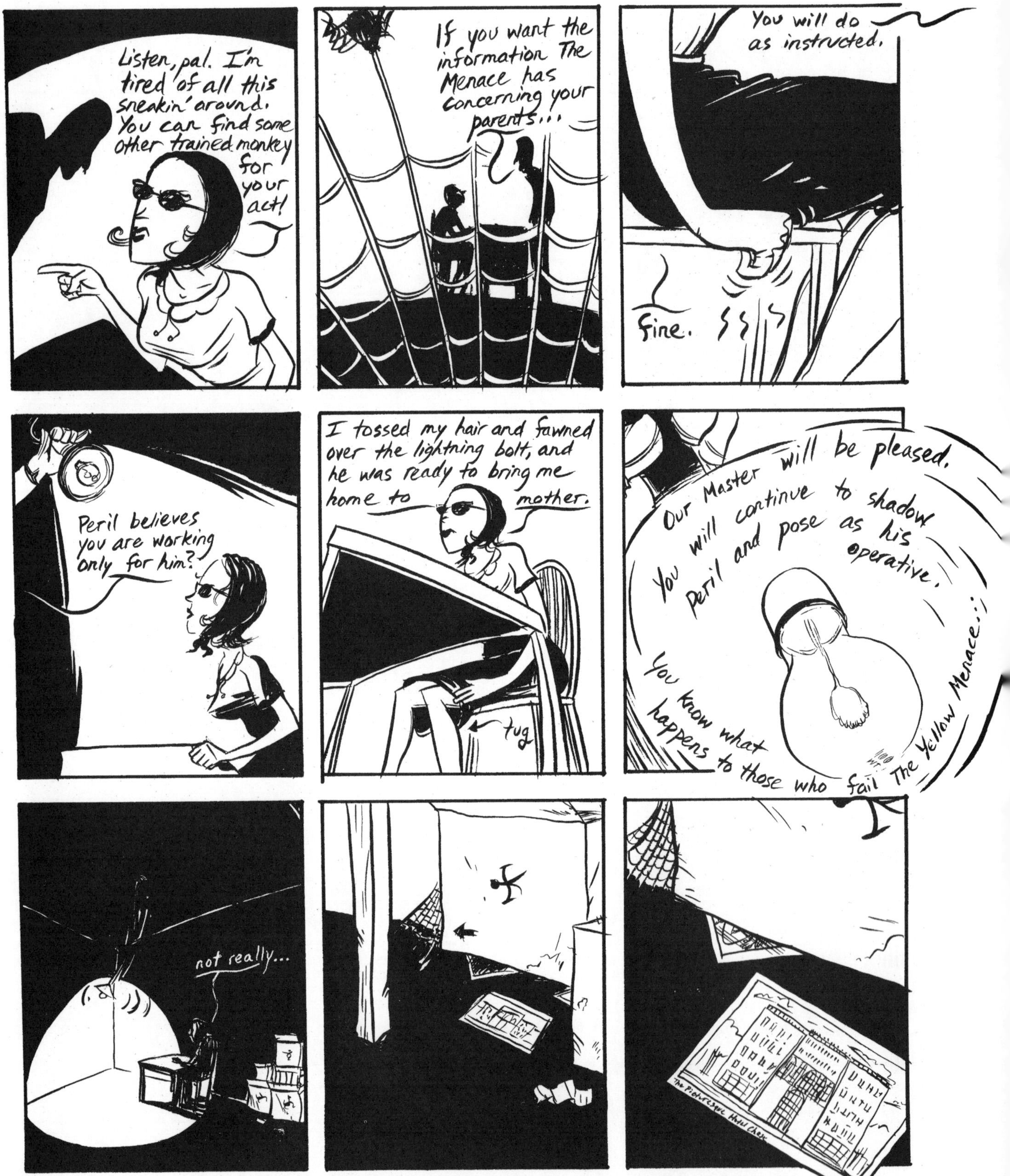

Listen, pal. I'm tired of all this sneakin' around. You can find some other trained monkey for your act!
If you want the information The Menace has concerning your parents...
You will do as instructed.
Fine.
Peril believes you are working only for him?
I tossed my hair and fawned over the lightning bolt, and he was ready to bring me home to mother.
tug
Our Master will be pleased. You will continue to shadow Peril and pose as his operative.
You know what happens to those who fail The Yellow Menace...
not really...

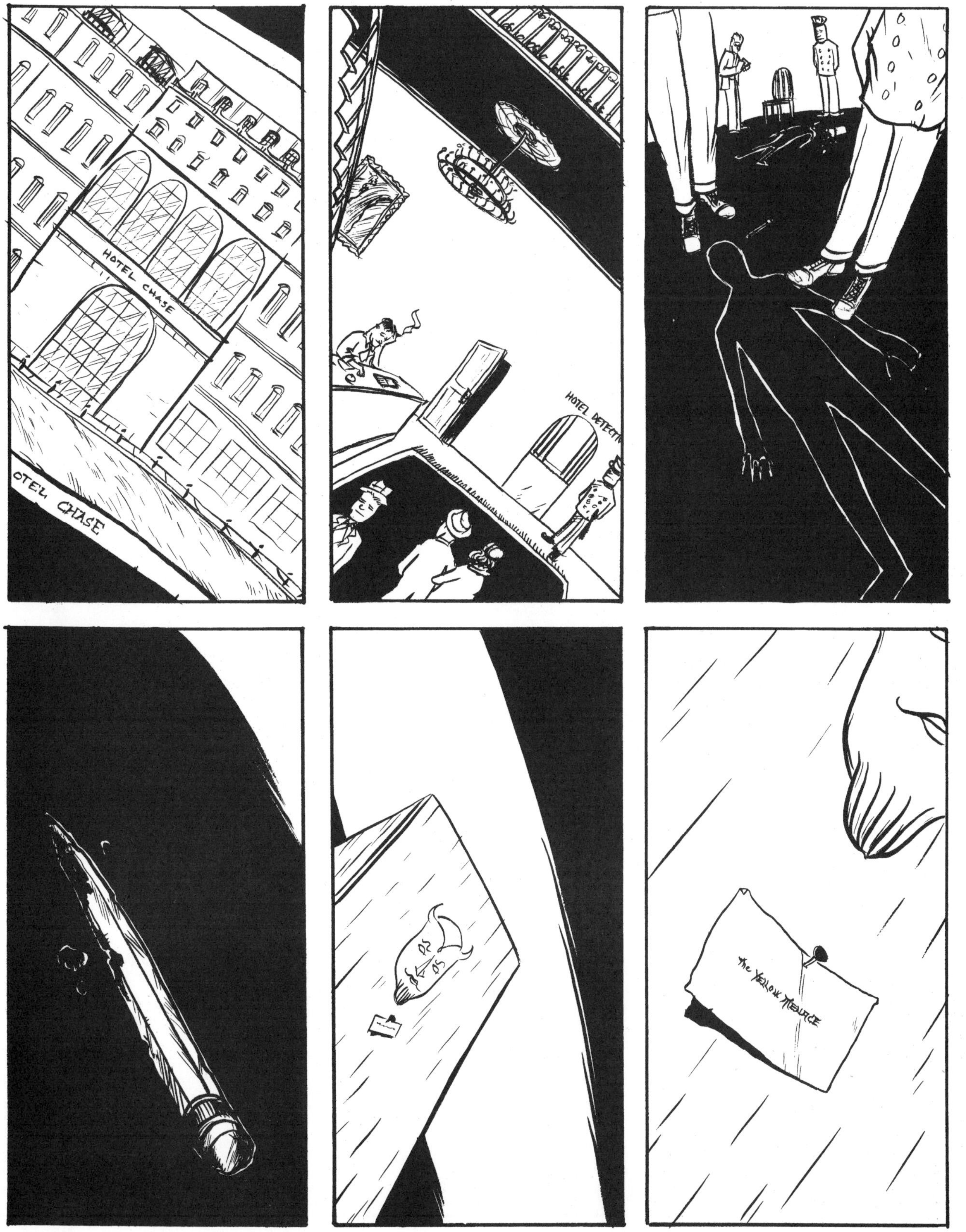
HOTEL CHASE
OTEL CHASE
HOTEL DETECTI
the YELLOW MENACE

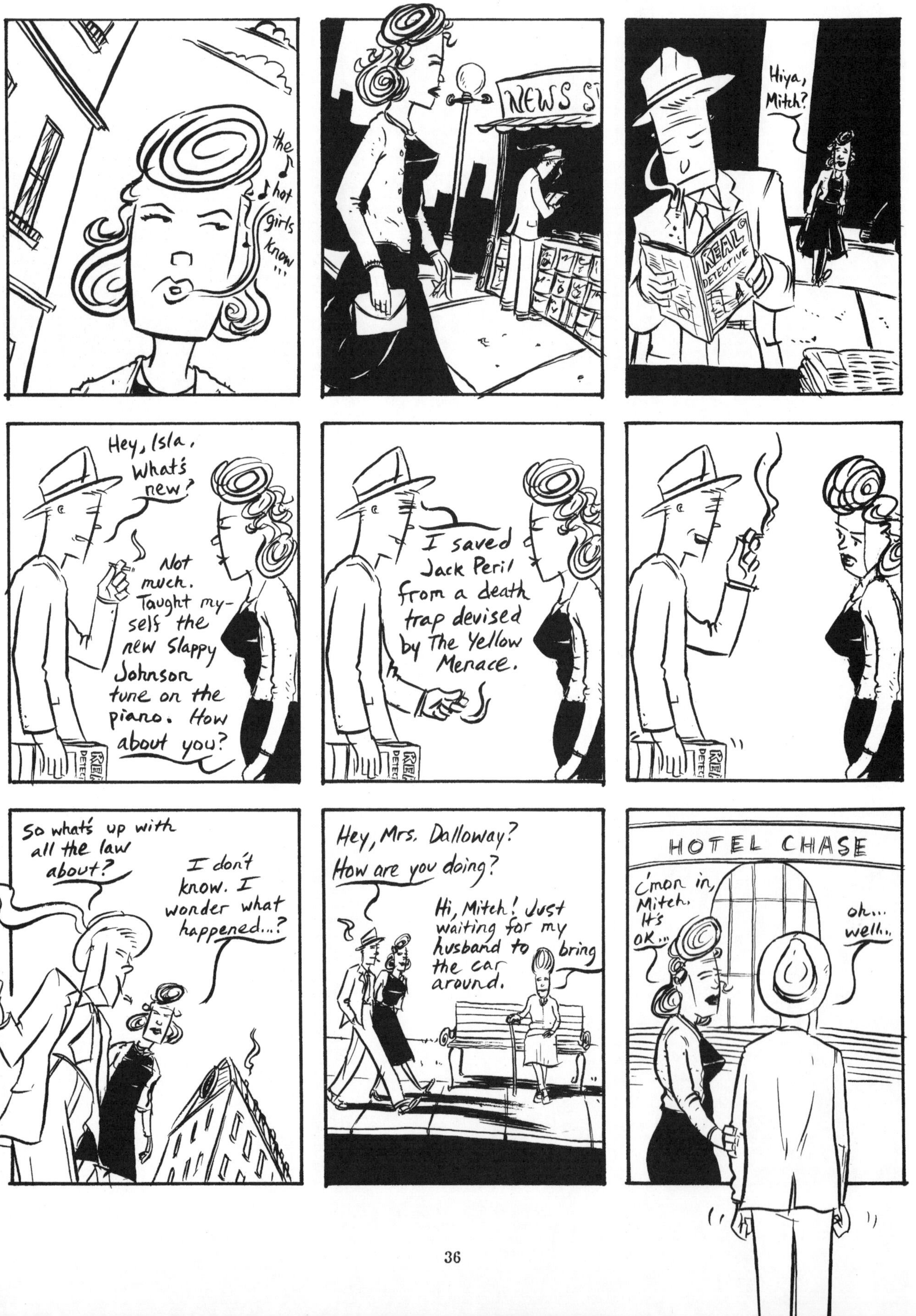
the hot girls know...
NEWS ST
Hiya, Mitch?
REAL DETECTIVE
Hey, Isla, What's new?
Not much. Taught myself the new Slappy Johnson tune on the piano. How about you?
I saved Jack Peril from a death trap devised by The Yellow Menace.
So what's up with all the law about?
I don't know. I wonder what happened...?
Hey, Mrs. Dalloway? How are you doing?
Hi, Mitch! Just waiting for my husband to bring the car around.
HOTEL CHASE
C'mon in, Mitch. It's OK...
oh... well...

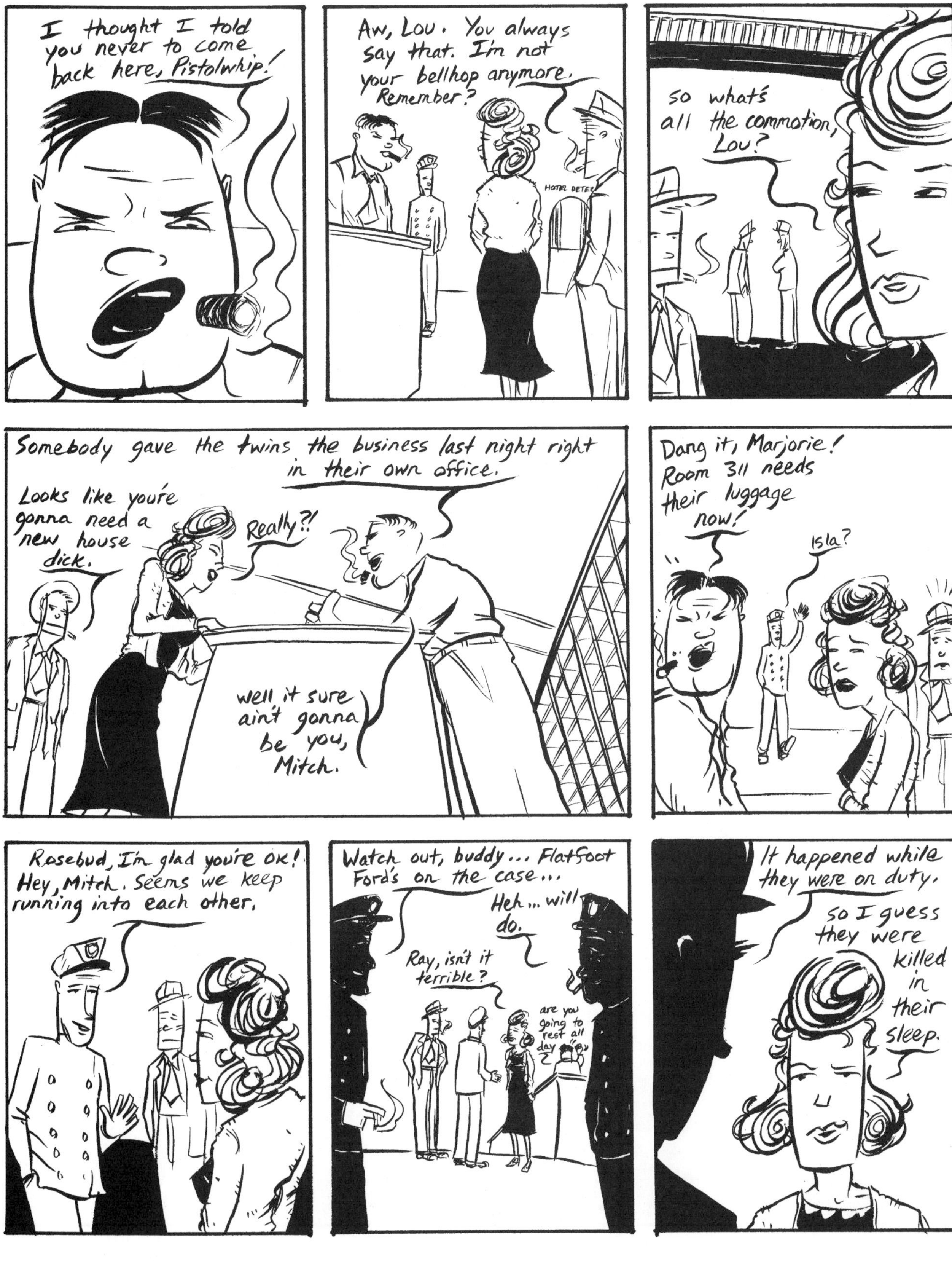
I thought I told you never to come back here, Pistolwhip!
Aw, Lou. You always say that. I'm not your bellhop anymore. Remember?
HOTEL DETEC
so what's all the commotion, Lou?
Somebody gave the twins the business last night right in their own office.
Looks like you're gonna need a new house dick.
Really?!
well it sure ain't gonna be you, Mitch.
Dang it, Marjorie! Room 311 needs their luggage now!
Isla?
Rosebud, I'm glad you're OK! Hey, Mitch. Seems we keep running into each other.
Watch out, buddy... Flatfoot Ford's on the case...
Heh... will do.
Ray, isn't it terrible?
are you going to rest all day?
It happened while they were on duty.
so I guess they were killed in their sleep.

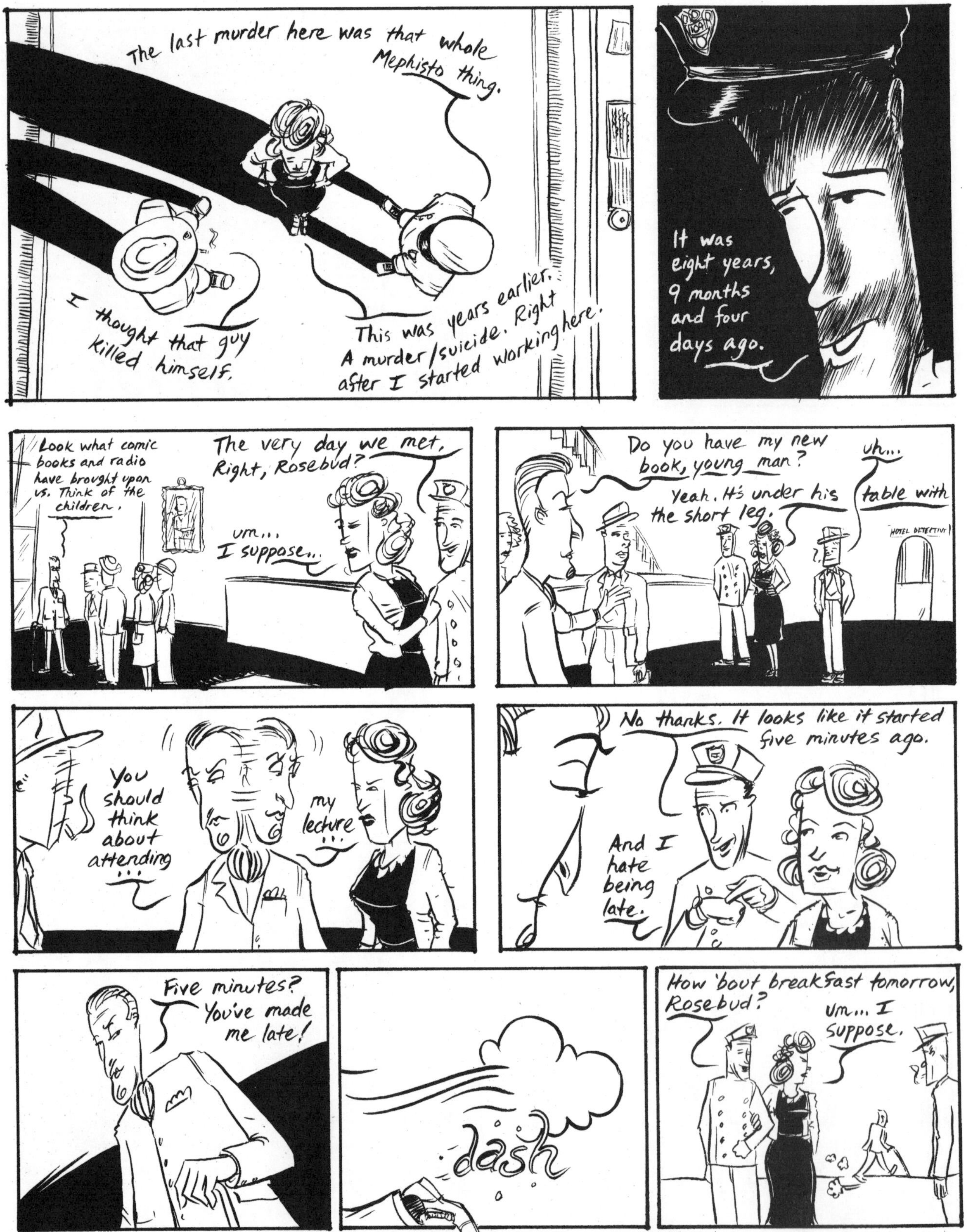

The last murder here was that whole Mephisto thing.
I thought that guy killed himself.
This was years earlier. A murder/suicide. Right after I started working here.
It was eight years, 9 months and four days ago.
Look what comic books and radio have brought upon us. Think of the children.
The very day we met, Right, Rosebud?
um... I suppose...
Do you have my new book, young man?
Yeah. It's under his table with the short leg.
uh...
HOTEL DETECTIVE
You should think about attending...
my lecture...
No thanks. It looks like it started five minutes ago.
And I hate being late.
Five minutes? You've made me late!
dash
How 'bout breakfast tomorrow, Rosebud?
um... I suppose.

See ya, guys. Keep me posted.
I thank you for attending under these circumstances...
Roderick Loom
How Immoral Amusements Unravel Our Moral Fiber
He's such a slowpoke. I've been waiting forever.
But these circumstances are my proof. A boy was murdered yesterday in the following manner...
How about a cup of coffee, Mrs. Dalloway?
P-Put it down.
from this children's comic book.
Oh... thank you, Mitch, but I don't want him to miss me.
Two brave detectives slain in this very hotel by an arch-villain impersonator!
I'LL KILL YOU AND YOUR FREE IDEALS, PERIL!
You hungry?
Not really.
A boat capsized and a boy drowned last week. No doubt mimicking "Gill-Man, Criminal Detective."
STICK 'EM UP Manipula!

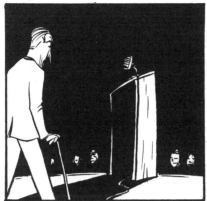

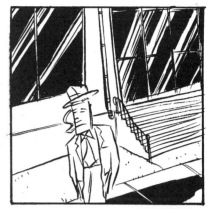

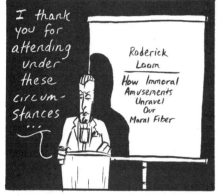

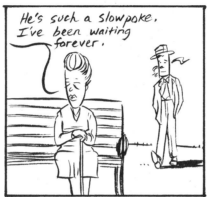

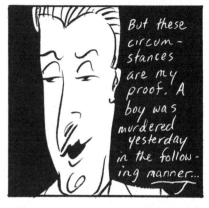

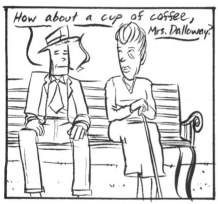

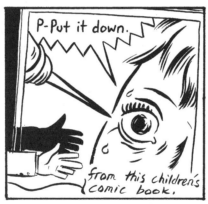

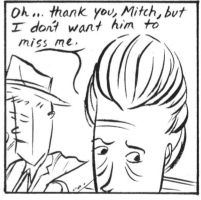

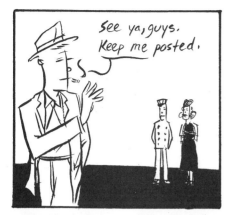

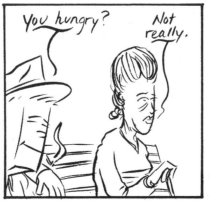

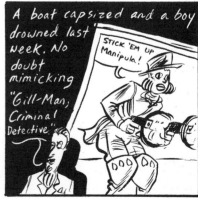

Well, I'm off then. I've got a hankerin' for some flapjacks.
All right, Mitch.
Boys and Girls call these "head-light" comics!
DON'T MOVE!
oh, brother.
BOAT REPAIR
There are pictures within pictures...
...for those who know how to look!
ESTLE'S BOAT REPAIR
Estle?
We are being bamboozled into buying this reprobate propaganda...
NO THANKS, SON, I'M FULL-UP ON PARTNERS.
Is this art?
Hey, Estle!
Hey, Mitchy!
Evelyn
The tyranny of these hacks surpasses even the nefarious threat of foreign dictators! Is this really "artistic" expression?
EXHIBIT C.I
REAL DETECTIVE fantasies
Gotcha' some-thing!
Thanks, Mitchy!

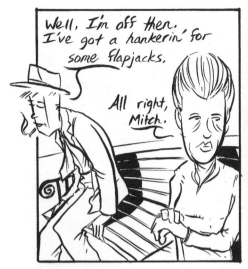

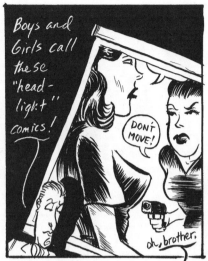

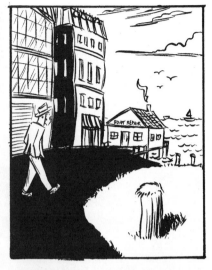

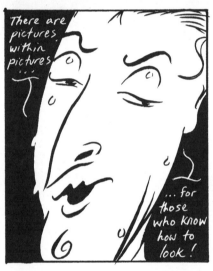

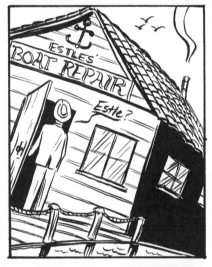

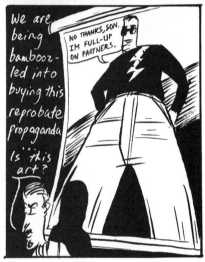

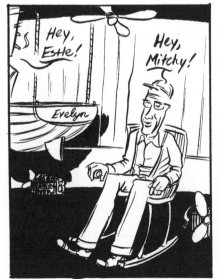

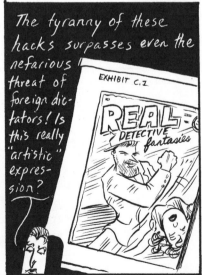

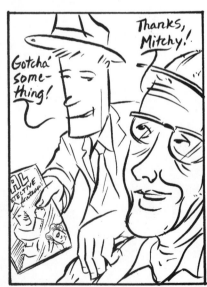

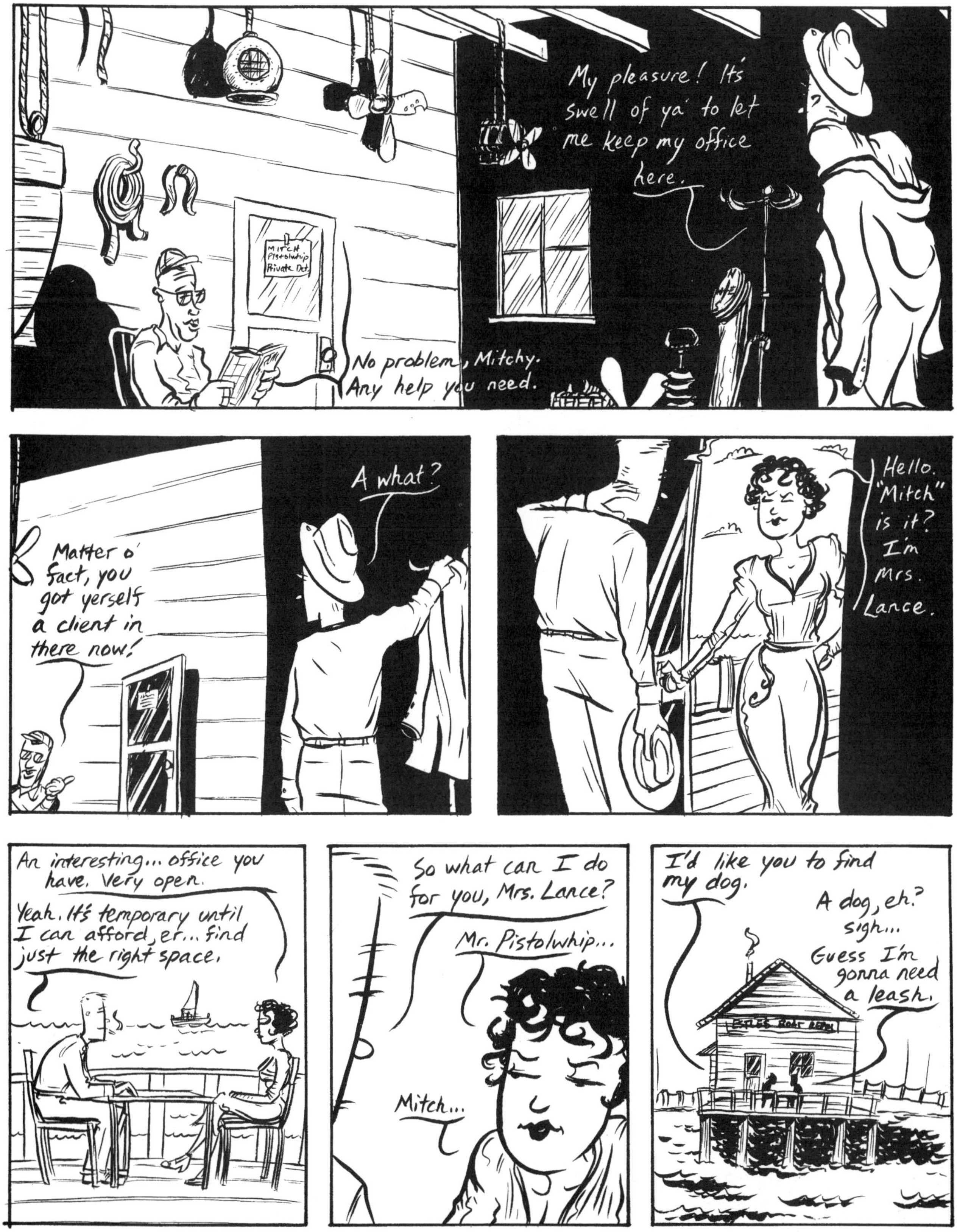
My pleasure! It's swell of ya' to let me keep my office here.
MITCH Pistolwhip Private Det.
No problem, Mitchy. Any help you need.
A what?
Matter o' fact, you got yerself a client in there now!
Hello. "Mitch" is it? I'm Mrs. Lance.
An interesting... office you have. Very open.
Yeah. It's temporary until I can afford, er... find just the right space.
So what can I do for you, Mrs. Lance?
Mr. Pistolwhip...
Mitch...
I'd like you to find my dog.
A dog, eh? sigh... Guess I'm gonna need a leash.

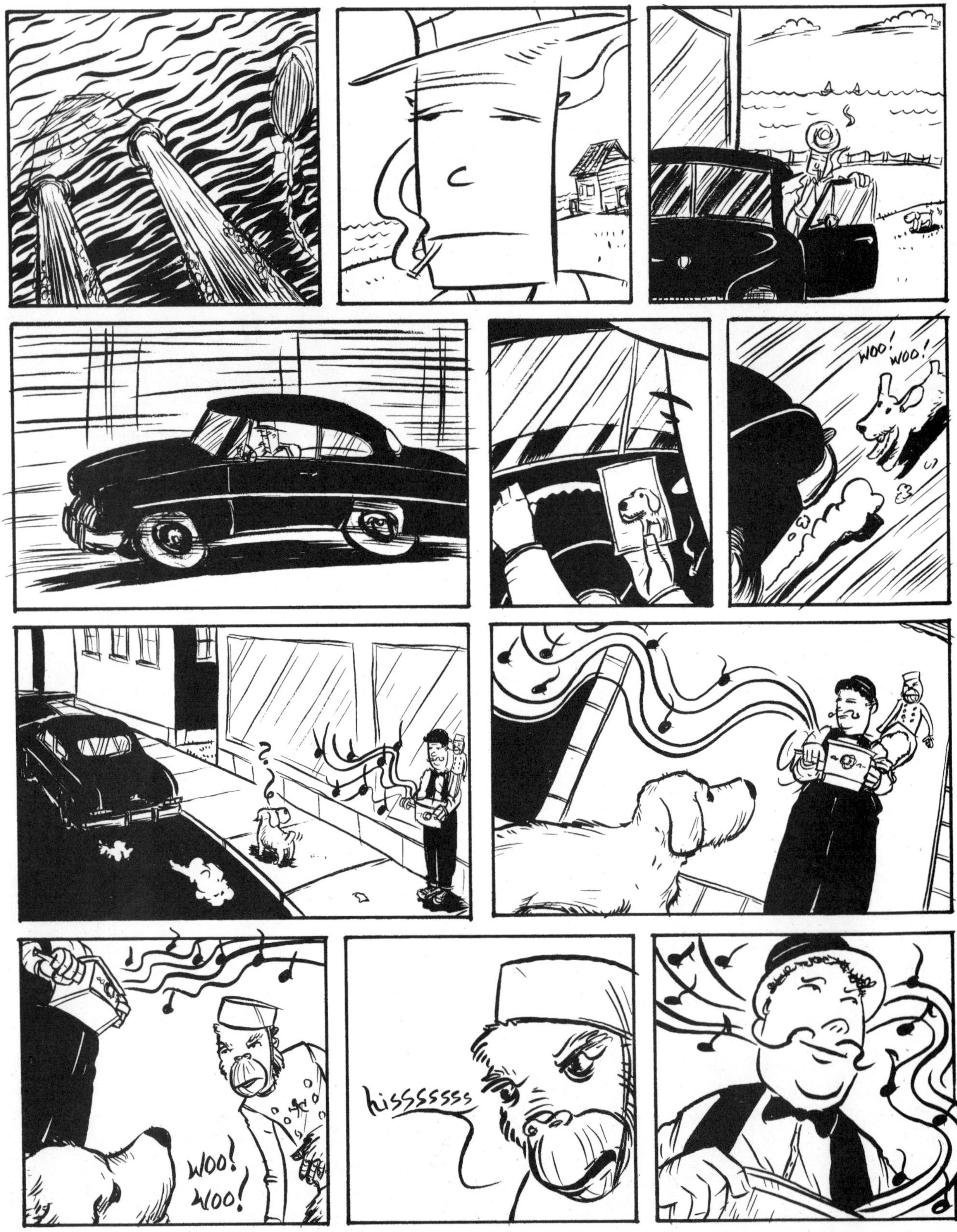
WOO! WOO!
WOO! WOO!
hissssss

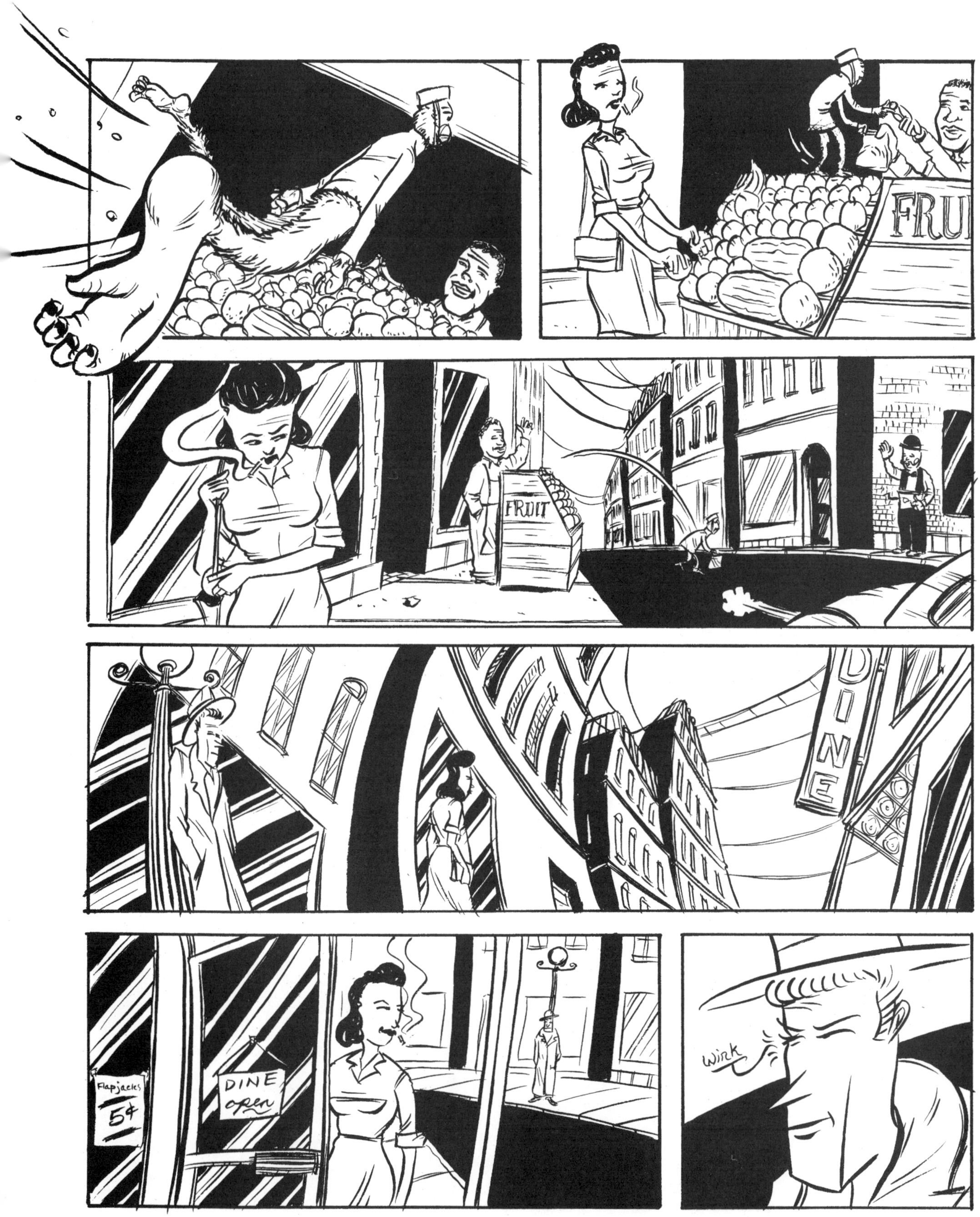
FRUI
FRUIT
DINE
Flapjacks
5¢
DINE
open
Wink

shove!
KRAK!
oof!
Le Chat People
SELL GRITTY NEWSPAPERS!

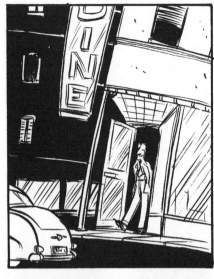

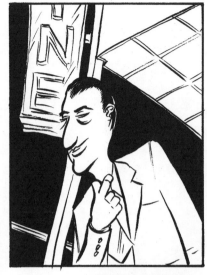

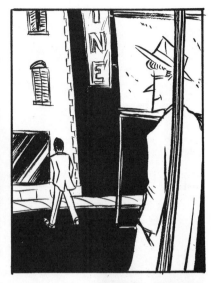

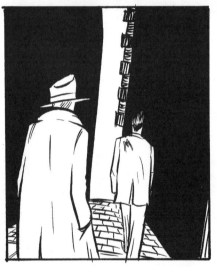

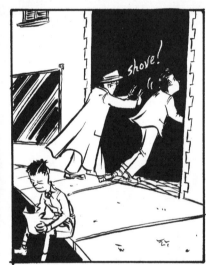

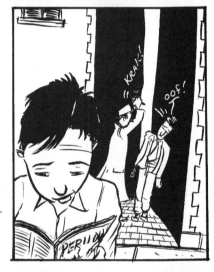

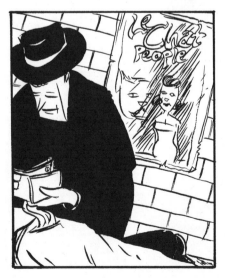

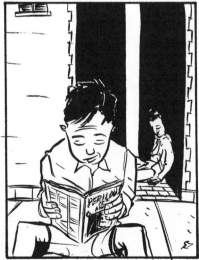

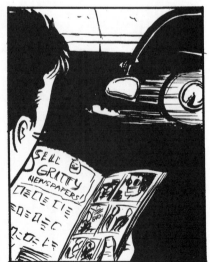

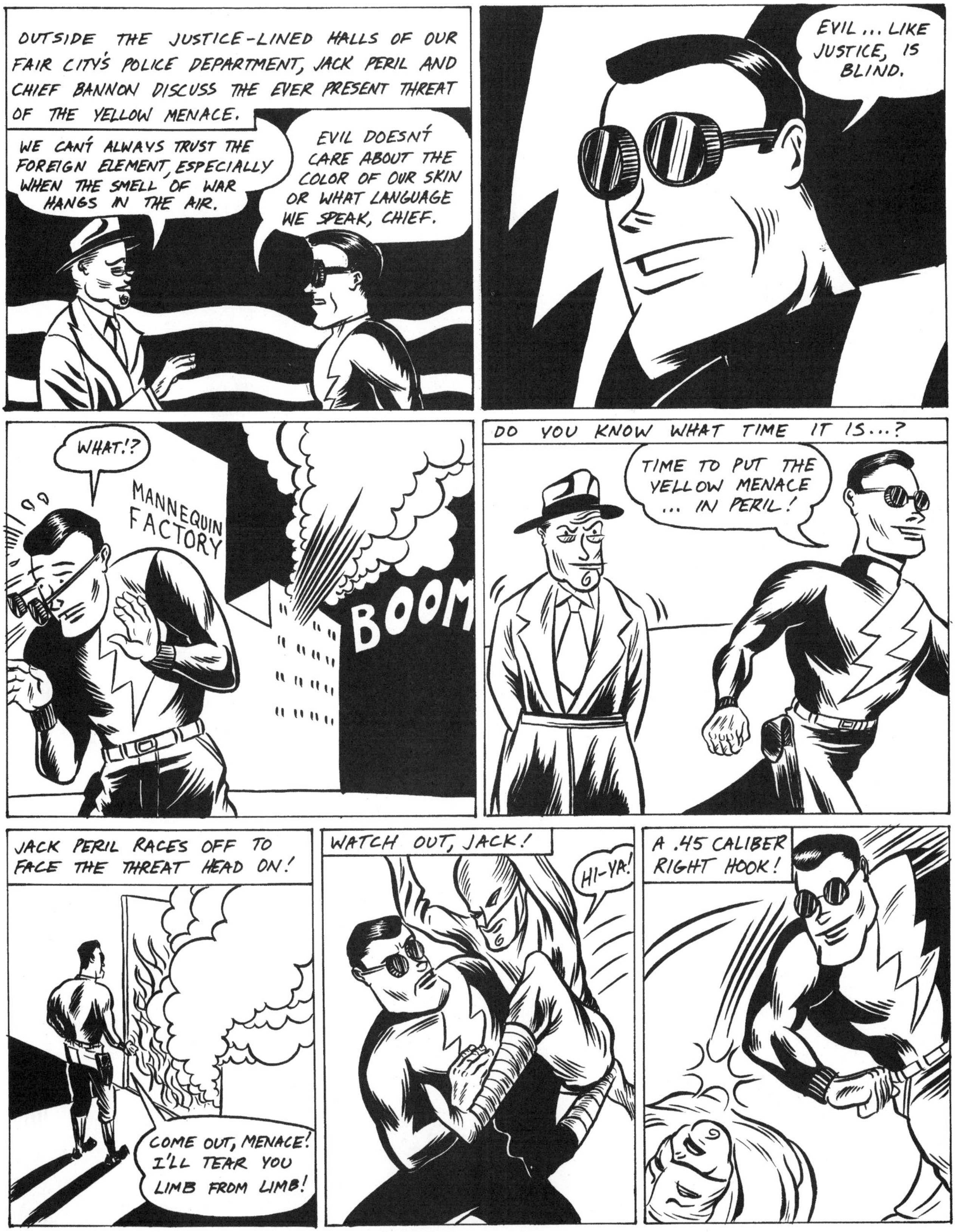
OUTSIDE THE JUSTICE-LINED HALLS OF OUR FAIR CITY'S POLICE DEPARTMENT, JACK PERIL AND CHIEF BANNON DISCUSS THE EVER PRESENT THREAT OF THE YELLOW MENACE.
WE CAN'T ALWAYS TRUST THE FOREIGN ELEMENT, ESPECIALLY WHEN THE SMELL OF WAR HANGS IN THE AIR.
EVIL DOESN'T CARE ABOUT THE COLOR OF OUR SKIN OR WHAT LANGUAGE WE SPEAK, CHIEF.
EVIL... LIKE JUSTICE, IS BLIND.
WHAT!?
MANNEQUIN FACTORY
BOOM
DO YOU KNOW WHAT TIME IT IS...?
TIME TO PUT THE YELLOW MENACE ... IN PERIL!
JACK PERIL RACES OFF TO FACE THE THREAT HEAD ON!
COME OUT, MENACE! I'LL TEAR YOU LIMB FROM LIMB!
WATCH OUT, JACK!
HI-YA!
A .45 CALIBER RIGHT HOOK!

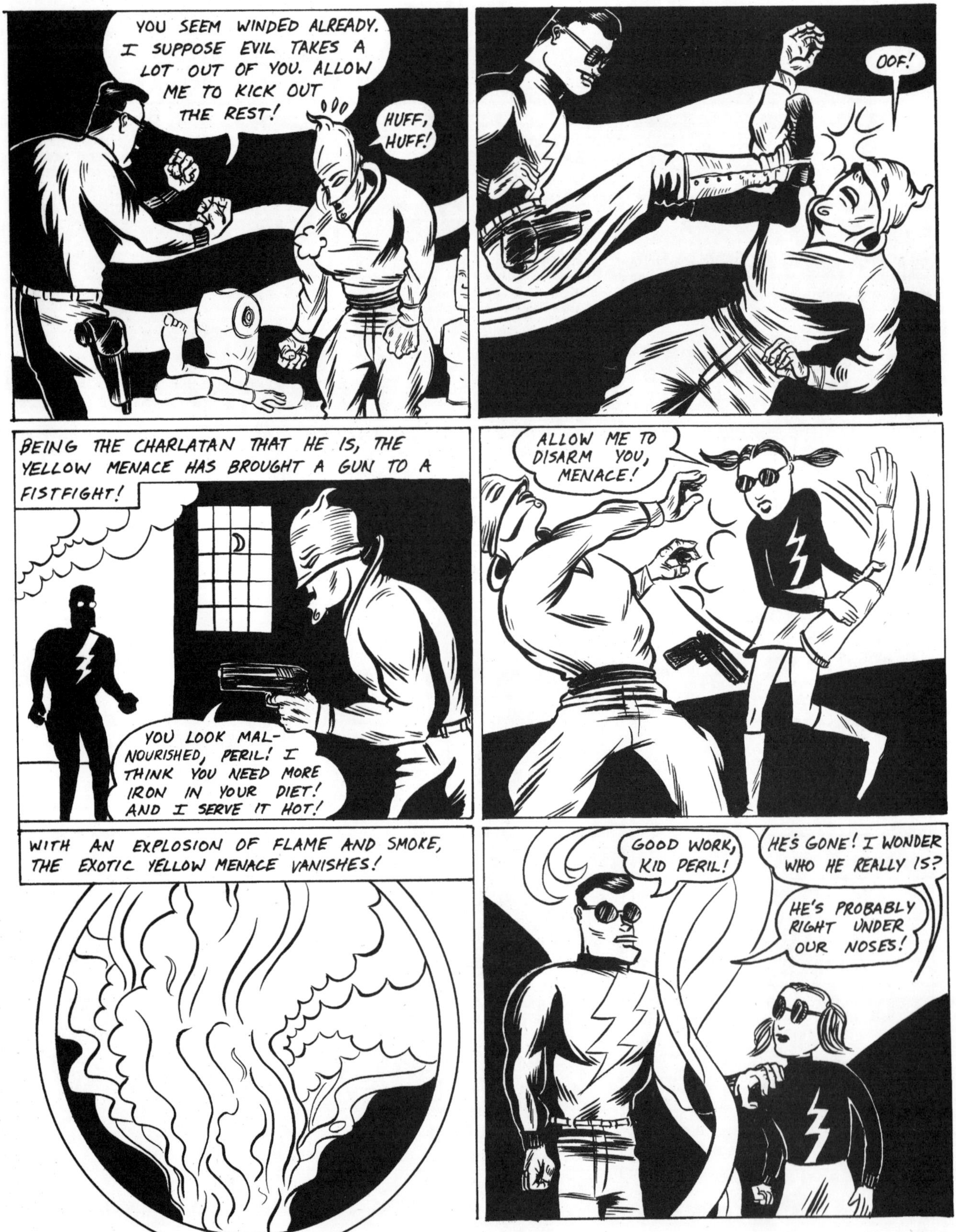
YOU SEEM WINDED ALREADY. I SUPPOSE EVIL TAKES A LOT OUT OF YOU. ALLOW ME TO KICK OUT THE REST!
HUFF, HUFF!
OOF!
BEING THE CHARLATAN THAT HE IS, THE YELLOW MENACE HAS BROUGHT A GUN TO A FISTFIGHT!
YOU LOOK MAL-NOURISHED, PERIL! I THINK YOU NEED MORE IRON IN YOUR DIET! AND I SERVE IT HOT!
ALLOW ME TO DISARM YOU, MENACE!
WITH AN EXPLOSION OF FLAME AND SMOKE, THE EXOTIC YELLOW MENACE VANISHES!
GOOD WORK, KID PERIL!
HE'S GONE! I WONDER WHO HE REALLY IS?
HE'S PROBABLY RIGHT UNDER OUR NOSES!

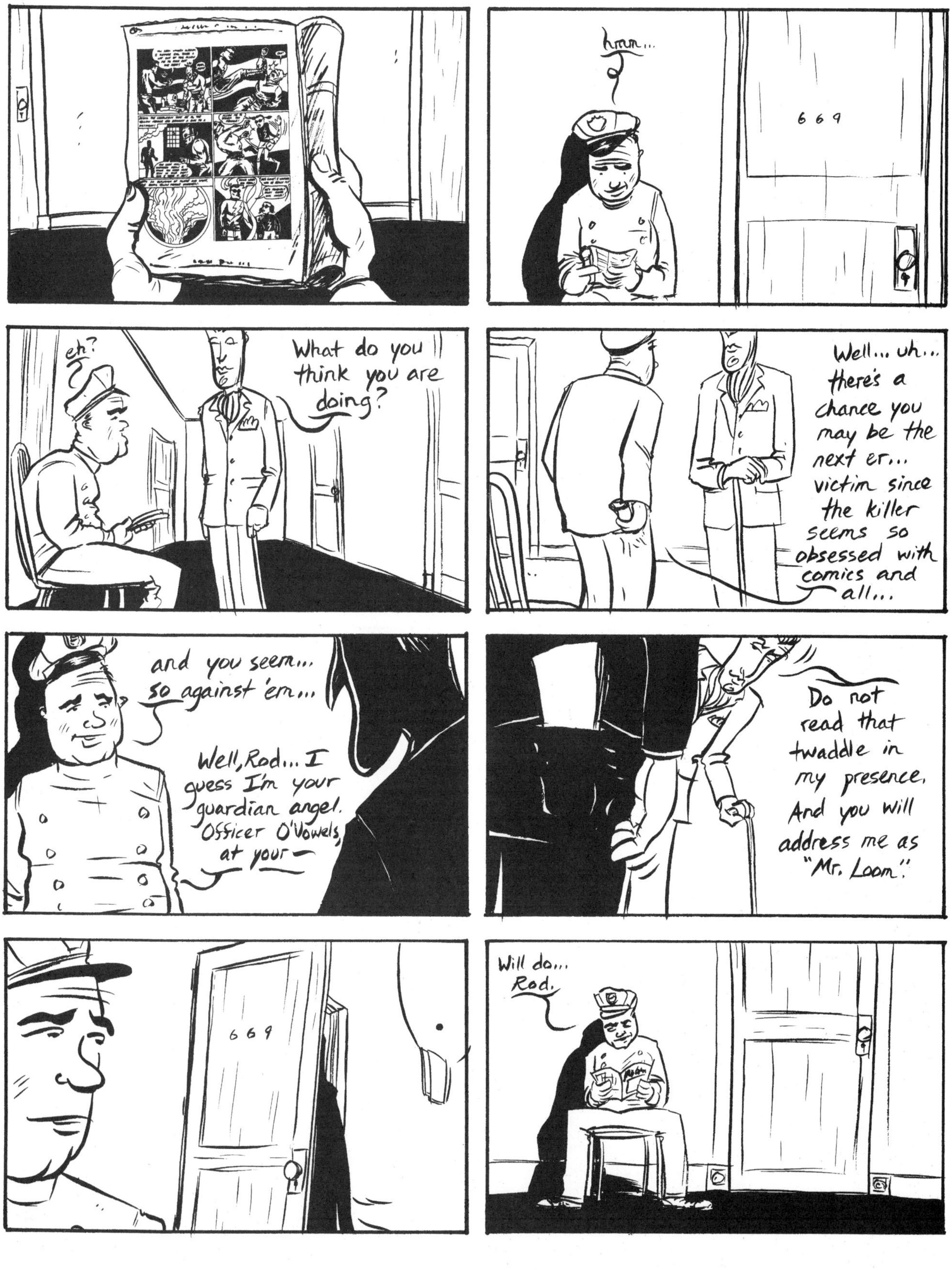
hmm...
eh?
What do you think you are doing?
Well... uh... there's a chance you may be the next er... victim since the killer seems so obsessed with comics and all...
and you seem... so against 'em...
Well, Rod... I guess I'm your guardian angel. Officer O'Vowels, at your—
Do not read that twaddle in my presence. And you will address me as "Mr. Loom".
669
Will do... Rod.

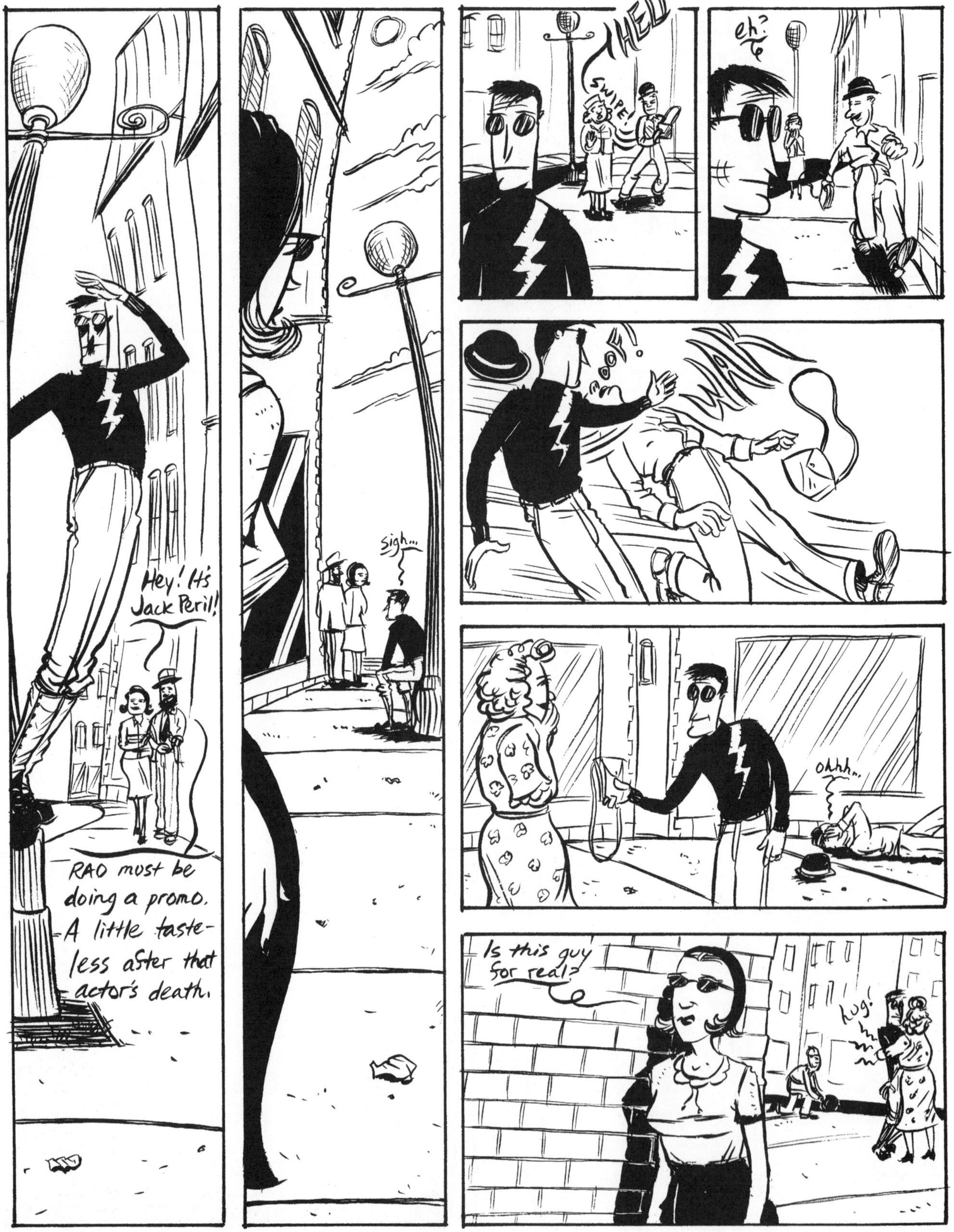
Hey! It's Jack Peril!
RAO must be doing a promo. A little tasteless after that actor's death.
Sigh...
HELP
SWIPE!
eh?
OOF!
Ohhh..
Is this guy for real?
hug!

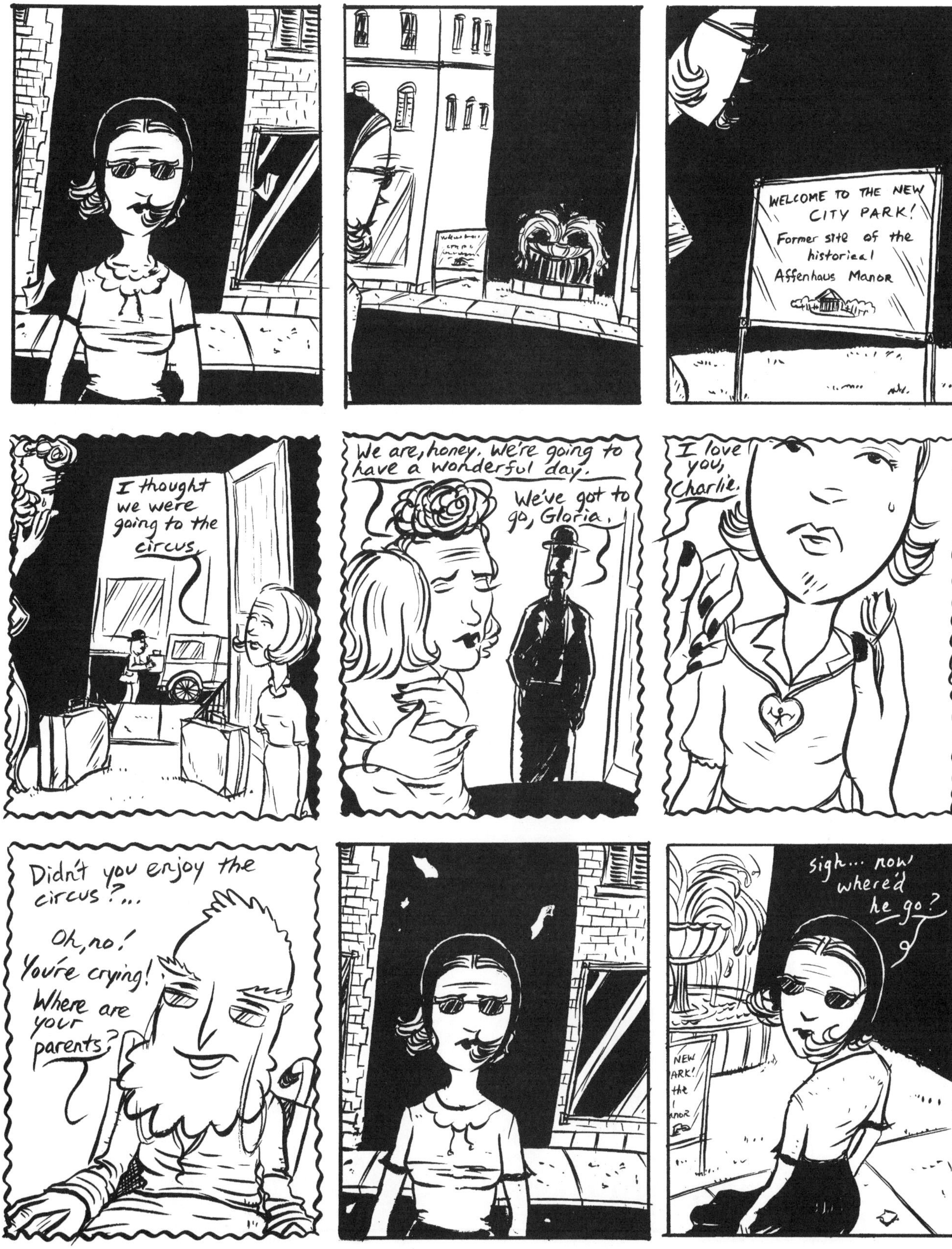

WELCOME TO THE NEW CITY PARK!
Former site of the historical Affenhaus Manor
I thought we were going to the circus.
We are, honey. We're going to have a wonderful day.
We've got to go, Gloria.
I love you, Charlie.
Didn't you enjoy the circus?...
Oh, no! You're crying! Where are your parents?
sigh... now where'd he go?

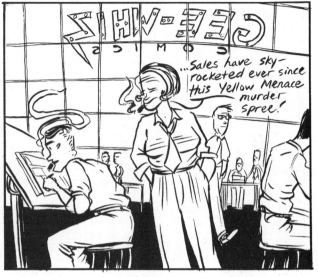

Kid?...
GEE-WHIZ COMICS
GEE-WHIZ COMICS
...Sales have sky-rocketed ever since this Yellow Menace murder spree!
That Lang fella gettin' bumped off was the best thing that's happened to us.
Jack Peril
This is bang-up stuff, King! Tell Eddie to keep up the swell dialogue and the Peril solo book is his!
Here's those two kids looking for jobs...
WHIP
Jobs? Those are even more scarce than good writing.
but... we'd kill to be in comics...
SHHH!

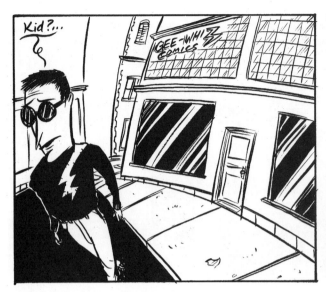

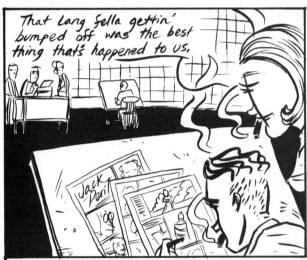

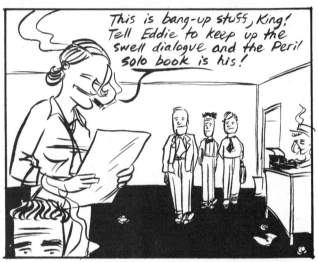

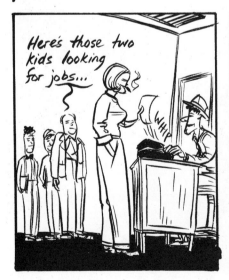

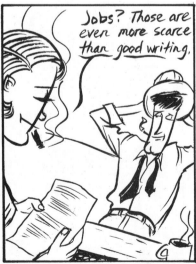

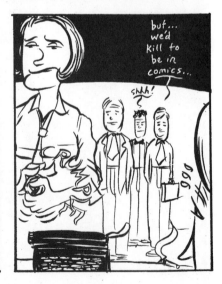

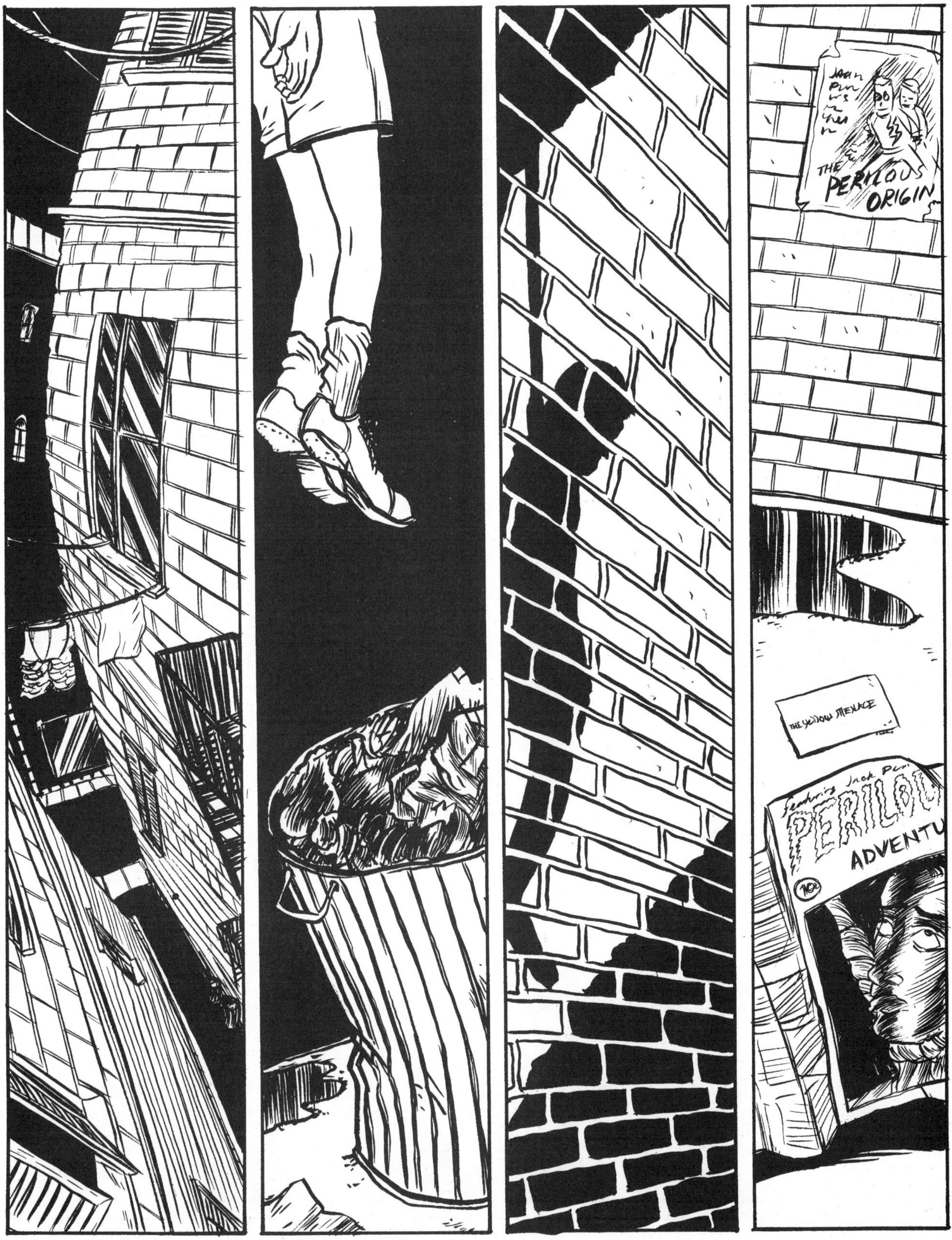
THE PERILOUS ORIGIN
THE YELLOW MENACE
featuring Jack
PERILOU
ADVENTU
10¢

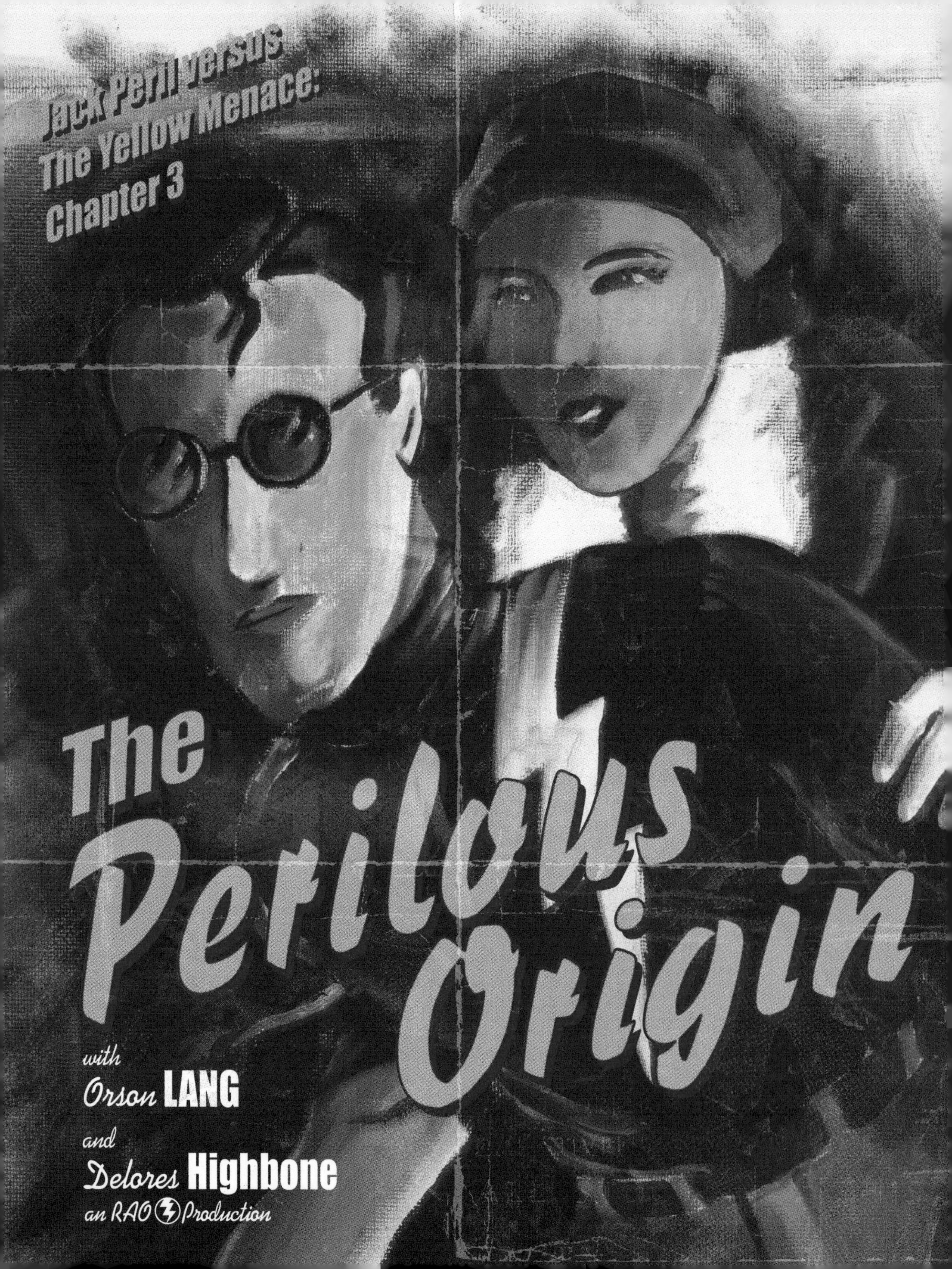
Jack Peril versus
The Yellow Menace:
Chapter 3
The
Perilous
Origin
with
Orson LANG
and
Delores Highbone
an RAO Production

Chapter Three

映画

Movies

SPLASH!

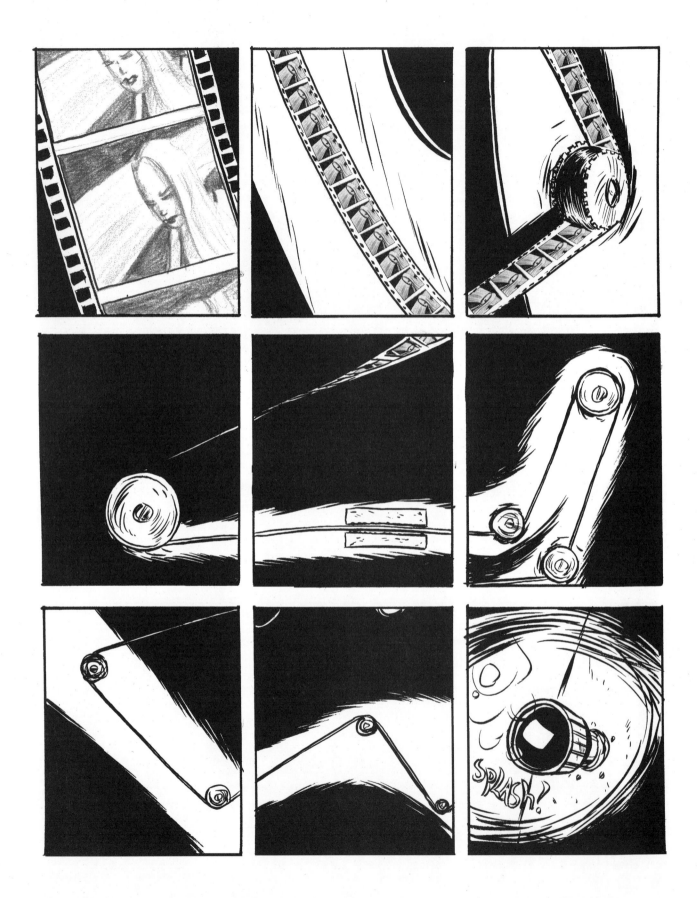

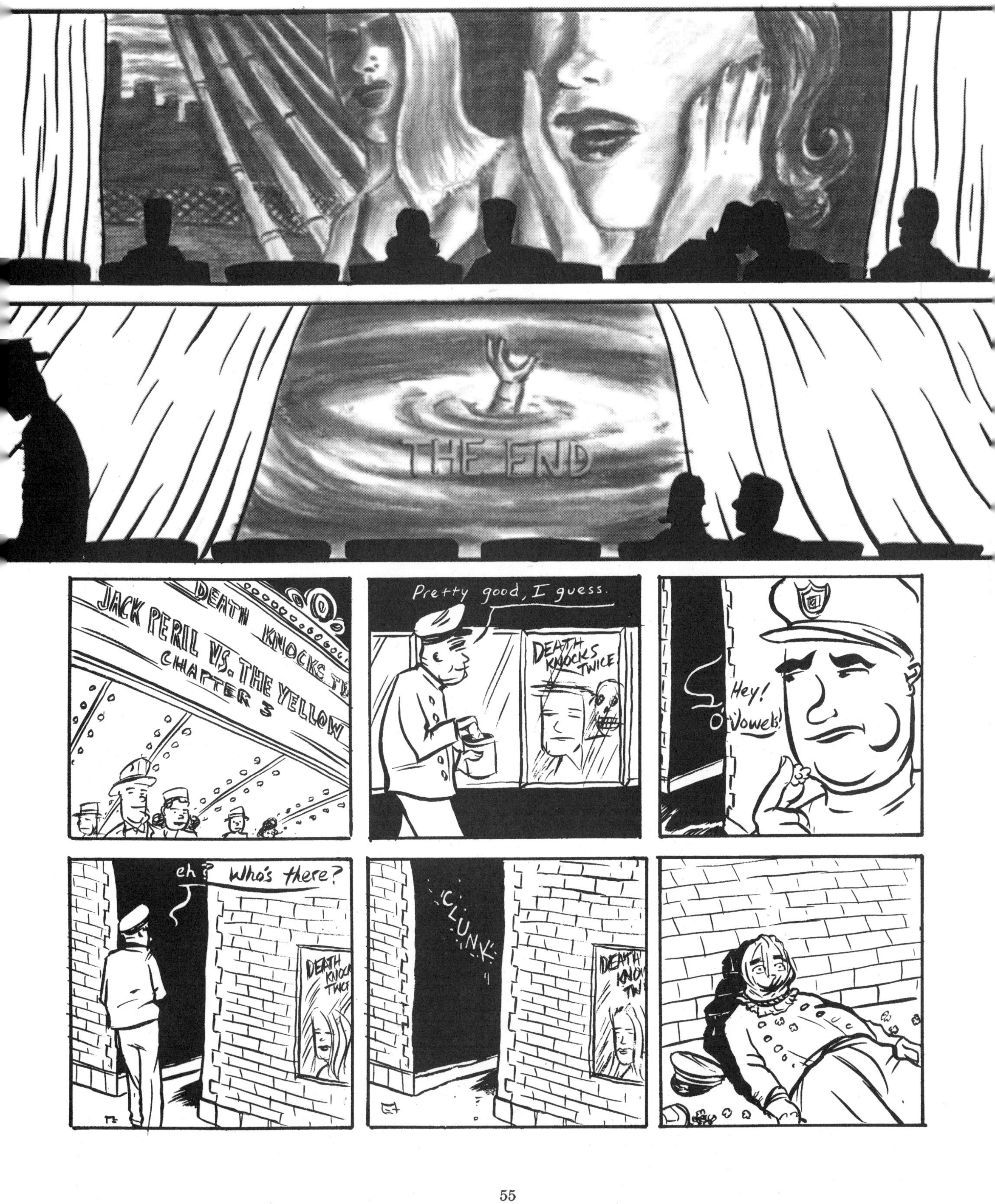
THE END
DEATH KNOCKS TW
JACK PERIL VS. THE YELLOW
CHAPTER 3
Pretty good, I guess.
DEATH KNOCKS TWICE
Hey! Jowels!
eh? Who's there?
DEATH KNOCK TWICE
CLUNK

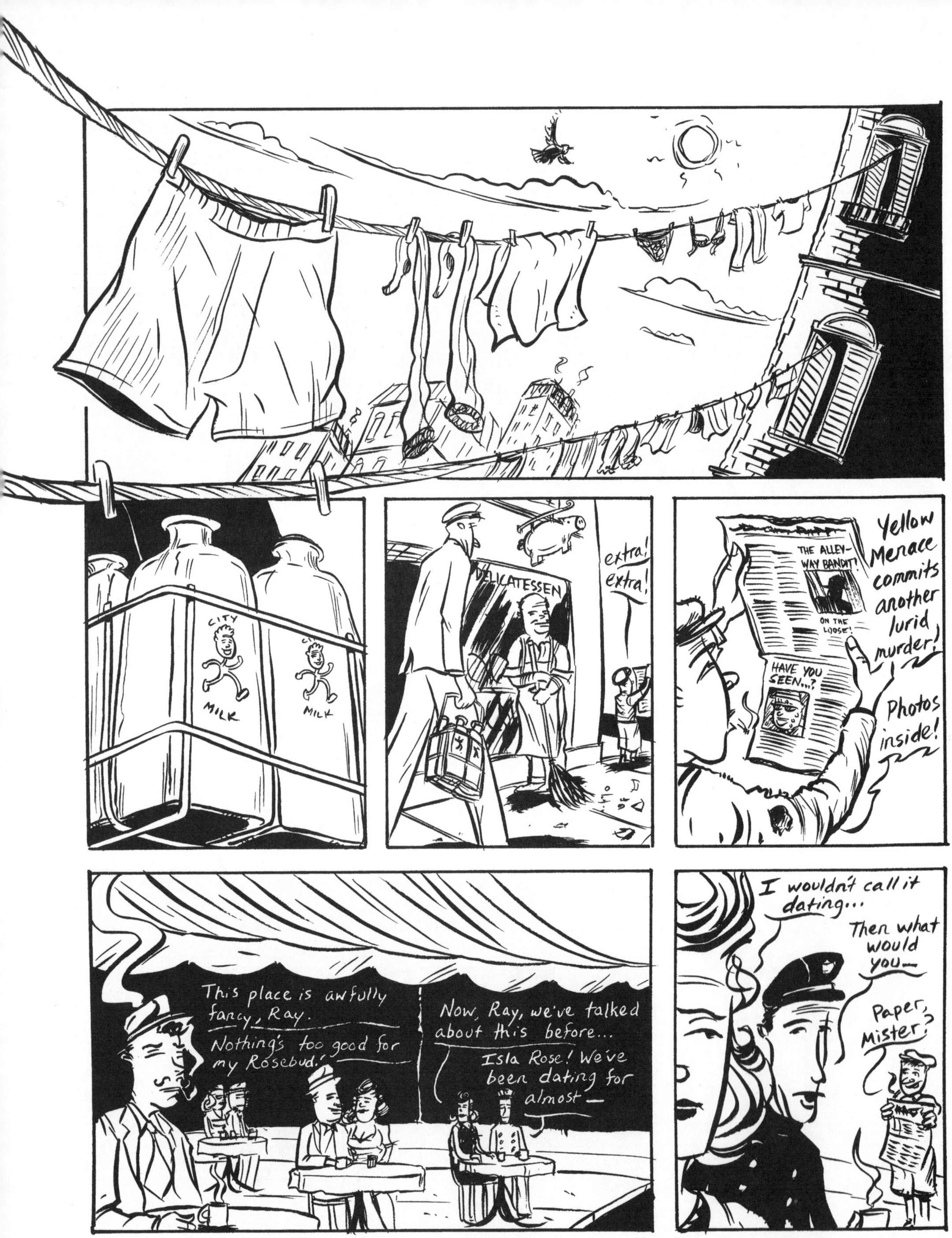
CITY MILK
CITY MILK
DELICATESSEN
extra! extra!
THE ALLEY-WAY BANDIT!
ON THE LOOSE!
HAVE YOU SEEN...?
Yellow Menace commits another lurid murder!
Photos inside!
This place is awfully fancy, Ray.
Nothing's too good for my Rosebud!
Now, Ray, we've talked about this before...
Isla Rose! We've been dating for almost —
I wouldn't call it dating...
Then what would you —
Paper, Mister?

I'll take one, kiddo.

Geez, another kid.

ALL THE NEWS

THE STANDARD

"COMIC KILLER" HANGS KID OUT TO DRY

Hmm...

This Lang fella looks familiar.

Well he IS the voice of Jack Peril.

CITY STILL MOURNING LANG DEATH

I didn't say he sounded familiar. I said he looks familiar.

Anyway, I don't listen to sham-hero silliness. The radio's for music.

You probably recognize him from The Chase.

LANG CONT.

Private Eye cheap. Call 349 that. ask for Mitri

Did he stay there?   No, his wife sang at The Cave.

His wife is Pidgeon Lang?

Yup.

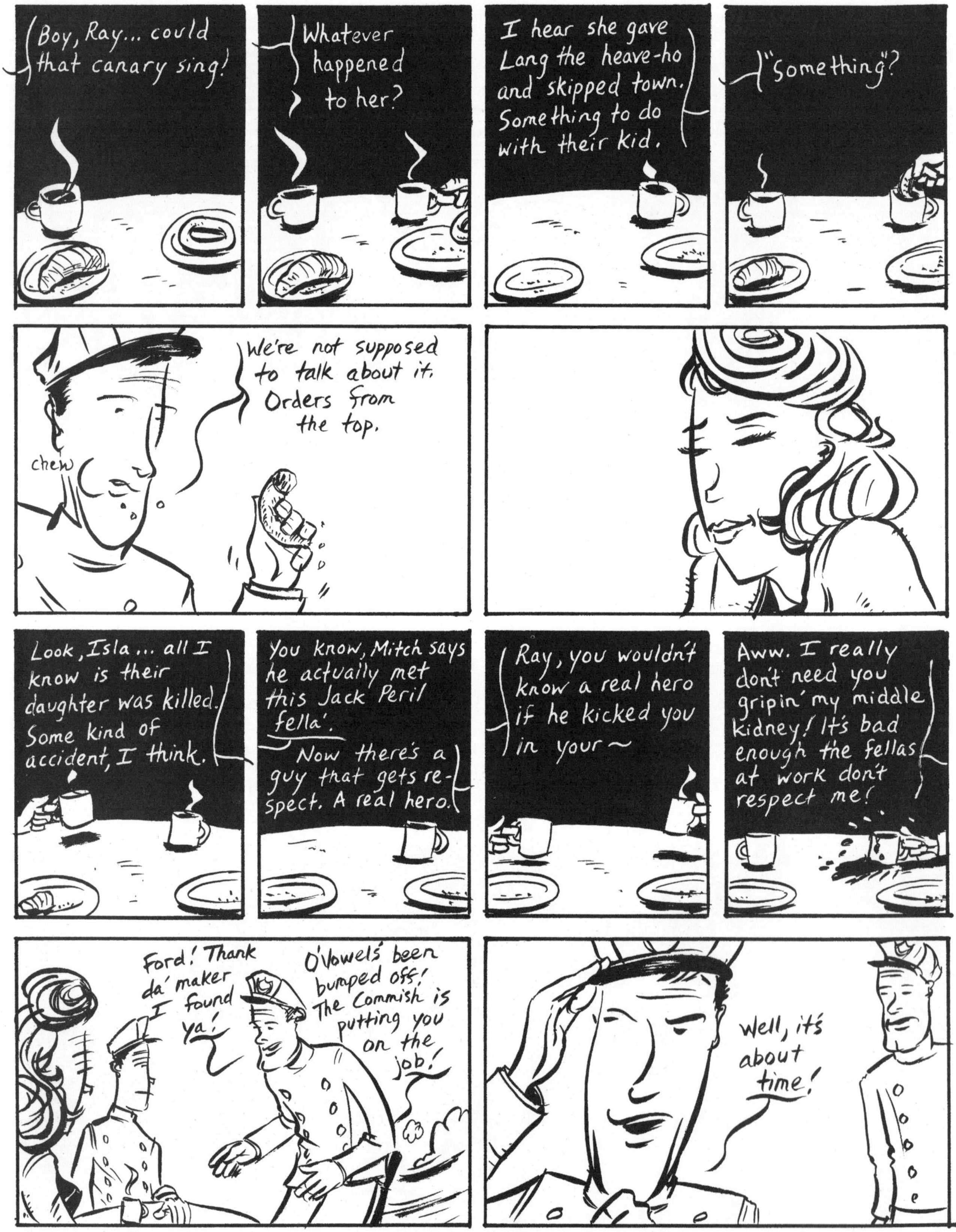
Boy, Ray... could that canary sing!
Whatever happened to her?
I hear she gave Lang the heave-ho and skipped town. Something to do with their kid.
"Something"?
We're not supposed to talk about it. Orders from the top.
chew
Look, Isla... all I know is their daughter was killed. Some kind of accident, I think.
You know, Mitch says he actually met this Jack Peril fella'.
Now there's a guy that gets respect. A real hero.
Ray, you wouldn't know a real hero if he kicked you in your~
Aww. I really don't need you gripin' my middle kidney! It's bad enough the fellas at work don't respect me!
Ford! Thank da' maker I found ya!
O'Vowels' been bumped off! The Commish is putting you on the job!
Well, it's about time!

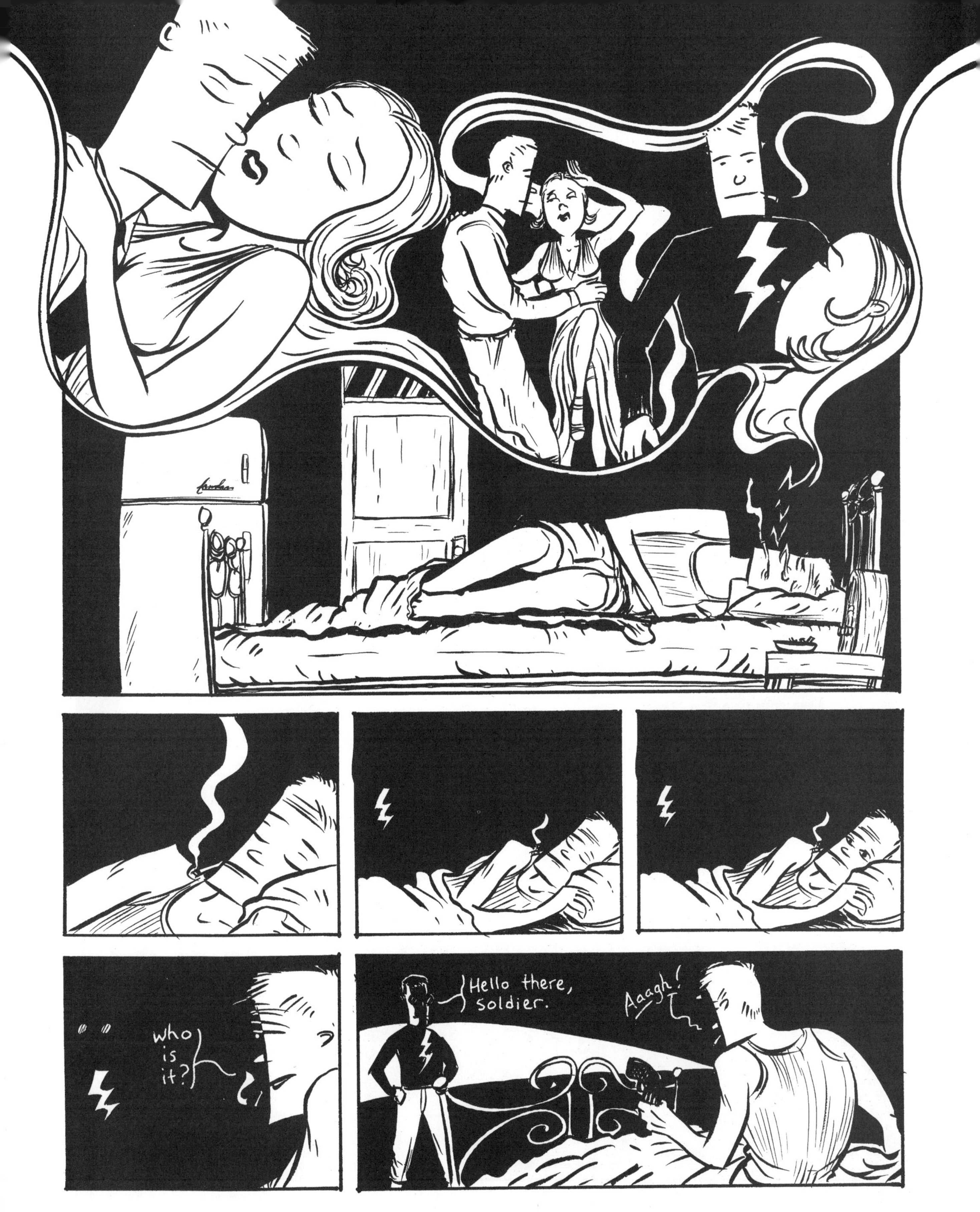
who is it?
Hello there, soldier.
Aaagh!

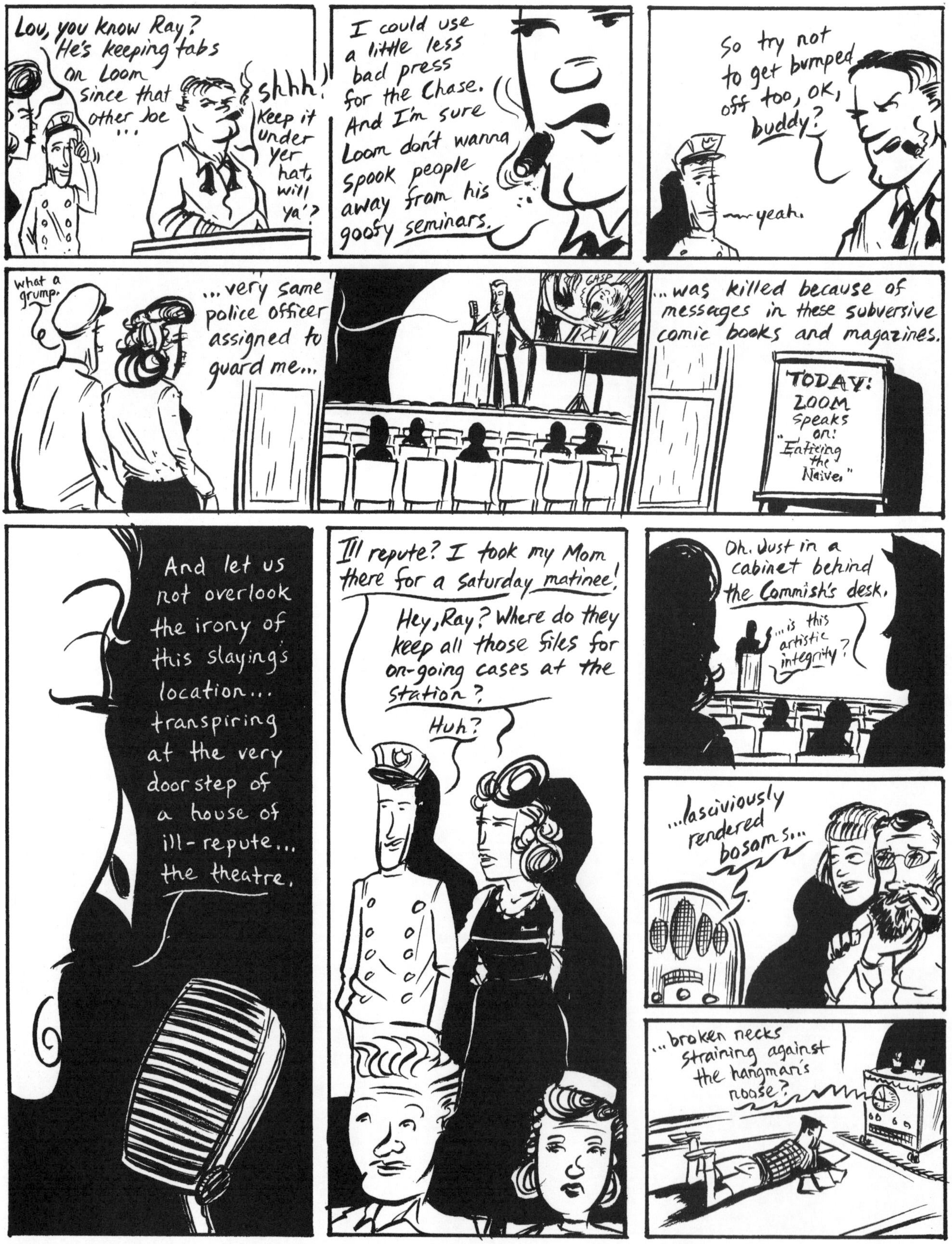
Lou, you know Ray? He's keeping tabs on Loom since that other Joe ...
Shhh! Keep it under yer hat, will ya'?
I could use a little less bad press for the Chase. And I'm sure Loom don't wanna spook people away from his goofy seminars.
So try not to get bumped off too, OK, buddy?
~~yeah.
what a grump.
...very same police officer assigned to guard me...
GASP
...was killed because of messages in these subversive comic books and magazines.
TODAY: ZOOM Speaks on: "Enticing the Naive."
And let us not overlook the irony of this slaying's location... transpiring at the very doorstep of a house of ill-repute... the theatre.
Ill repute? I took my Mom there for a saturday matinee!
Hey, Ray? Where do they keep all those files for on-going cases at the station?
Huh?
Oh. Just in a cabinet behind the Commish's desk.
...is this artistic integrity?
...lasciviously rendered bosoms...
...broken necks straining against the hangman's noose?

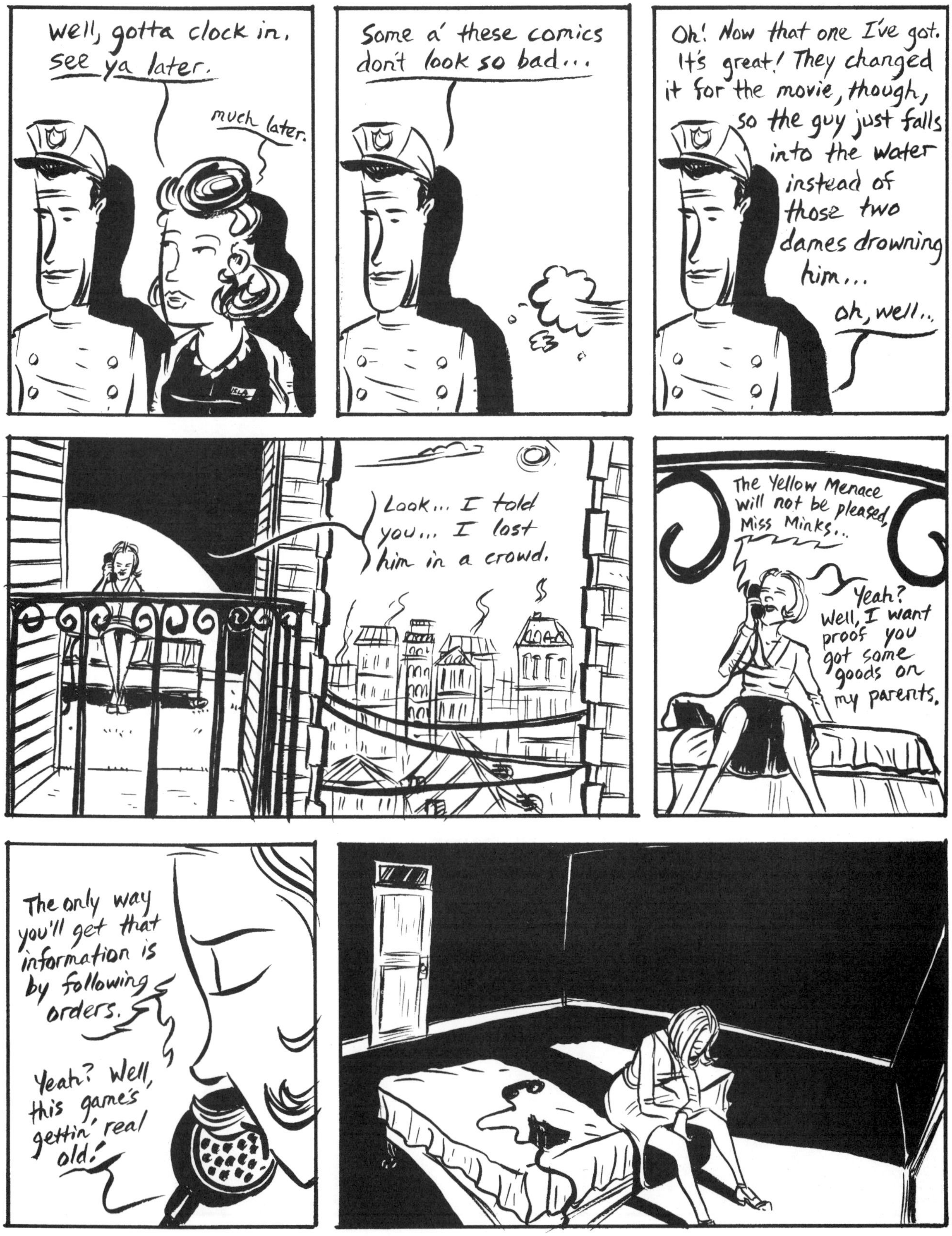
Well, gotta clock in. see ya later.
much later.
Some a' these comics don't look so bad...
Oh! Now that one I've got. It's great! They changed it for the movie, though, so the guy just falls into the water instead of those two dames drowning him...
oh, well...
Look... I told you... I lost him in a crowd.
The Yellow Menace will not be pleased, Miss Minks...
Yeah? Well, I want proof you got some goods on my parents.
The only way you'll get that information is by following orders.
Yeah? Well, this game's gettin' real old!

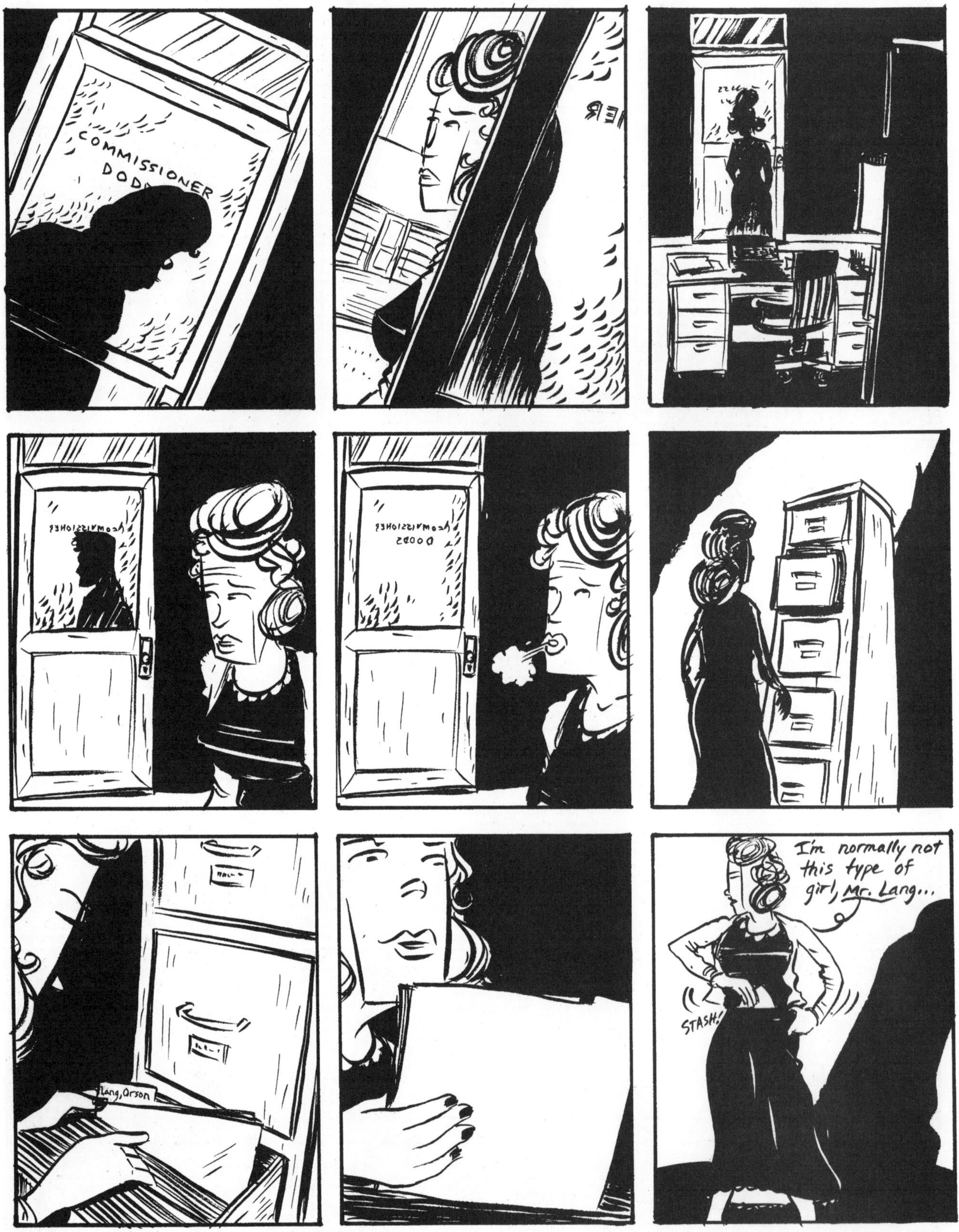
COMMISSIONER
Lang, Orson
I'm normally not this type of girl, Mr. Lang...
STASH!

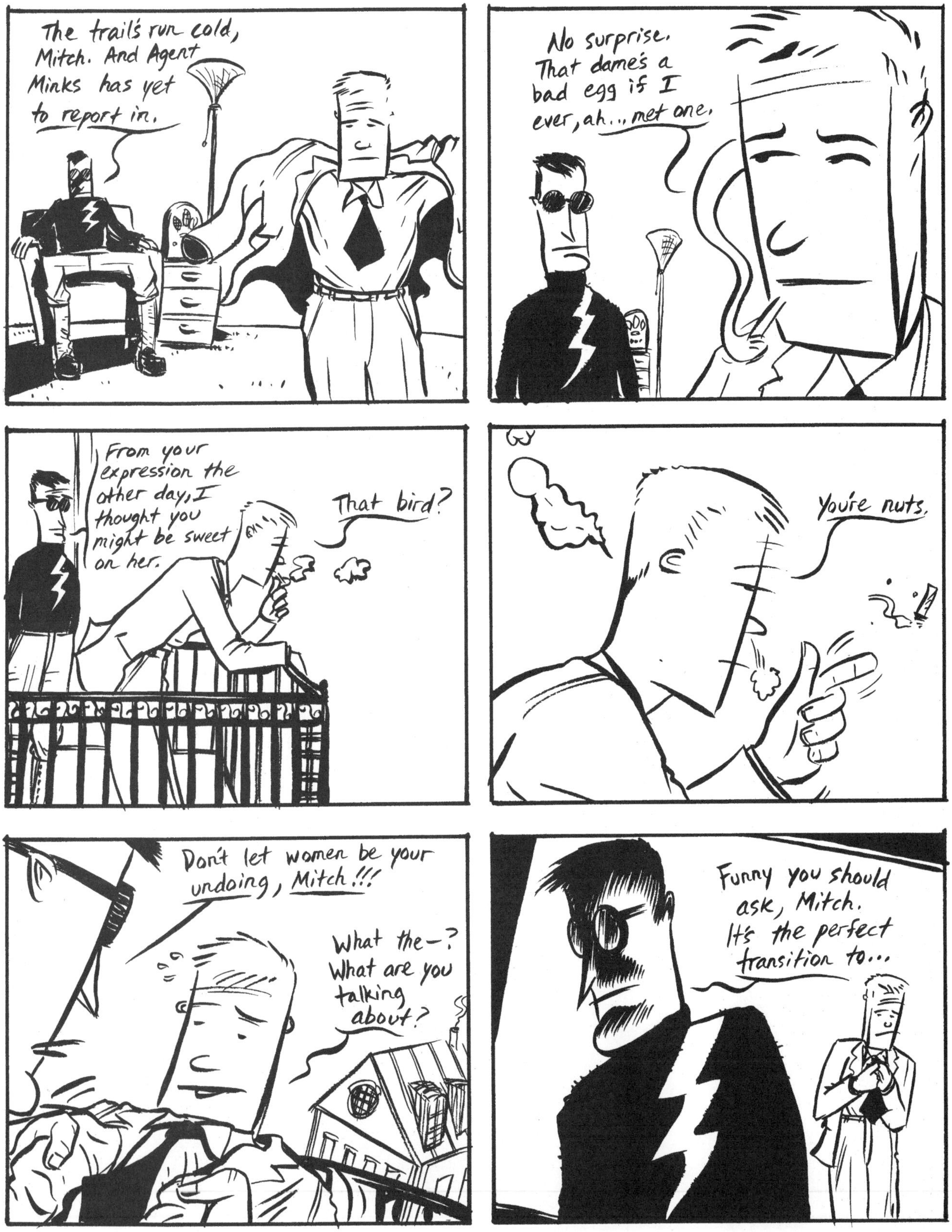
The trail's run cold, Mitch. And Agent Minks has yet to report in.
No surprise. That dame's a bad egg if I ever, ah... met one.
From your expression the other day, I thought you might be sweet on her.
That bird?
You're nuts.
Don't let women be your undoing, Mitch!!!
What the—? What are you talking about?
Funny you should ask, Mitch. It's the perfect transition to...

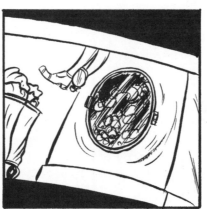

...dramatic pause...

Victim: Orson Lang, Jack Peril

The Adventures of Jack Peril
Chapter 3:
The Perilous Origin

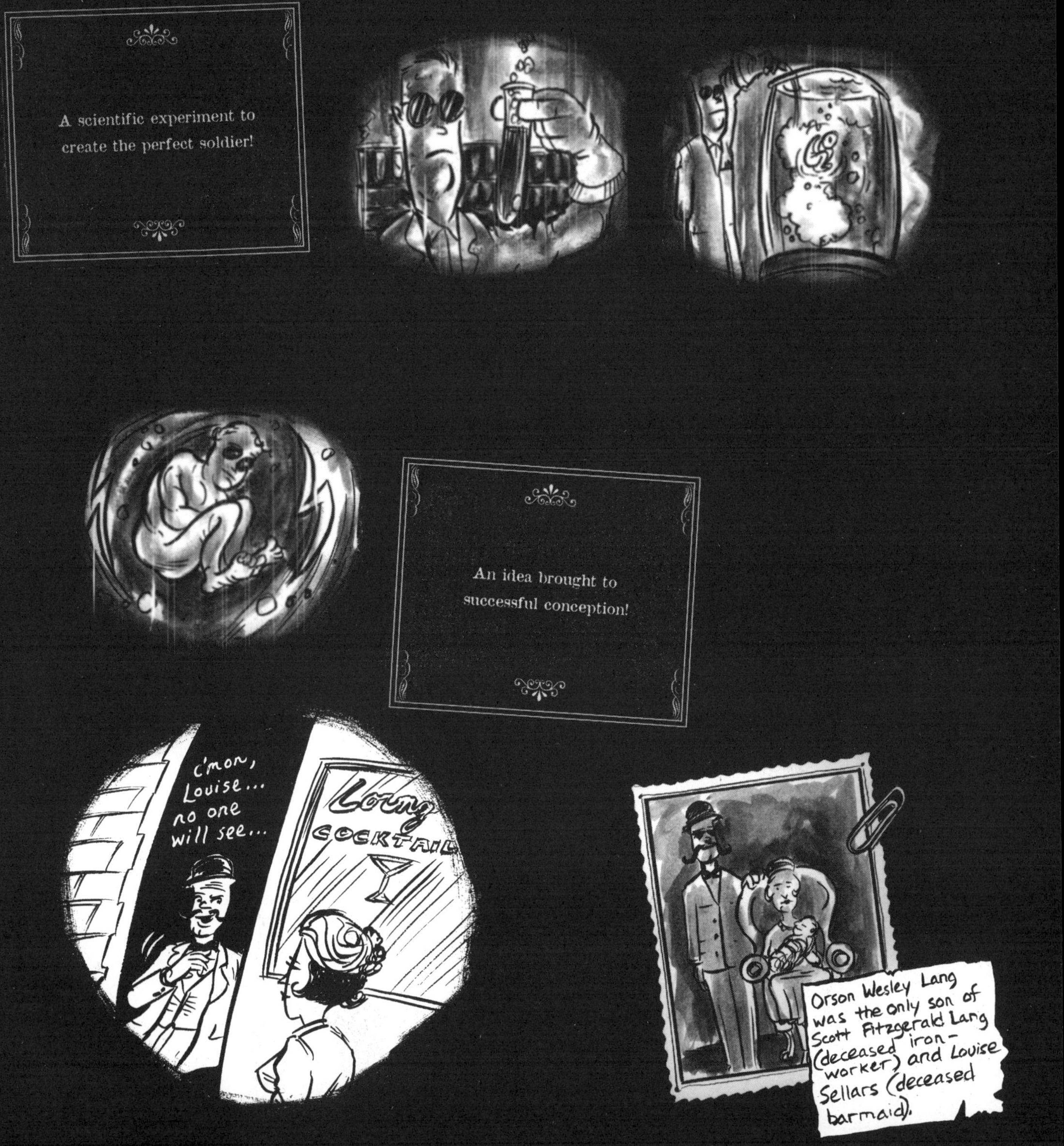
A scientific experiment to create the perfect soldier!
An idea brought to successful conception!
c'mon, Louise... no one will see...
Orson Wesley Lang was the only son of Scott Fitzgerald Lang (deceased iron-worker) and Louise Sellars (deceased barmaid).

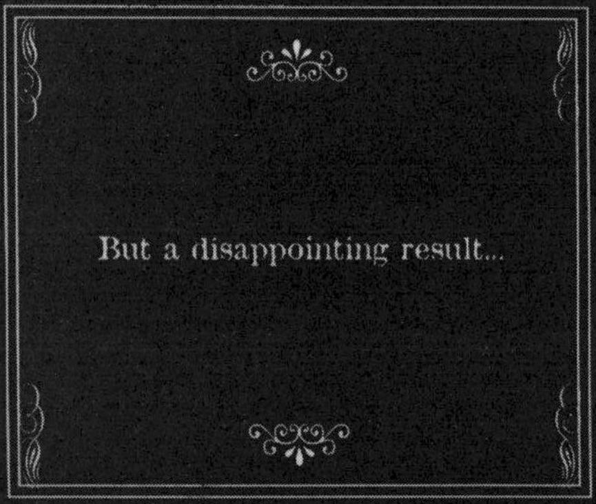
But a disappointing result...

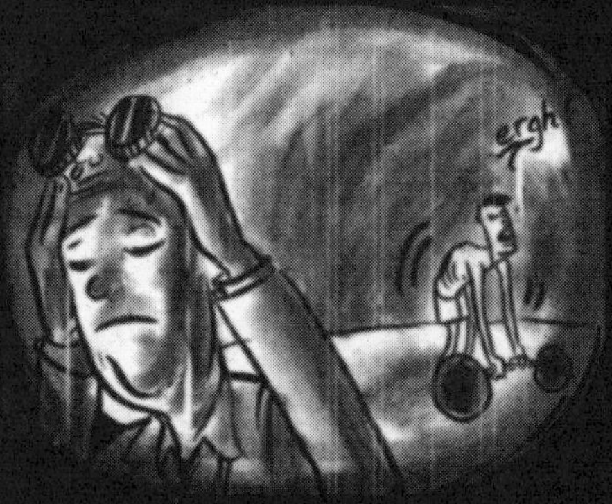
ergh!

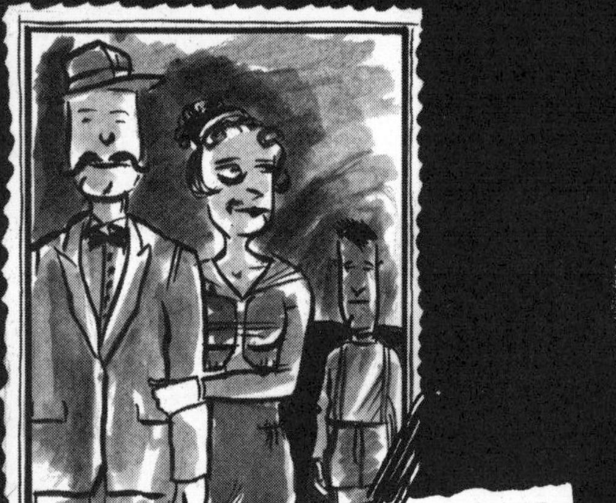
Not much is known about the early years of the family except for a few visits from the Dept. for domestic disturbance & an inquiry by the father to the hospital as to the paternity of the child. (Orson)

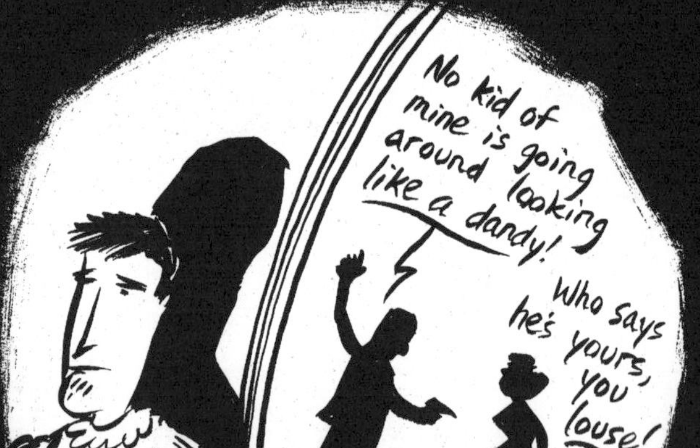
No kid of mine is going around looking like a dandy!
Who says he's yours, you louse!
HAMLET

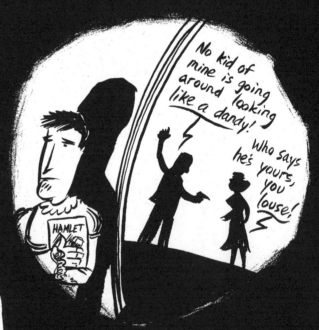

Young Jack, hurt and confused, runs away and falls in love!

Pidgeon Lily

singing jass nightly

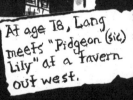

At age 18, Lang meets "Pidgeon (sic) Lily" at a tavern out west.

So... do you come here often?

well... I sing here every night...

Four months later, they are married.

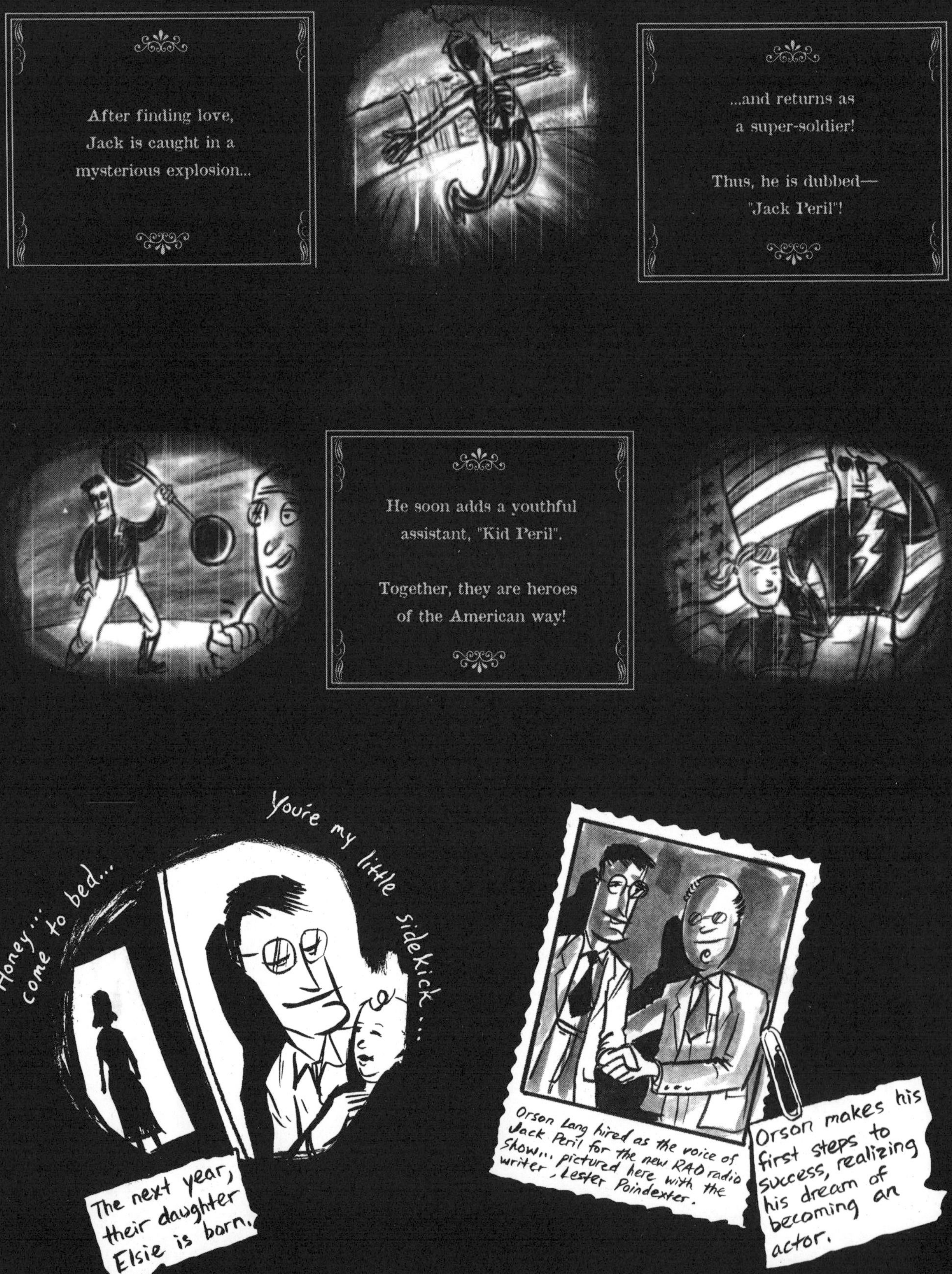
After finding love, Jack is caught in a mysterious explosion...
...and returns as a super-soldier!
Thus, he is dubbed— "Jack Peril"!
He soon adds a youthful assistant, "Kid Peril".
Together, they are heroes of the American way!
Honey... come to bed...
You're my little sidekick...
The next year, their daughter Elsie is born.
Orson Lang hired as the voice of Jack Peril for the new RAO radio show... pictured here with the writer, Lester Poindexter.
Orson makes his first steps to success, realizing his dream of becoming an actor.

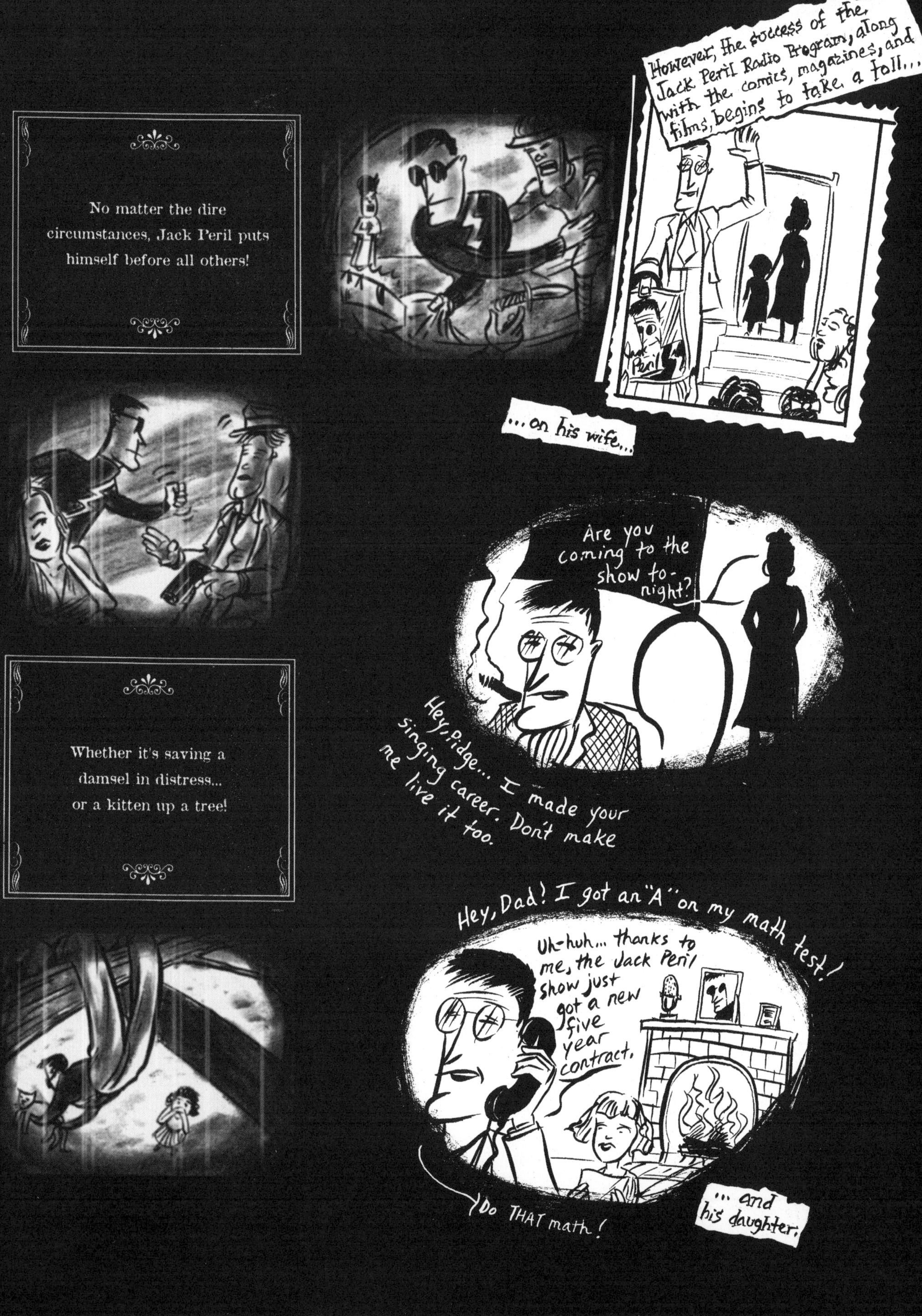

No matter the dire circumstances, Jack Peril puts himself before all others!
Whether it's saving a damsel in distress... or a kitten up a tree!
However, the success of the Jack Peril Radio Program, along with the comics, magazines, and films, begins to take a toll...
...on his wife...
Are you coming to the show to-night?
Hey, Pidge... I made your singing career. Don't make me live it too.
Hey, Dad! I got an "A" on my math test!
Uh-huh... thanks to me, the Jack Peril show just got a new five year contract.
Do THAT math!
...and his daughter.

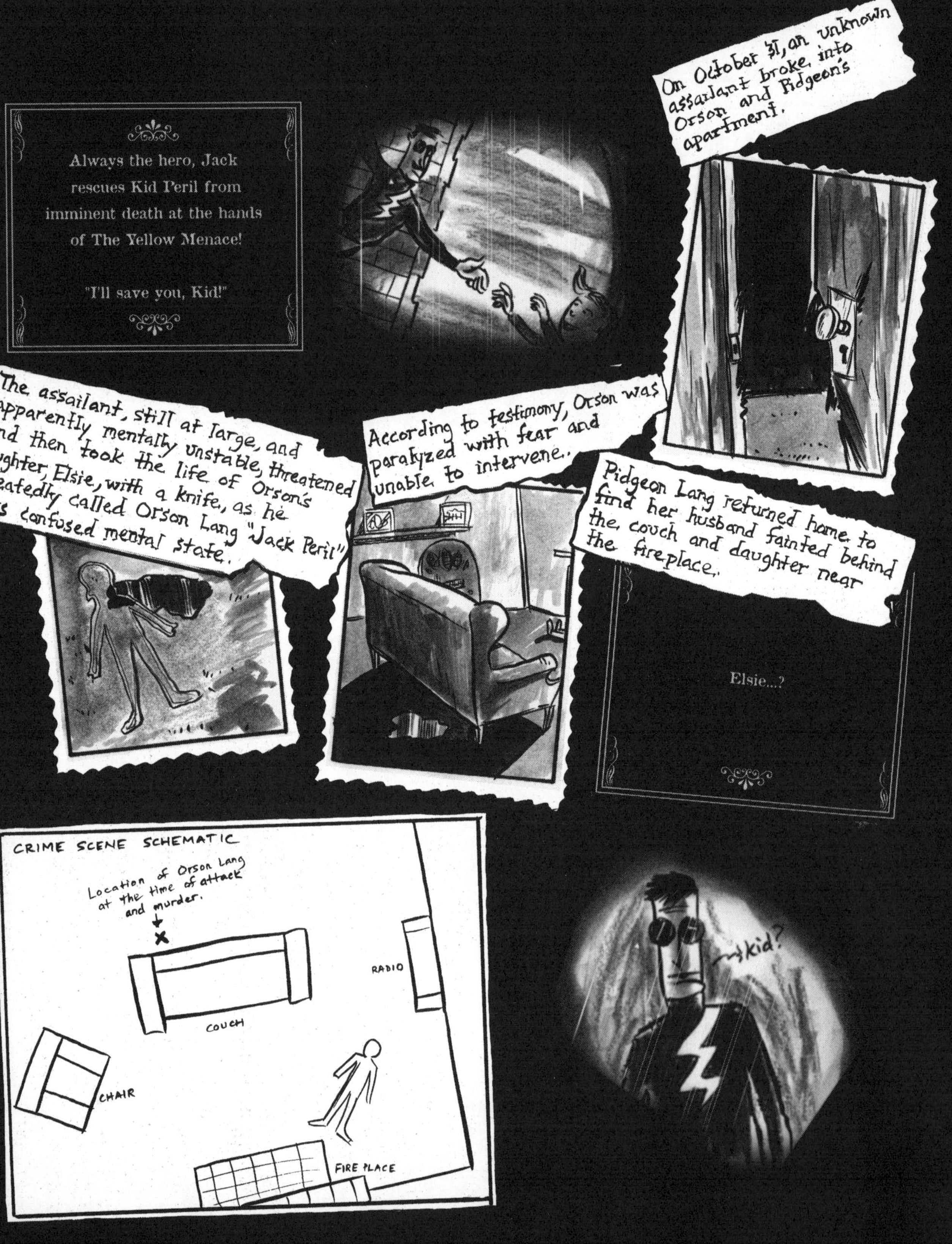
Always the hero, Jack rescues Kid Peril from imminent death at the hands of The Yellow Menace!
"I'll save you, Kid!"
On October 31, an unknown assailant broke into Orson and Pidgeon's apartment.
The assailant, still at large, and apparently mentally unstable, threatened and then took the life of Orson's daughter, Elsie, with a knife, as he repeatedly called Orson Lang "Jack Peril" in his confused mental state.
According to testimony, Orson was paralyzed with fear and unable to intervene.
Pidgeon Lang returned home to find her husband fainted behind the couch and daughter near the fireplace.
Elsie...?
CRIME SCENE SCHEMATIC
Location of Orson Lang at the time of attack and murder.
RADIO
COUCH
CHAIR
FIRE PLACE
...kid?

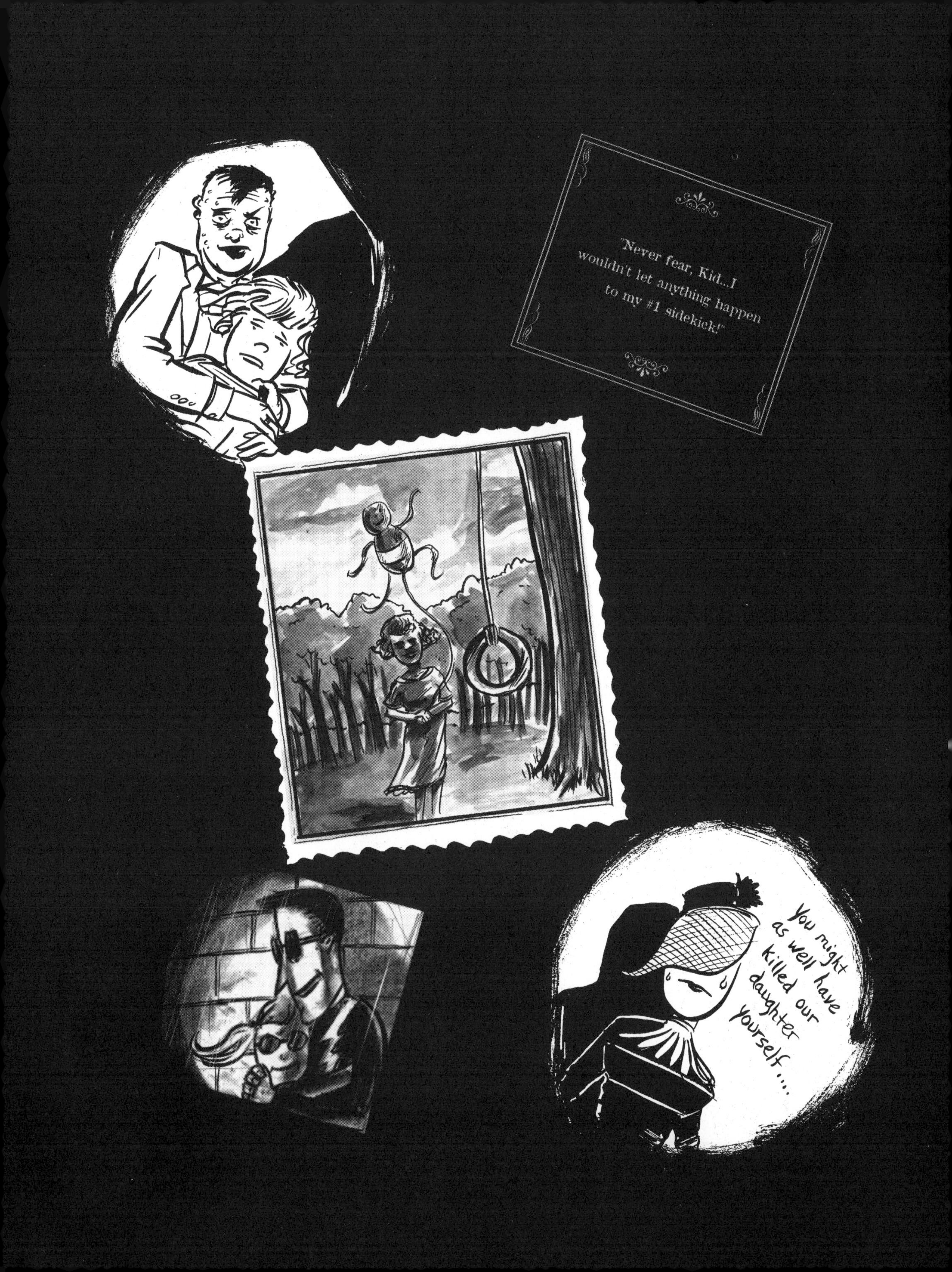
"Never fear, Kid...I wouldn't let anything happen to my #1 sidekick!"
You might as well have killed our daughter yourself....

But then Jack's gypsy love betrays him and becomes the villainess, Madame Cauchemar!

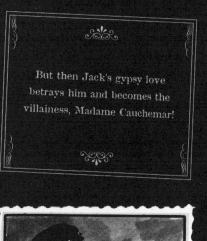

Orson Long - one week before divorce proceedings.

No doubt due in part to the murder of their daughter, Pidgeon (sic) files for divorce, citing... cowardice.

However, Jack Peril soon recovers from his heartbreak as parades in his honor become a common practice!

But what is the secret connection between The Yellow Menace and Jack Peril's origin?

Orson's drinking and work performance continue to get worse...

until his death along with 47 others...

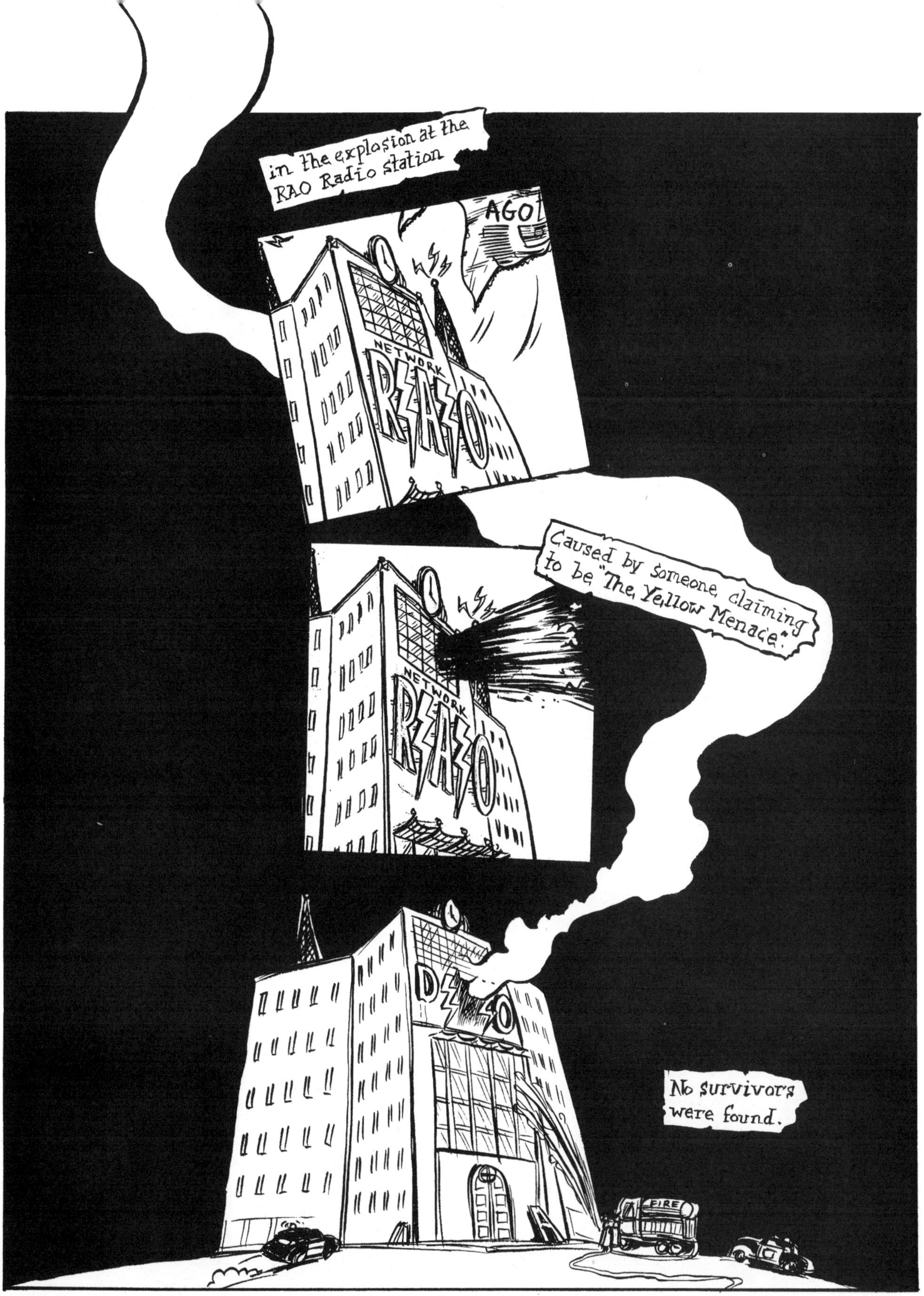
in the explosion at the RAO Radio station
AGO
NETWORK
RAO
Caused by someone claiming to be "The Yellow Menace".
NETWORK
RAO
No survivors were found.
FIRE

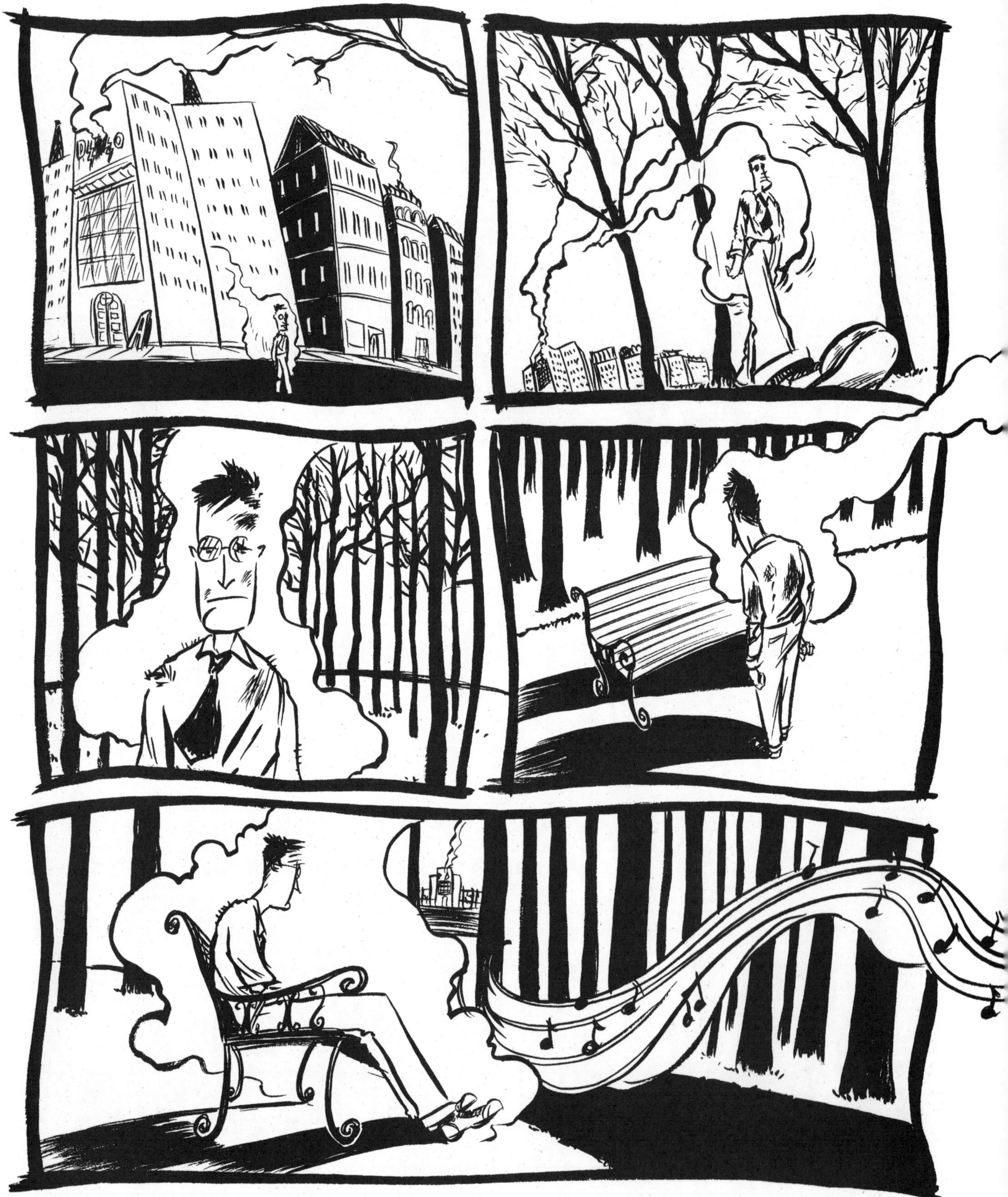

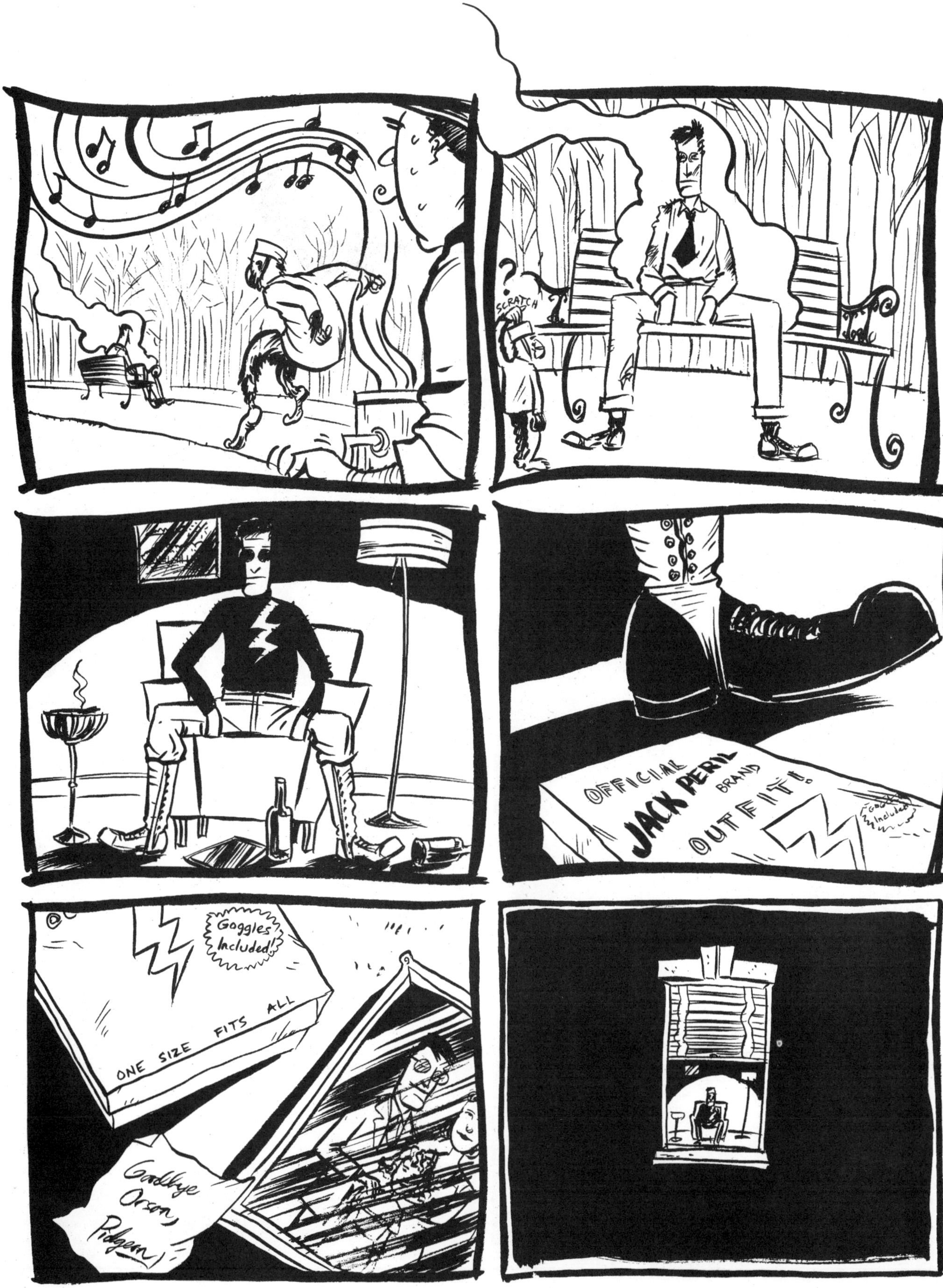
?
SCRATCH
OFFICIAL JACK PERIL BRAND OUTFIT!
Goggles Included!
ONE SIZE FITS ALL
Goodbye Orson,
Pidgeon

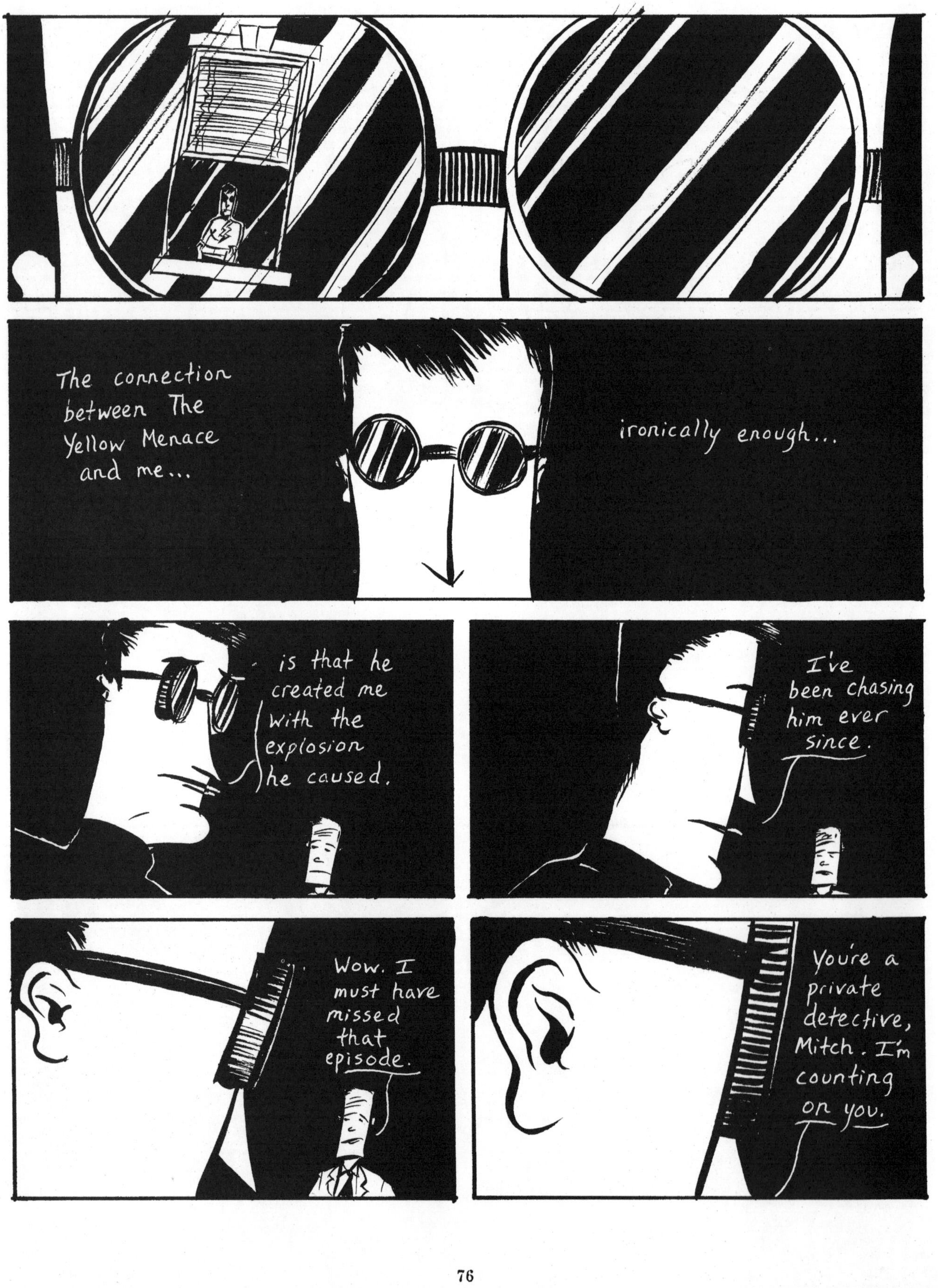
The connection between The Yellow Menace and me...
ironically enough...
is that he created me with the explosion he caused.
I've been chasing him ever since.
Wow. I must have missed that episode.
You're a private detective, Mitch. I'm counting on you.

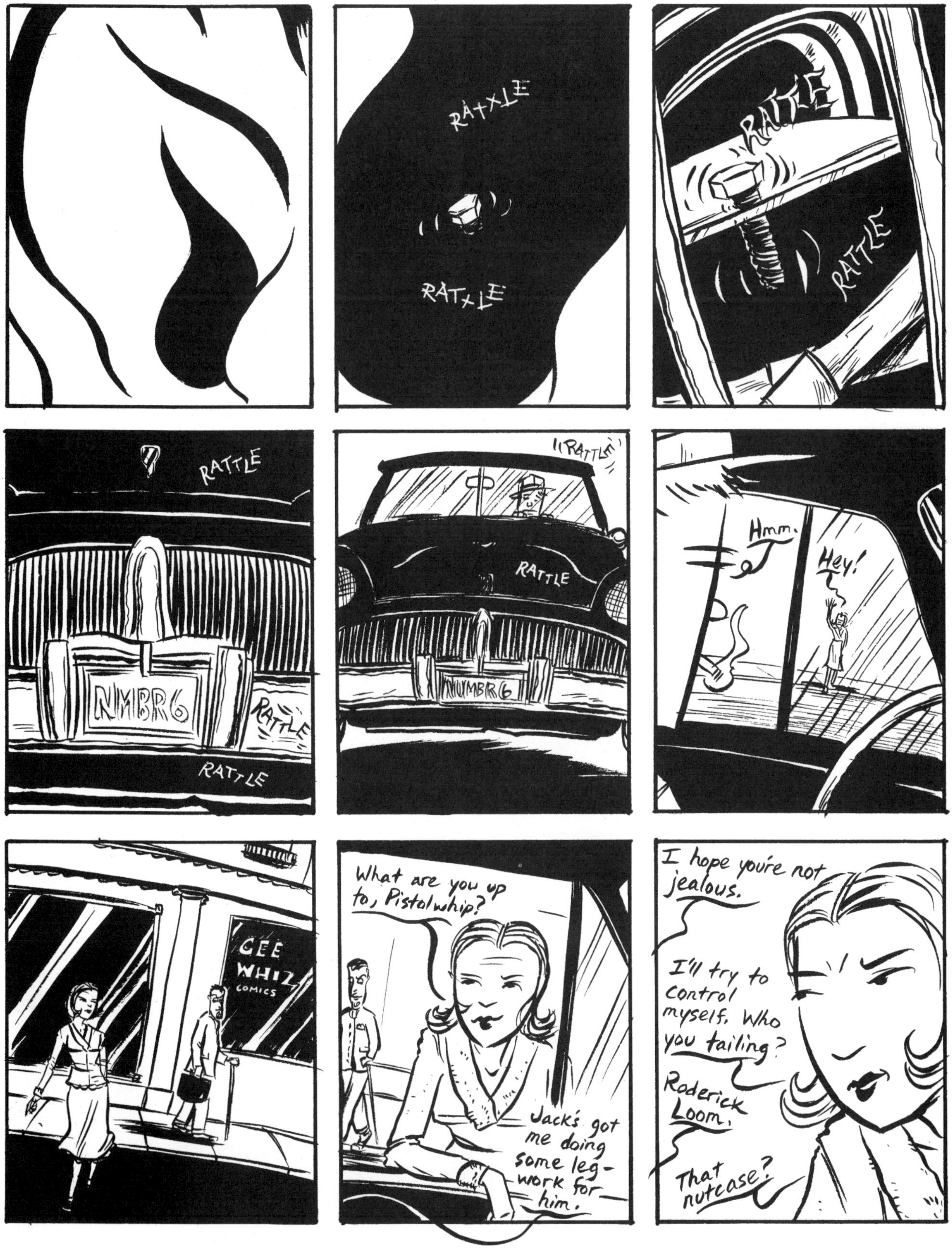

RATTLE
RATTLE
RATTLE
RATTLE
RATTLE
NMBR6
RATTLE
RATTLE
RATTLE
RATTLE
NMBR6
Hmm.
Hey!
GEE WHIZ COMICS
What are you up to, Pistolwhip?
Jack's got me doing some leg-work for him.
I hope you're not jealous.
I'll try to control myself. Who you tailing?
Roderick Loom.
That nutcase?

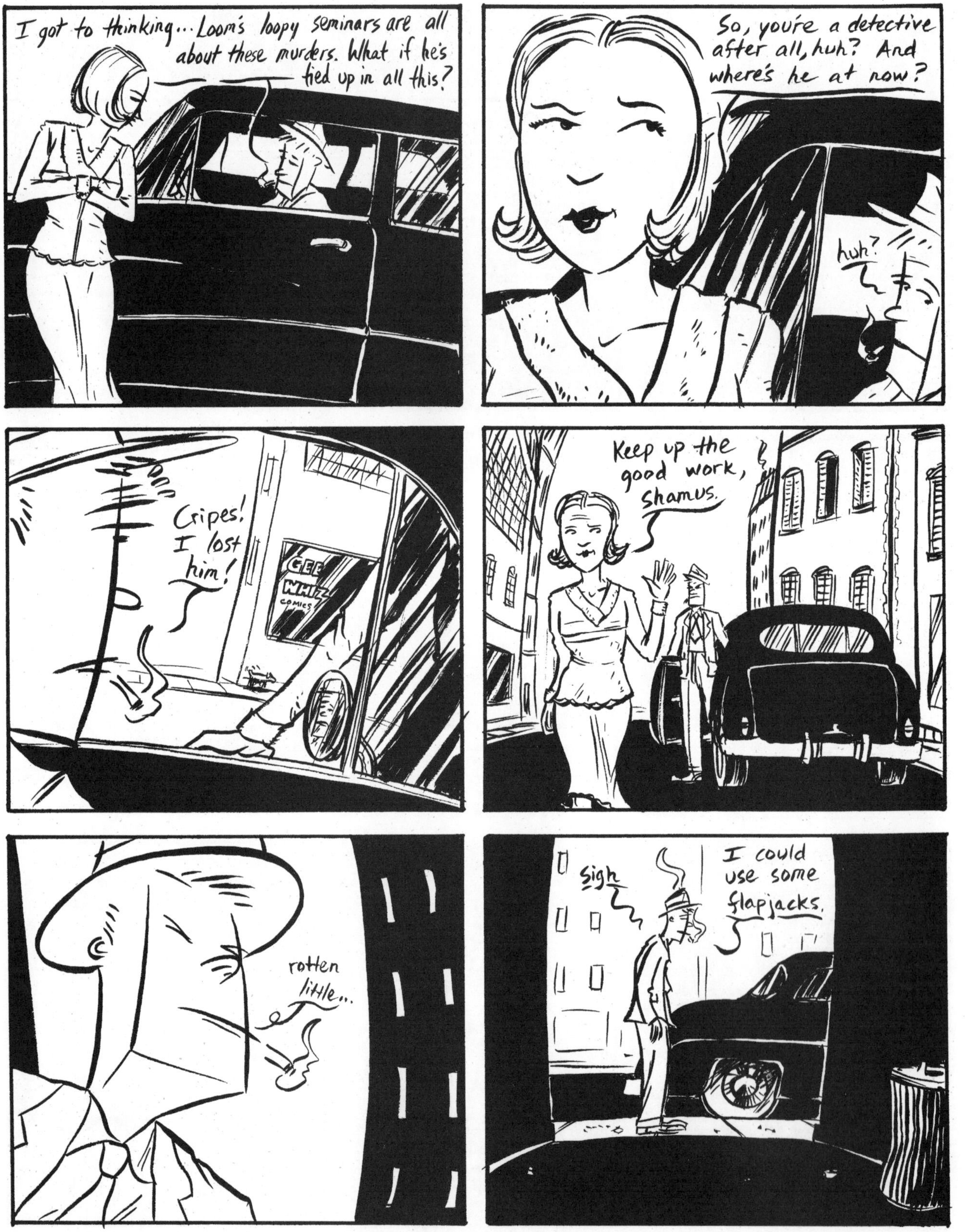
I got to thinking... Loom's loopy seminars are all about these murders. What if he's tied up in all this?
So, you're a detective after all, huh? And where's he at now?
huh?
Cripes! I lost him!
GEE WHIZ COMICS
Keep up the good work, shamus.
rotten little...
Sigh
I could use some flapjacks.

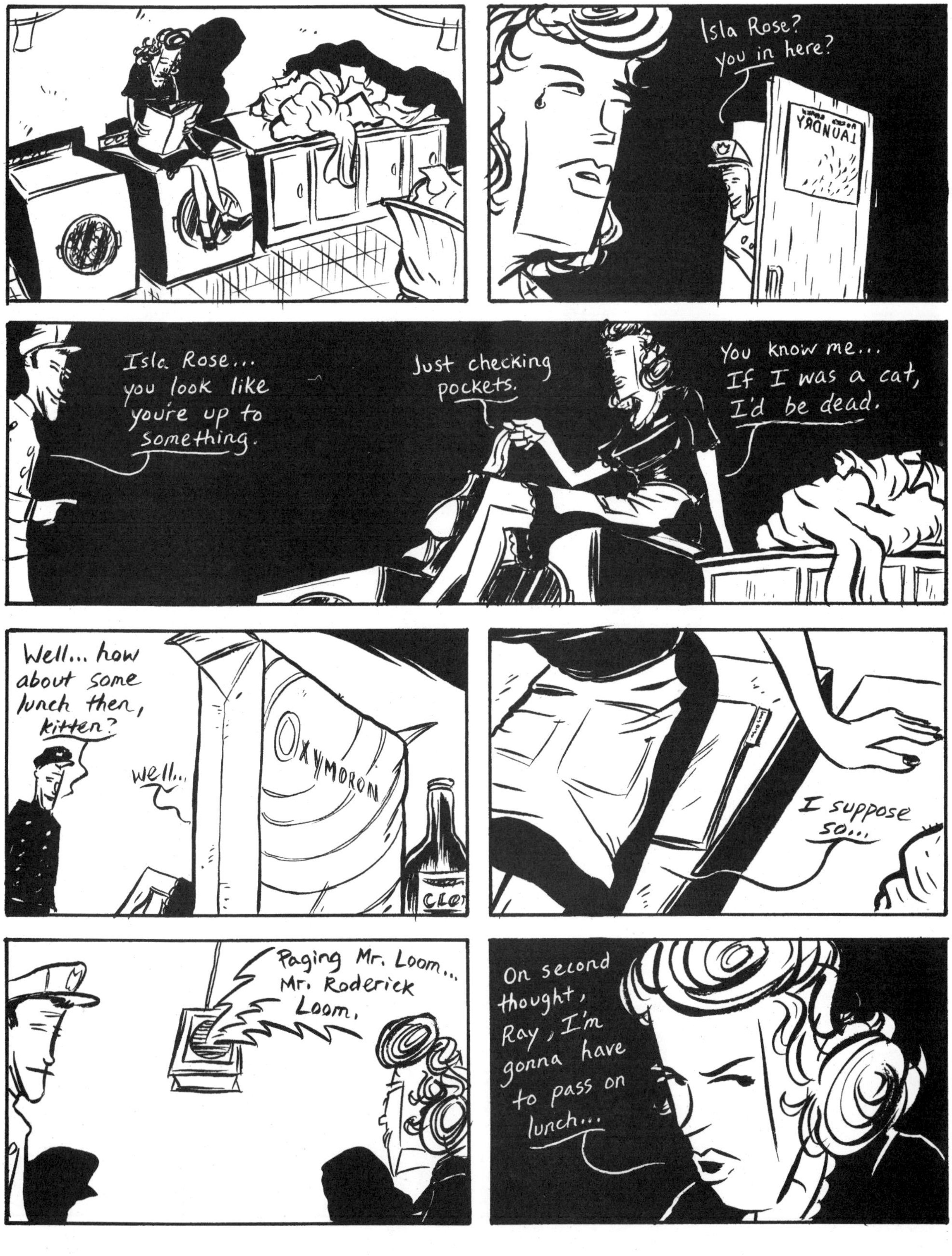

LAUNDRY
Isla Rose? you in here?
Isla Rose... you look like you're up to something.
Just checking pockets.
You know me... If I was a cat, I'd be dead.
Well... how about some lunch then, kitten?
well...
OXYMORON
I suppose so...
Paging Mr. Loom... Mr. Roderick Loom.
On second thought, Ray, I'm gonna have to pass on lunch...

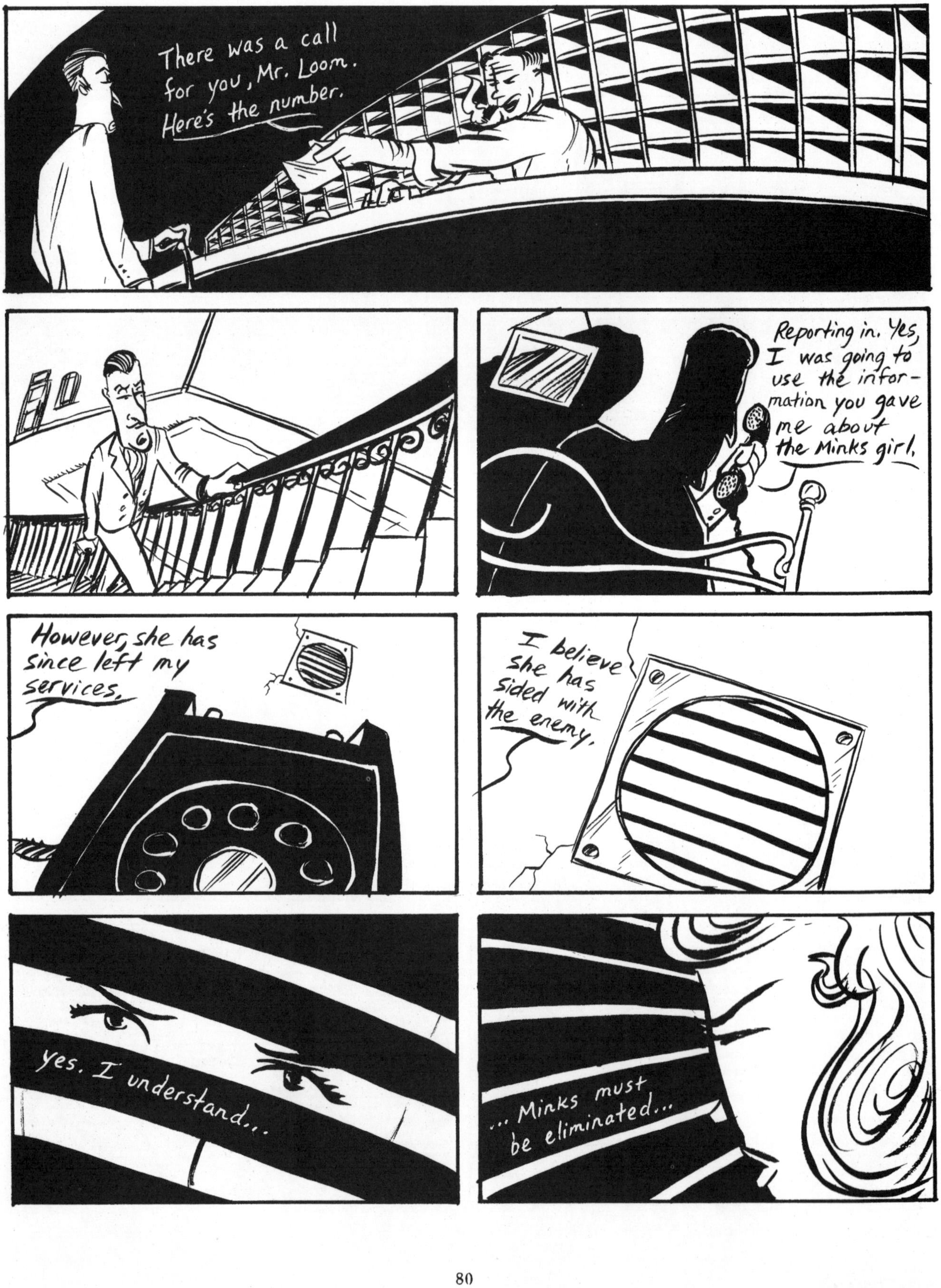
There was a call for you, Mr. Loom. Here's the number.
Reporting in. Yes, I was going to use the information you gave me about the Minks girl.
However, she has since left my services.
I believe she has sided with the enemy.
yes. I understand...
...Minks must be eliminated...

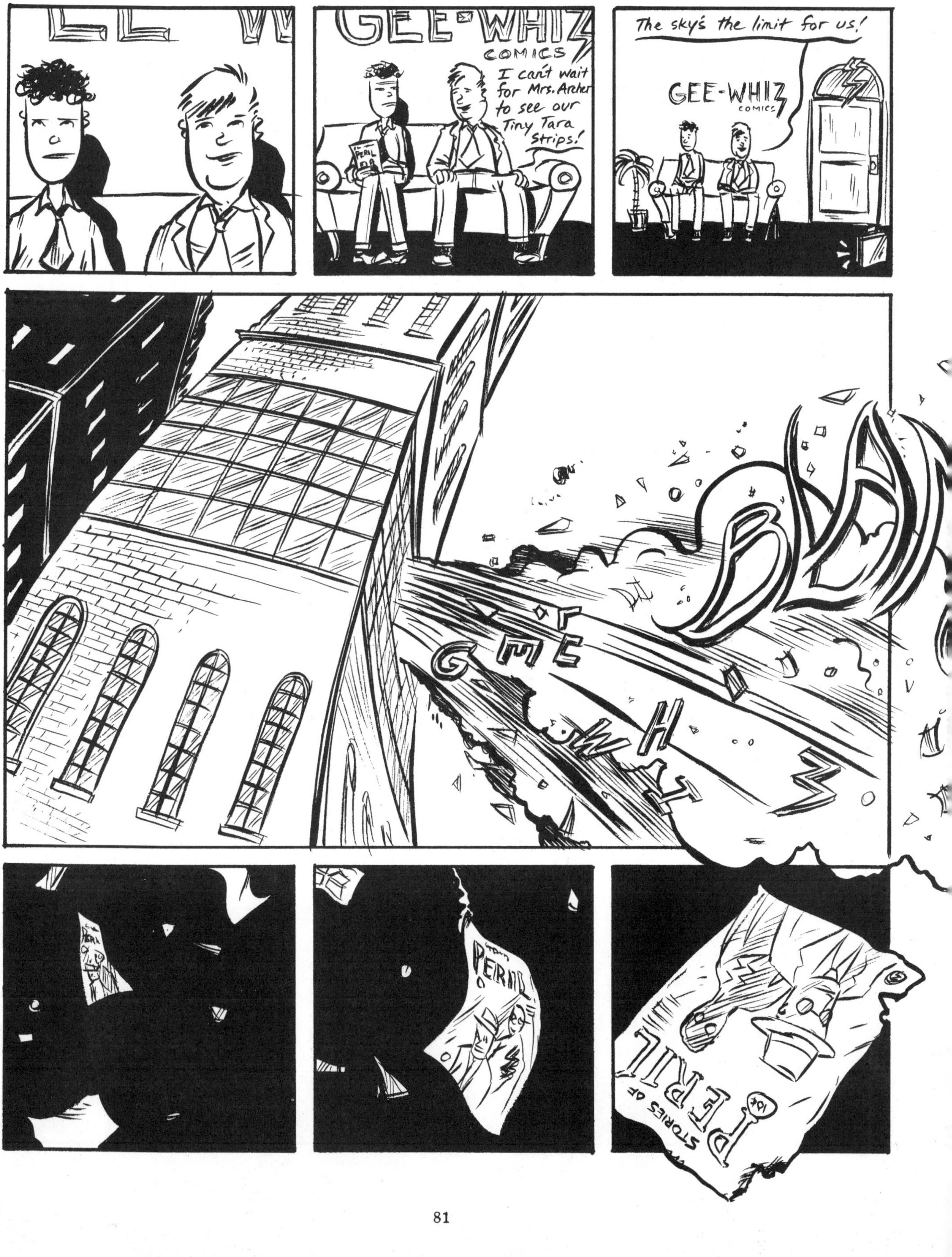

GEE-WHIZ COMICS
I can't wait for Mrs. Archer to see our Tiny Tara Strips!
The sky's the limit for us!
GEE-WHIZ COMICS
BLAM
PERIL
PERIL
STORIES OF PERIL 10¢

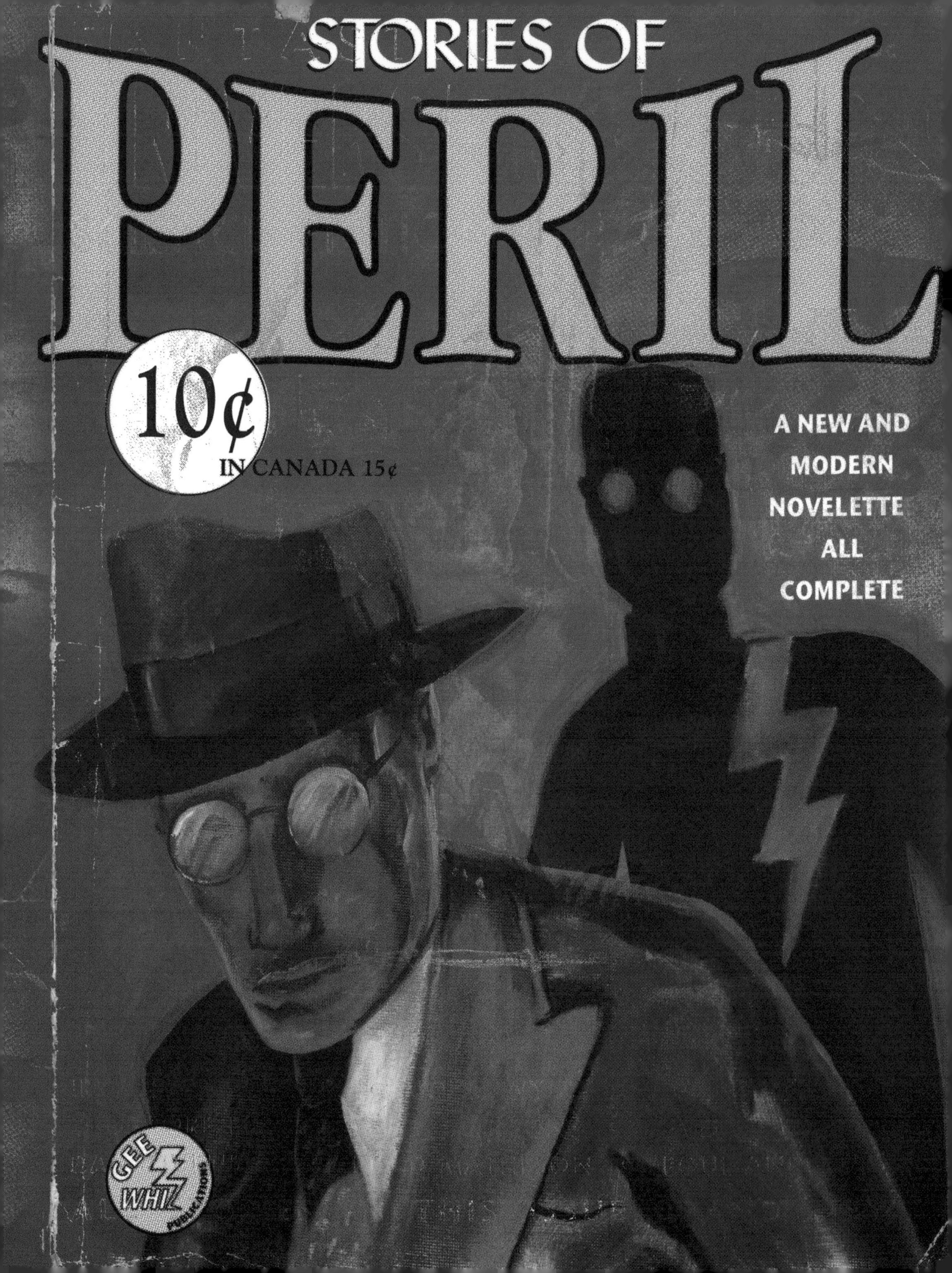

STORIES OF
PERIL
10¢
IN CANADA 15¢
A NEW AND
MODERN
NOVELETTE
ALL
COMPLETE
GEE
WHIZ
PUBLICATIONS

Chapter Four

赤本

Pulps

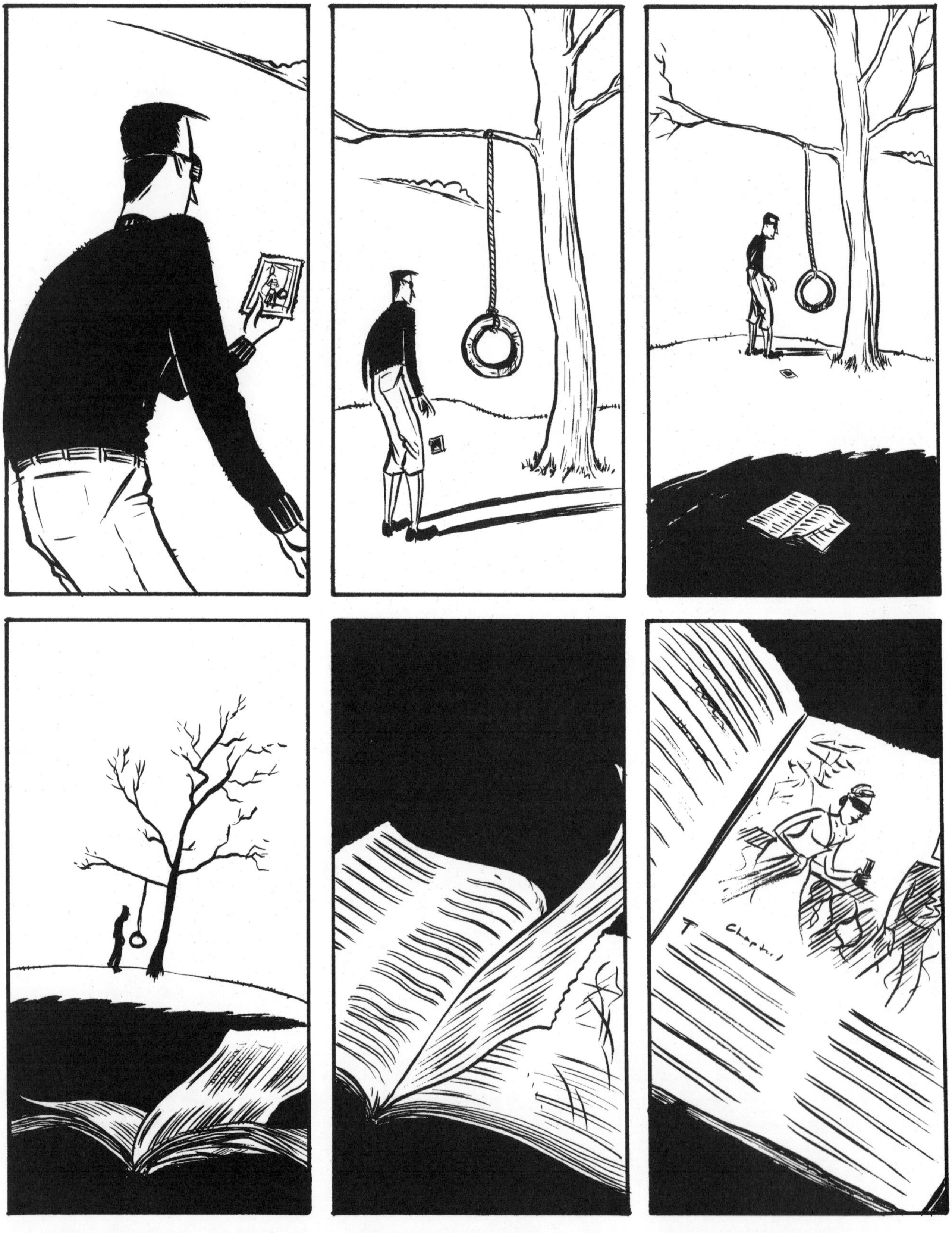
Chapter 1

— hours earlier he had been boot-deep in battle with the seductive Madame Cauchemar...

CHAPTER I

Perilous Slumber

The lightning strike was but a flash of memory quickly followed by a thunderous warning not to ignore its promised secrets. The sound of the storm's child-like tantrum pulled Jack Peril from the clutching grasp of a nightmare, waking him with a start. Marble-sized raindrops showered the window like bullets in an insane melody of violent taps. Jack's entire body, including his white lightning-bolt clad black shirt, was soaked to the bone—his dark goggles still firmly in place over his eyes. He was in his own bed, of that much he was certain. But how had he gotten there? Those memories were as vague and distant as the hazy dreadful dream the raging storm had just rescued him from.

He knew hours earlier he had been boot-deep in battle with the venomous, yet seductive, Madame Cauchemar. She was on the verge of poisoning the city's reservoir with a mind-altering toxin when Jack found her, having successfully solved her final self-incriminating clue. He had prayed she wasn't the responsible culprit, because against all better judgment...he was in love with her.

She had stood there before him in her inky-black dress, the crushed velvet a wet sheet clinging to the sinful contours of her body, the vial of hallucinogen precariously poised over the water. A single wispy tress of blood-red hair, like a flame barely under control, hung in front of her left eye—the same eye that then became home to one of Jack Peril's .45 caliber right hooks! There was no time to be a gentleman when lives were at stake.

And she had betrayed him...

But at least she wasn't as maniacal as The Yellow Menace, whom Jack, with the help of his trusty sidekick, Kid Peril, had finally done away with months earlier when the two titans tussled

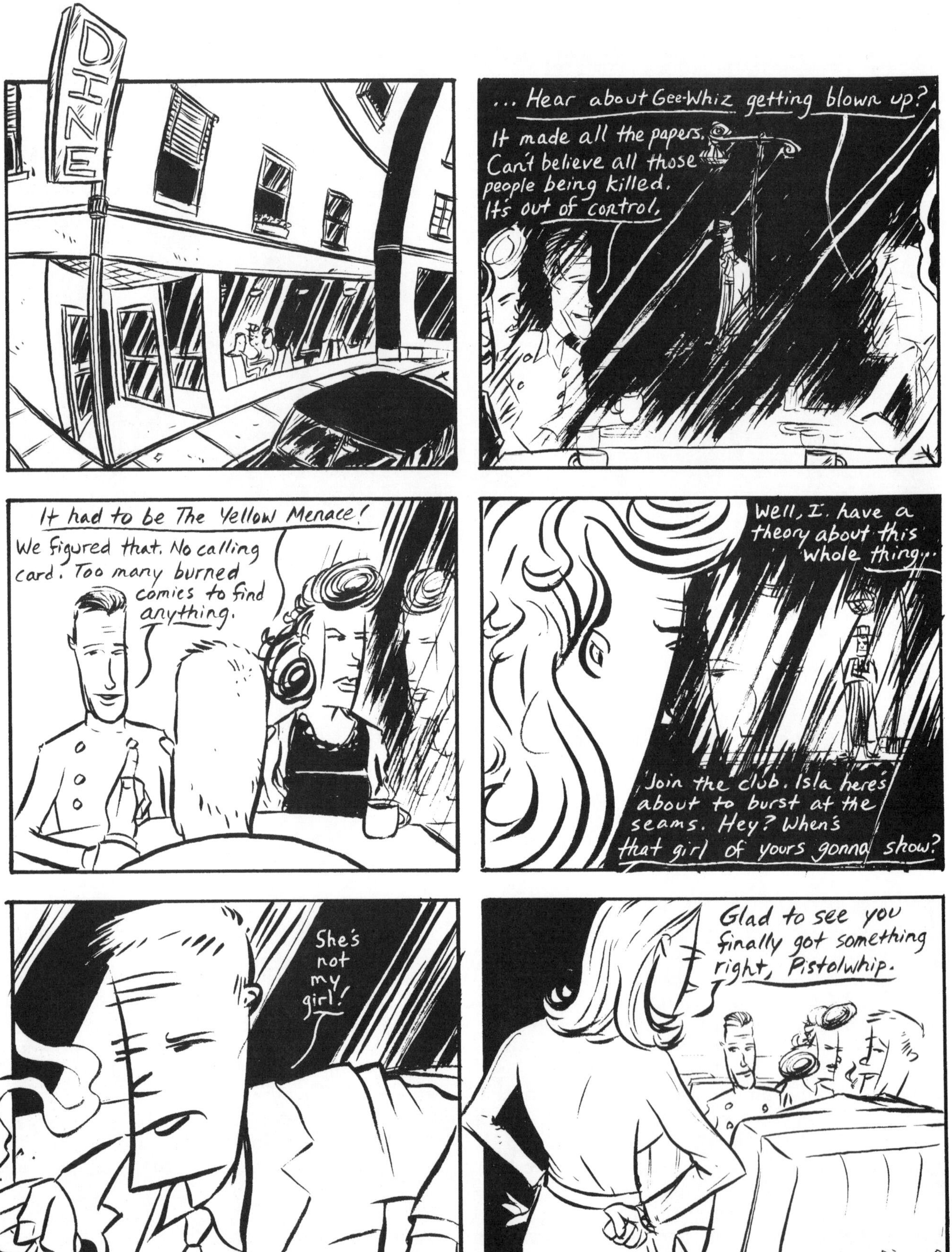
DINE
... Hear about Gee-Whiz getting blown up?
It made all the papers. Can't believe all those people being killed. It's out of control.
It had to be The Yellow Menace!
We figured that. No calling card. Too many burned comics to find anything.
Well, I have a theory about this whole thing...
Join the club. Isla here's about to burst at the seams. Hey? When's that girl of yours gonna show?
She's not my girl!
Glad to see you finally got something right, Pistolwhip.

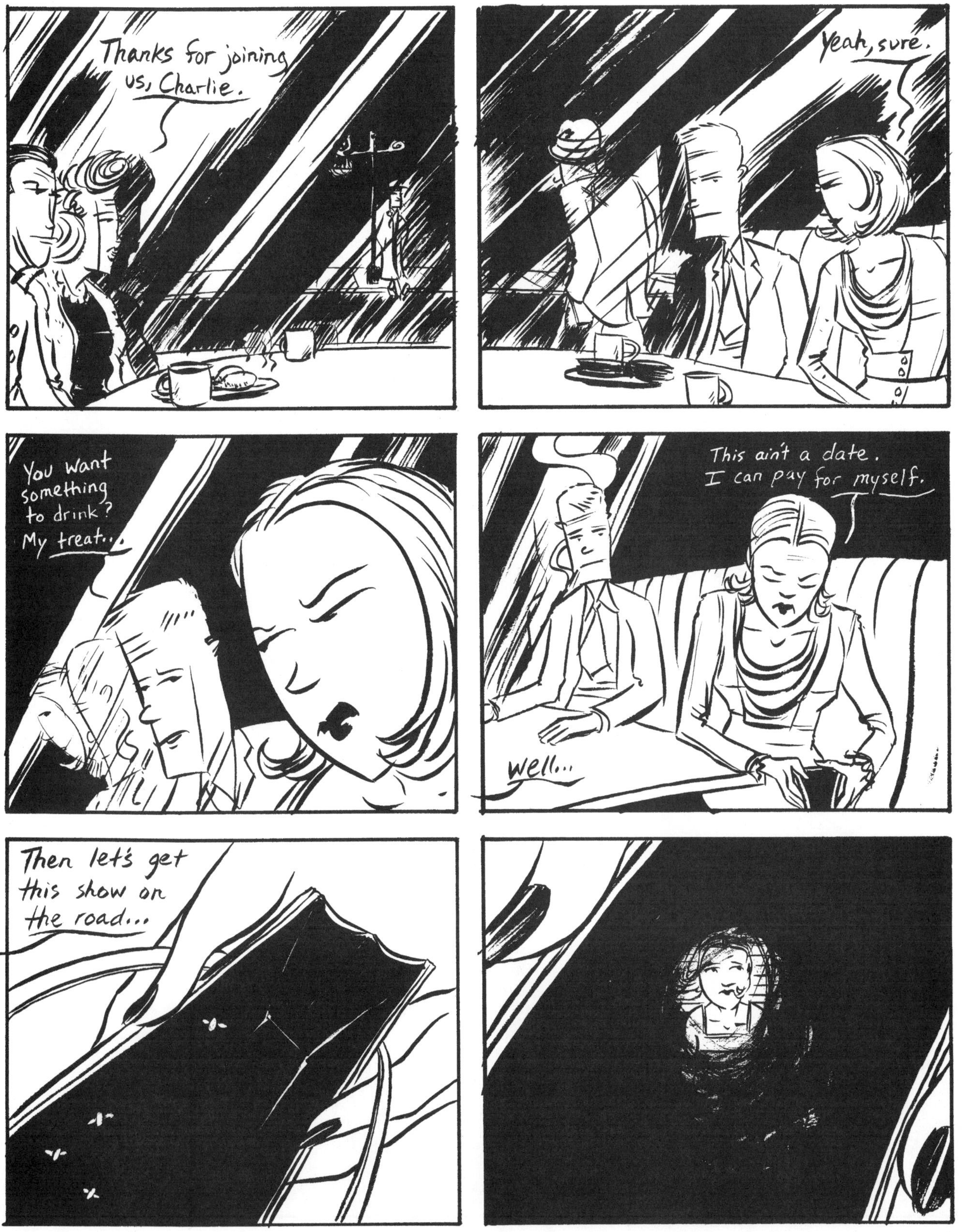
Thanks for joining us, Charlie.
Yeah, sure.
You want something to drink? My treat...
This ain't a date. I can pay for myself.
Well...
Then let's get this show on the road...

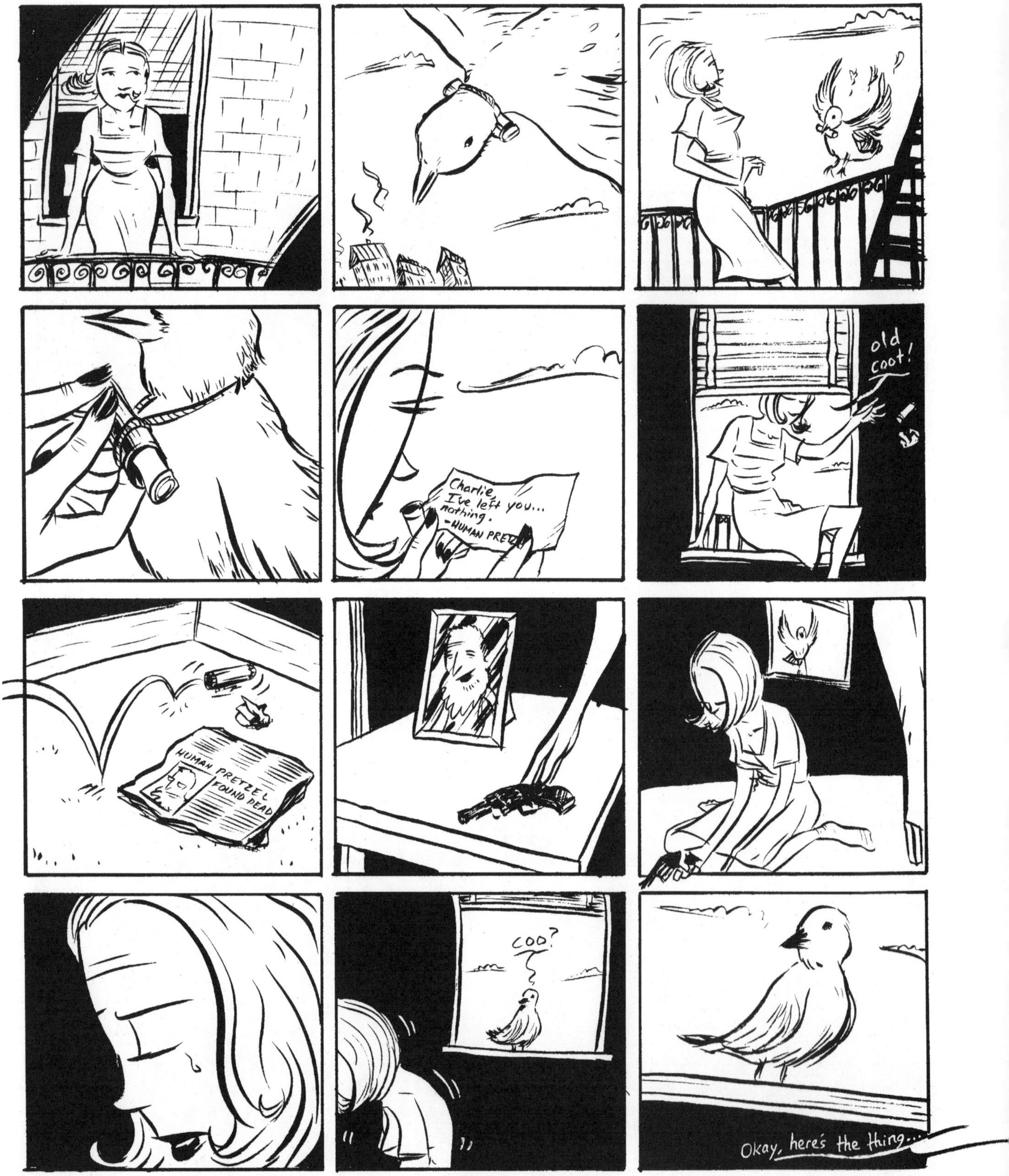

Charlie, I've left you... nothing. -HUMAN PRETZ
old coot!
HUMAN PRETZEL FOUND DEAD
coo?
Okay, here's the thing...

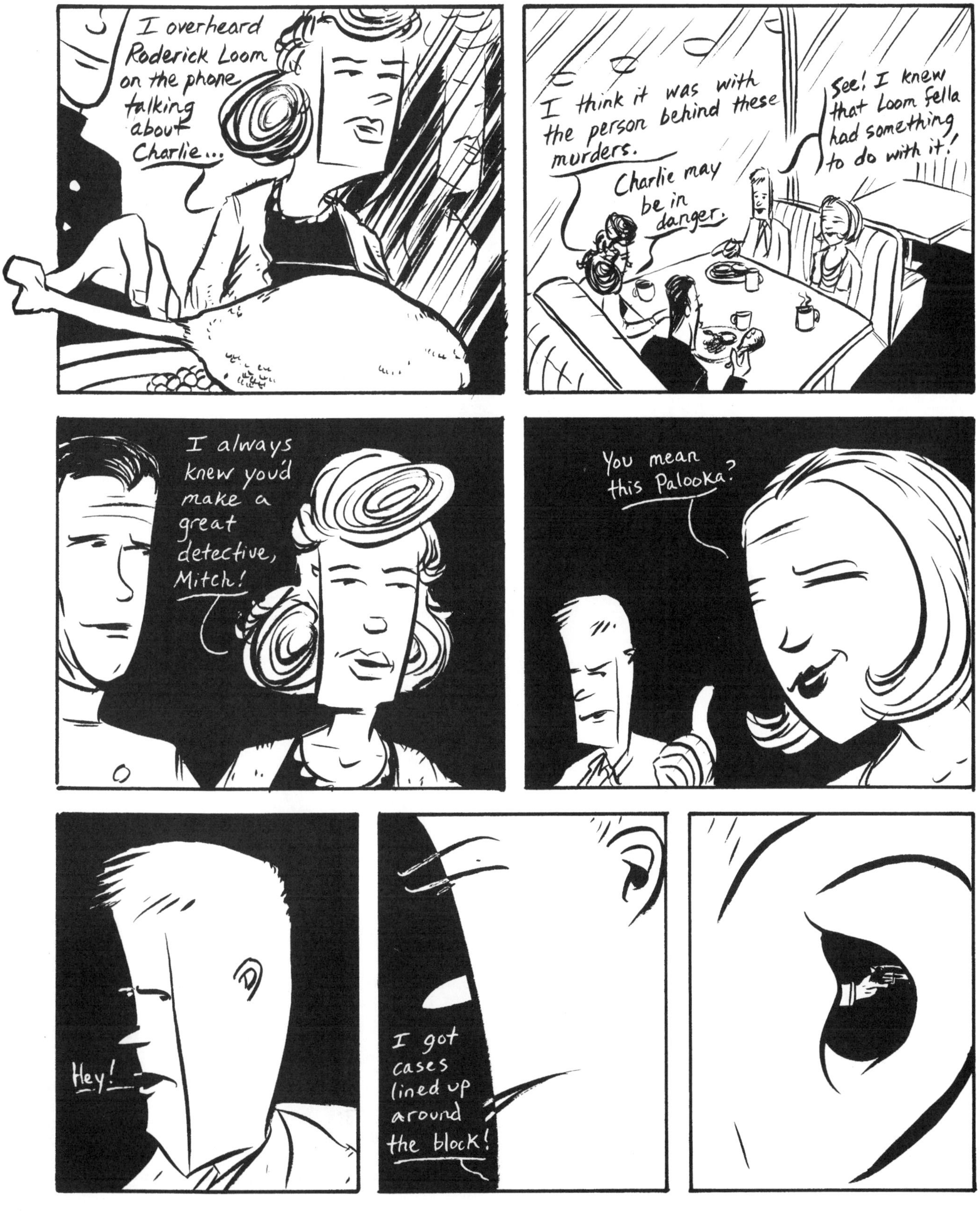
I overheard Roderick Loom on the phone talking about Charlie...
I think it was with the person behind these murders.
Charlie may be in danger.
See! I knew that Loom fella had something to do with it!
I always knew you'd make a great detective, Mitch!
You mean this Palooka?
Hey!
I got cases lined up around the block!

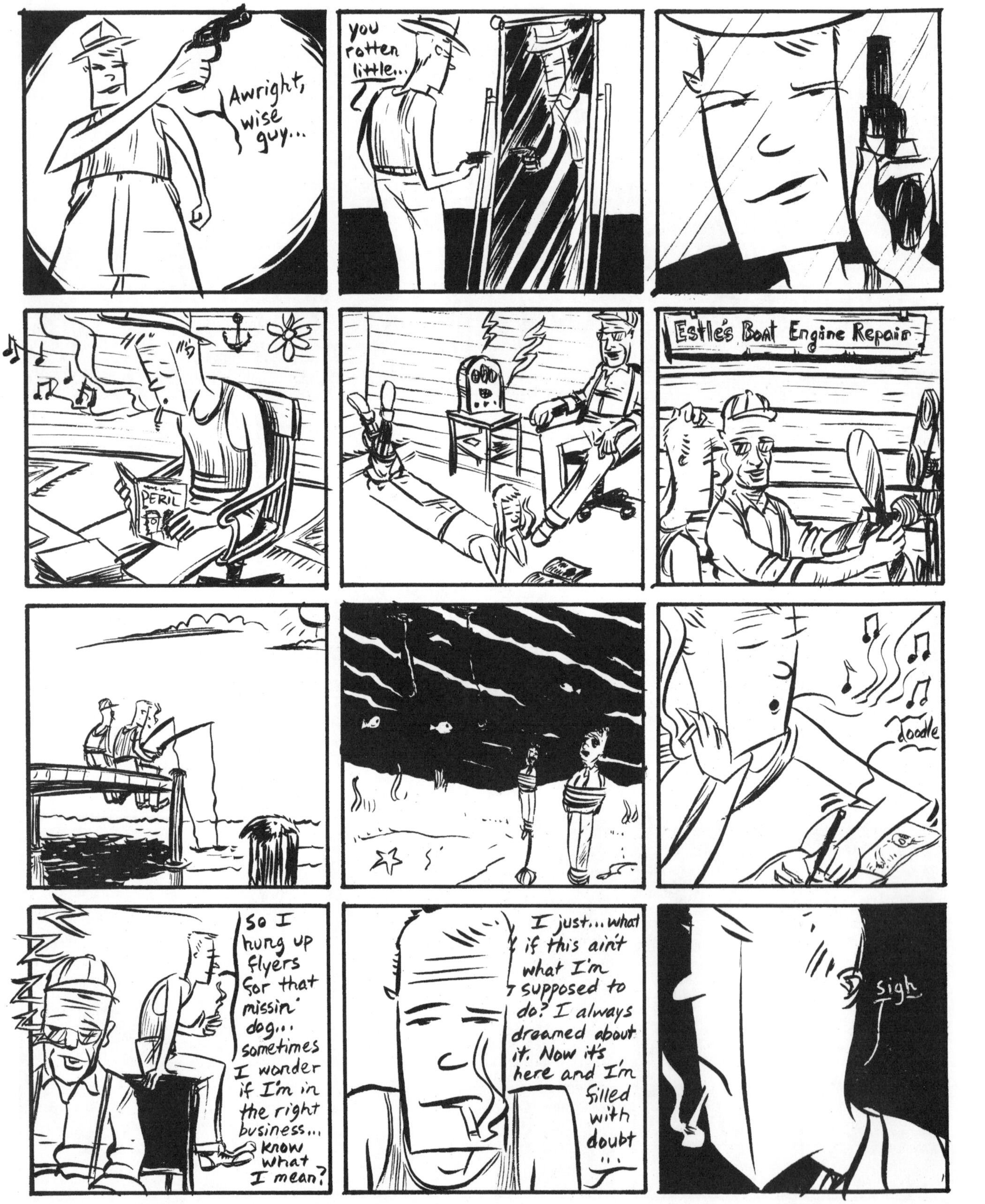
Awright, wise guy...
you rotten little...
Estle's Boat Engine Repair
PERIL
doodle
So I hung up flyers for that missin' dog... sometimes I wonder if I'm in the right business... know what I mean?
I just... what if this ain't what I'm supposed to do? I always dreamed about it. Now it's here and I'm filled with doubt...
sigh

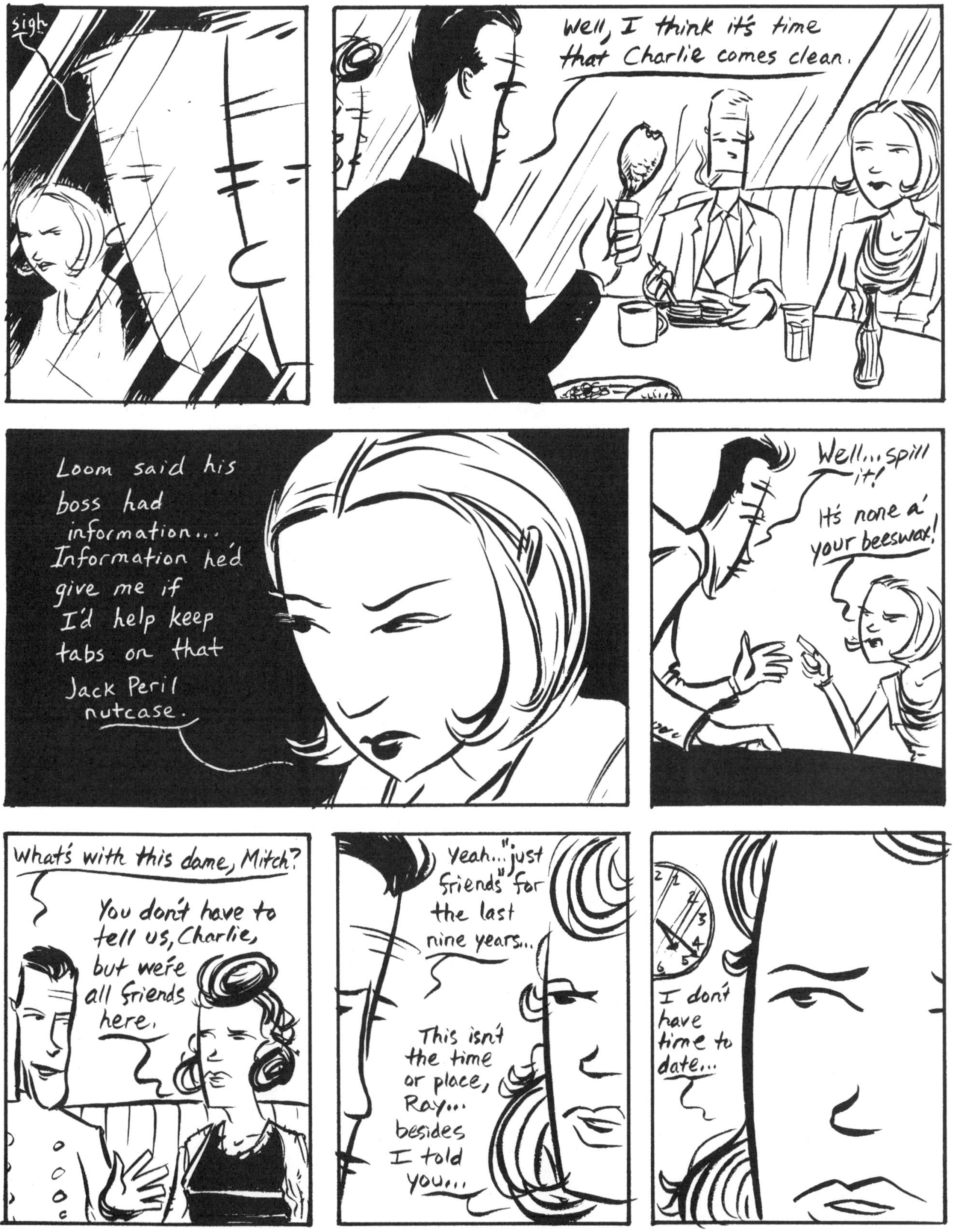
sigh
Well, I think it's time that Charlie comes clean.
Loom said his boss had information... Information he'd give me if I'd help keep tabs on that Jack Peril nutcase.
Well... spill it!
It's none a' your beeswax!
What's with this dame, Mitch?
You don't have to tell us, Charlie, but we're all friends here.
Yeah..."just friends" for the last nine years...
This isn't the time or place, Ray... besides I told you...
I don't have time to date...

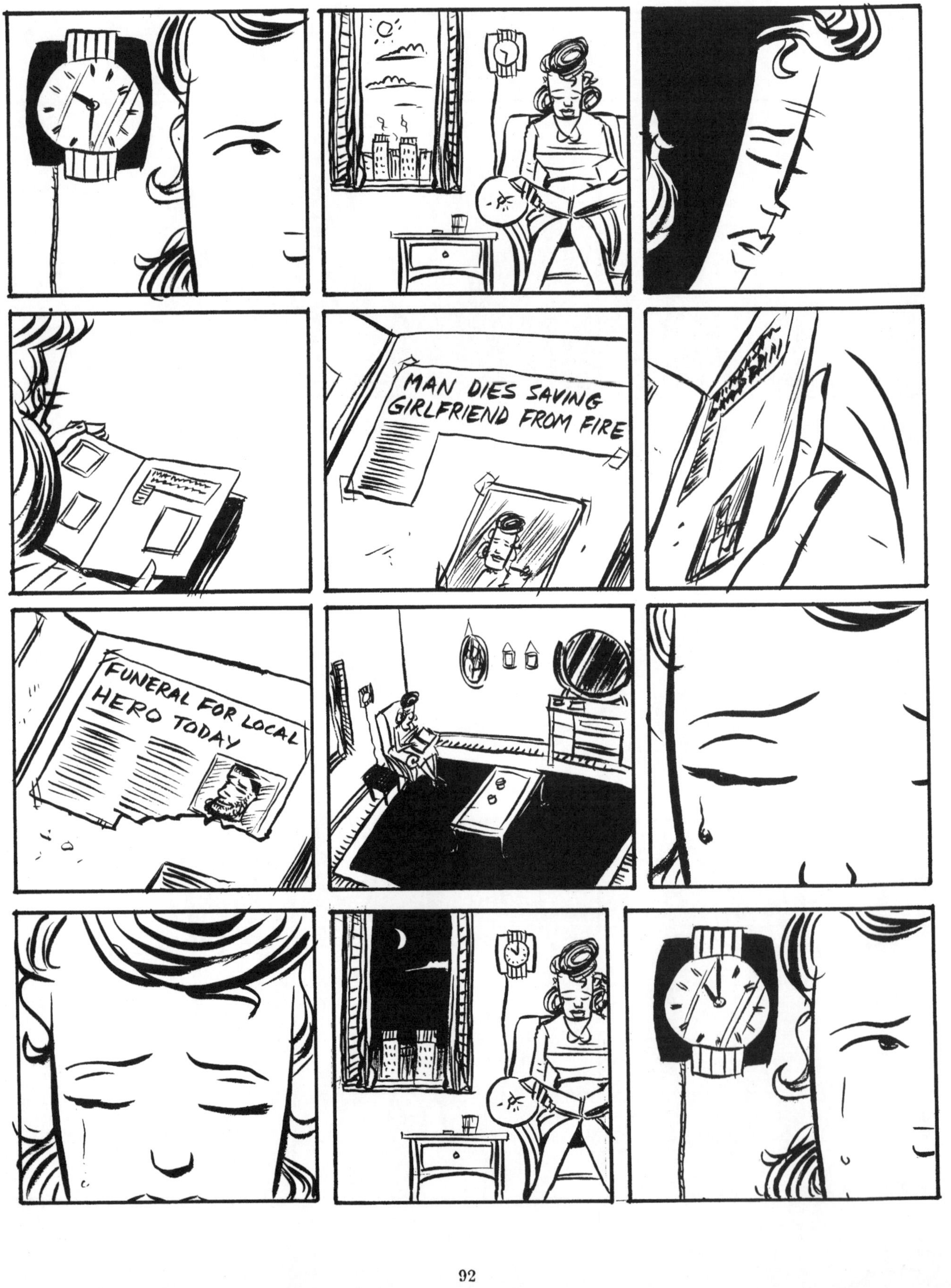
MAN DIES SAVING GIRLFRIEND FROM FIRE
FUNERAL FOR LOCAL HERO TODAY

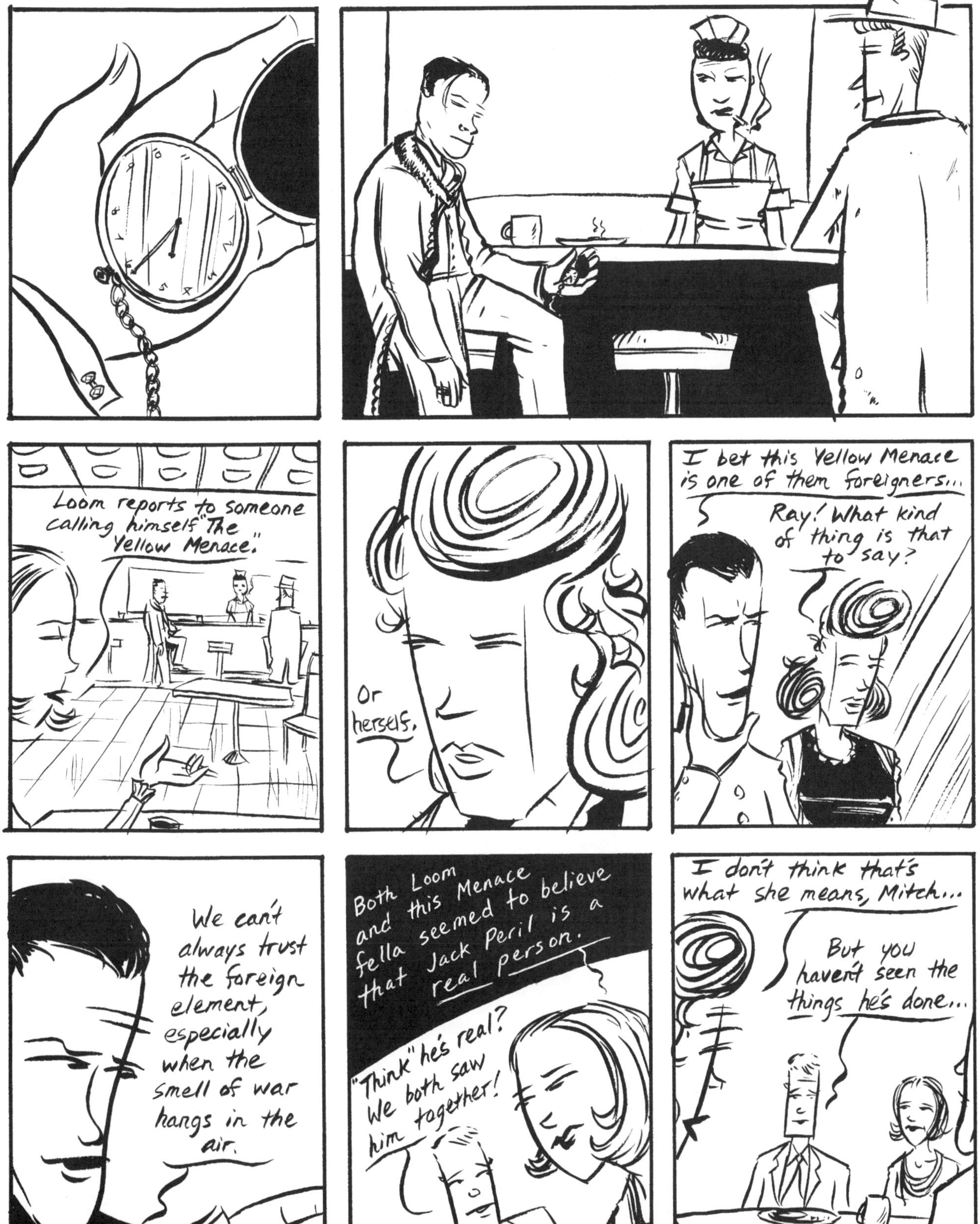
Loom reports to someone calling himself "The Yellow Menace."
Or herself.
I bet this Yellow Menace is one of them foreigners...
Ray! What kind of thing is that to say?
We can't always trust the foreign element, especially when the smell of war hangs in the air.
Both Loom and this Menace seemed to believe that Jack Peril is a real person.
"Think" he's real? We both saw him together!
I don't think that's what she means, Mitch...
But you haven't seen the things he's done...

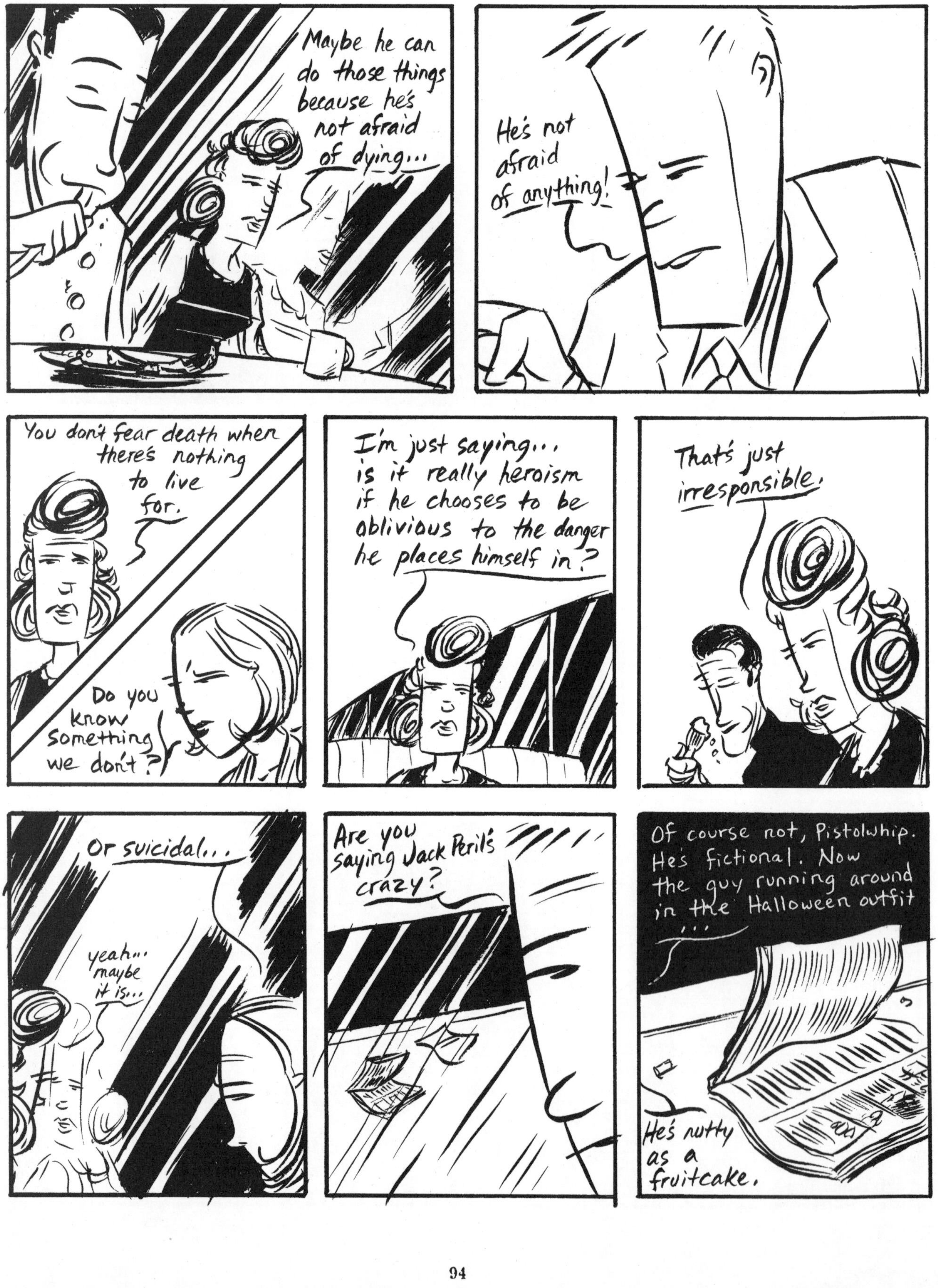

Maybe he can do those things because he's not afraid of dying...
He's not afraid of anything!
You don't fear death when there's nothing to live for.
Do you know something we don't?
I'm just saying... is it really heroism if he chooses to be oblivious to the danger he places himself in?
That's just irresponsible.
Or suicidal...
yeah... maybe it is...
Are you saying Jack Peril's crazy?
Of course not, Pistolwhip. He's fictional. Now the guy running around in the Halloween outfit ...
He's nutty as a fruitcake.

heavy feeling of foreboding Jack carried with him made him ponder his own sanity. Bannon had pleaded with Peril not to go up alone, but even though Bannon was the Chief-of-Police, Jack refused to put the life of another in jeopardy on his watch. The message left with police headquarters specifically stated that Jack was to come alone to the top of the lighthouse at Port des Ames. And it was signed....The Yellow Menace! "It has to be a fake..." Jack mused as he climbed the spiral stone staircase to the lighthouse's pinnacle.

The reason for his doubt was that Jack had killed The Yellow Menace months earlier atop this very lighthouse! After Kid Peril had lured The Menace there, a duel to the death between he and Jack Peril, the two archest-of-enemies, ensued. Mighty blows had flared in the revolving light of the lighthouse's beacon, until Jack's patented .45 caliber right hook knocked The Yellow Menace from the summit. The Menace's body was crushed against the waiting rocks below and washed out to the unforgiving sea.

Suddenly, Jack's reminiscing was pierced by a blood-curdling scream from below. Jack leaped down the granite steps three at a time, but it wasn't fast enough. Bannon was gone! Just then, a familiar vicious laugh echoed from above. As the searching light passed the cloud cover overhead, it cast the shadow of what appeared to be a hanging body! Once again, Jack Peril ascended the stairs with lightning speed. What he found there was pure horror...

Chief Bannon was dangling from a hangman's noose, neck broken; his swelled tongue protruding from his sagging head. The rotating light mockingly illuminated his lifeless eyes in a sinister rhythmic pattern. A note violently stabbed to his chest with a knife read, "I'm back, Jack! And guess who's next?—The Yellow Menace". Jack's thoughts turned to Kid Peril and his world

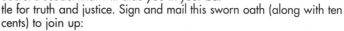

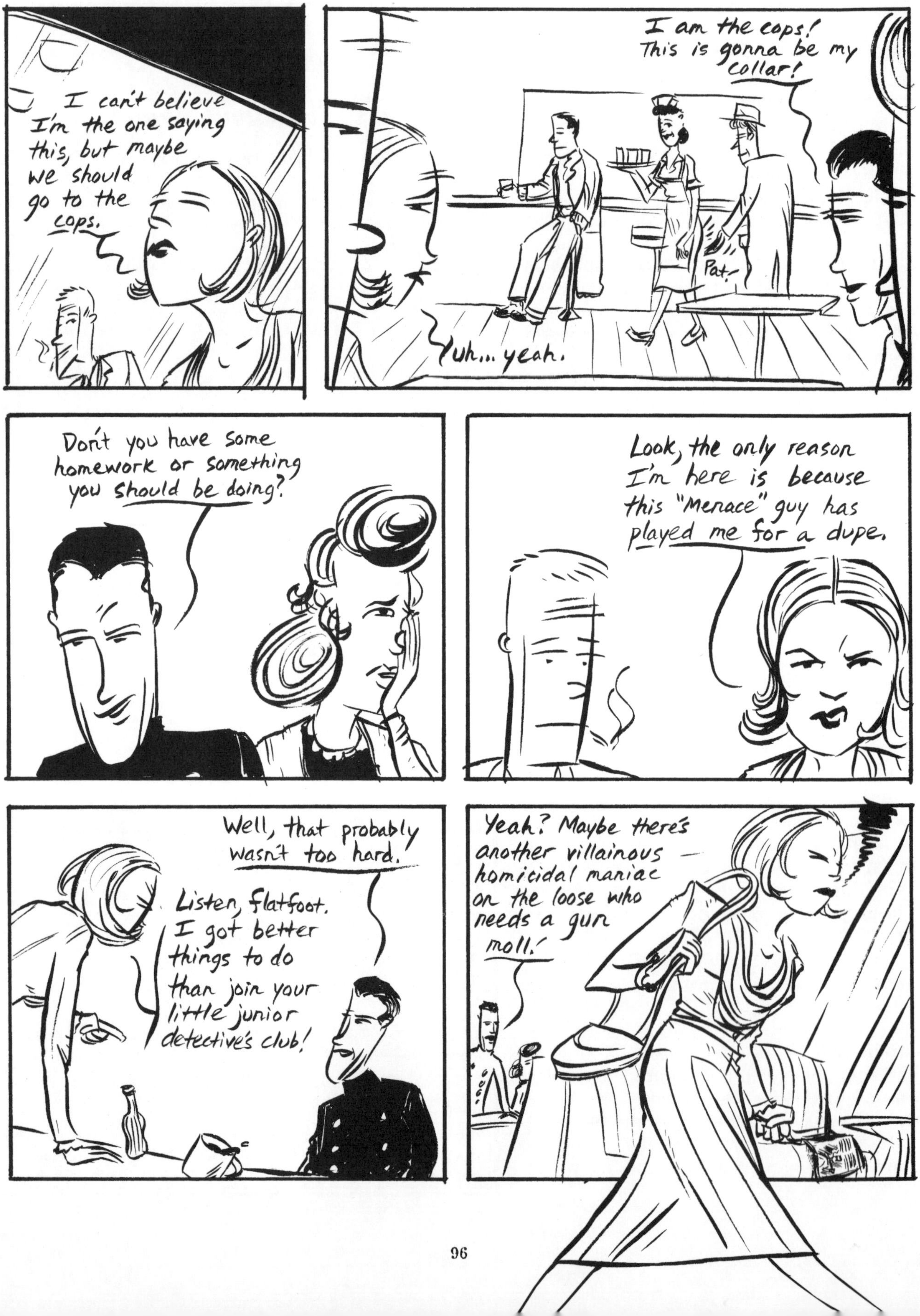
I can't believe I'm the one saying this, but maybe we should go to the cops.
I am the cops! This is gonna be my collar!
Pat-
Uh... yeah.
Don't you have some homework or something you should be doing?
Look, the only reason I'm here is because this "Menace" guy has played me for a dupe.
Well, that probably wasn't too hard.
Listen, flatfoot. I got better things to do than join your little junior detective's club!
Yeah? Maybe there's another villainous homicidal maniac on the loose who needs a gun moll!

saw his yellow robes whisking around the corner, like the tail of a serpent retreating to its nest with fresh kill. Jack was hot in pursuit, his thoughts on fire, his eyes burning with rage. Kid Peril had now been missing for two weeks without a word, until The Yellow Menace's cryptic message arrived once again at police headquarters. Jack's steel trap of a mind quickly snapped closed on its meaning, but its implications were something he never dared think possible.

Jack Peril burst through the rotted cellar door, stepping into a foot of murky water. "It's time to put you in—". Jack stopped short, finding himself face to face with a nightmare come to life.

Kid Peril was hanging by her wrists, tied by thick rope descending from the cellar's shadowy rafters. Her feet were submersed in the filthy water spread throughout the room. The Yellow Menace stood poised on a small platform above the water level. Next to him was a giant electrical contraption—a work of horrific art created from an insane man's dream. A thick metal wire led down into the water from the base of the machine. Kid Peril's goggles dangled around her neck, her eyes red and swollen with frightful tears.

"Jack...save me!" she cried in a hoarse whisper. Jack's knuckles turned white, his fingernails drawing blood from his own palms.

"You guessed right, Jack!" The Menace cackled...and then he threw the switch.

CHAPTER XVII

Peril Undone

Twelve thousand volts of unbiased electricity surged into the water. Jack Peril had no choice but to jump back out of the room, helpless to save his young partner. After what seemed like an eternity, the taunting hum of the electrical device ceased, and The Yellow Menace's mocking laughter faded into the distance.

Jack leaped into the room, rushing to free Kid Peril from her bonds, refusing to accept he was too late. Her youthful face was burnt and blackened, smoke still rising off her small frame. His goggles filled with tears as he held her ten-year-old lifeless body in his arms.

"I couldn't save you...it's all my fault..." he sobbed quietly, clutching her against his shattered heart. "Kid... "

And in that moment, Jack Peril's world became undone. He would see The Menace's yellow robes soaked red with the villain's own blood. There was absolutely nothing that could

"I couldn't save you...it's all my fault..." he sobbed quietly, clutching her against his shattered heart. "Kid... "

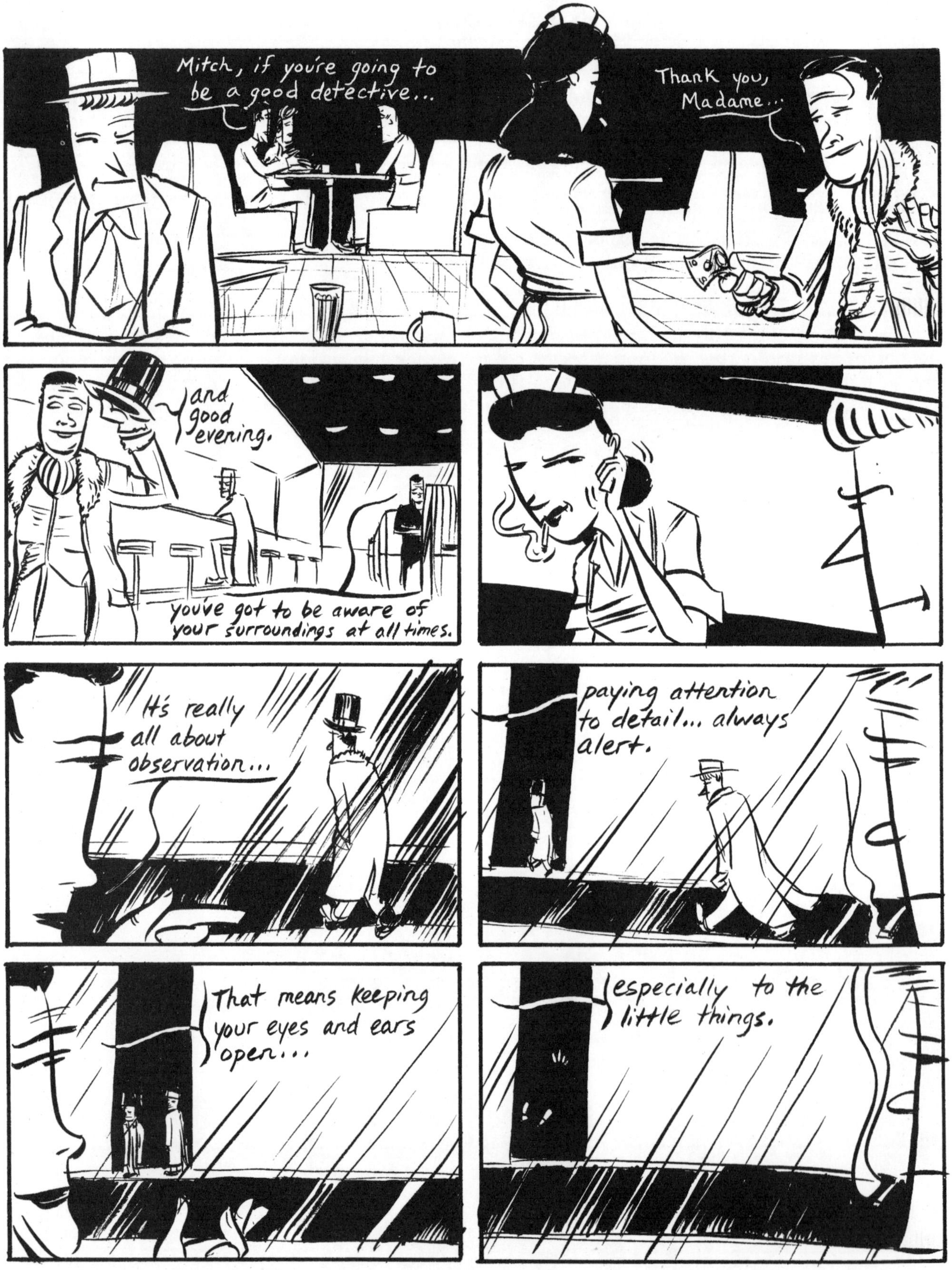

Mitch, if you're going to be a good detective...
Thank you, Madame...
and good evening.
you've got to be aware of your surroundings at all times.
It's really all about observation...
paying attention to detail... always alert.
That means keeping your eyes and ears open...
especially to the little things.

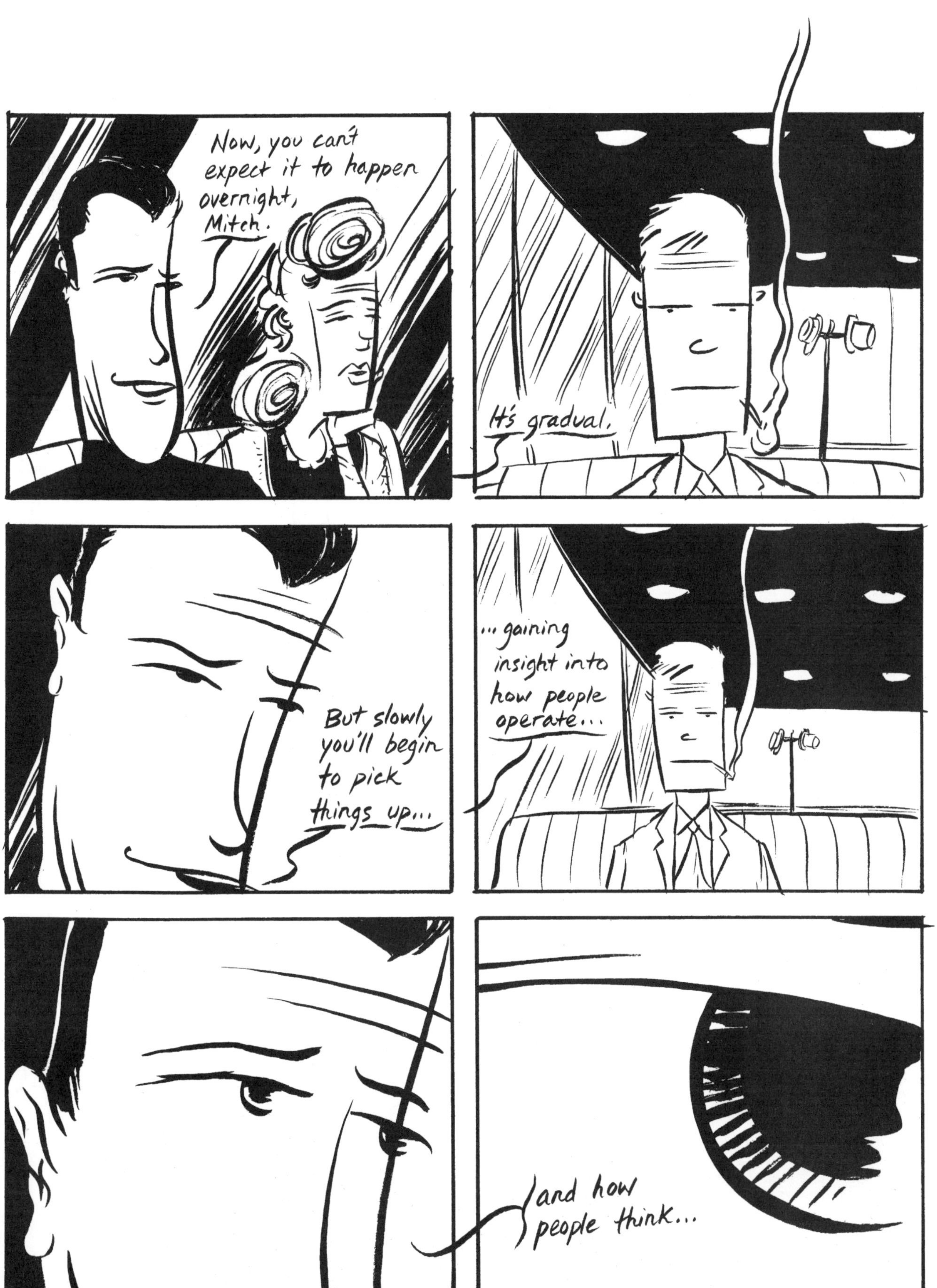
Now, you can't expect it to happen overnight, Mitch.
It's gradual.
But slowly you'll begin to pick things up...
...gaining insight into how people operate...
and how people think...

LOCKER ROOM
...can you believe it?
The Commish put Ford on the Menace case...
Flatfoot Ford?
yup.
Well, someone's gotta watch that Loom fruit.
Besides, since O'Vowels got bumped off, I hear the Commish is hoping the same thing happens to Ford.
See? I told ya'...
our Commish is one smart fella...
HA HA HA HA HA HA HA HA

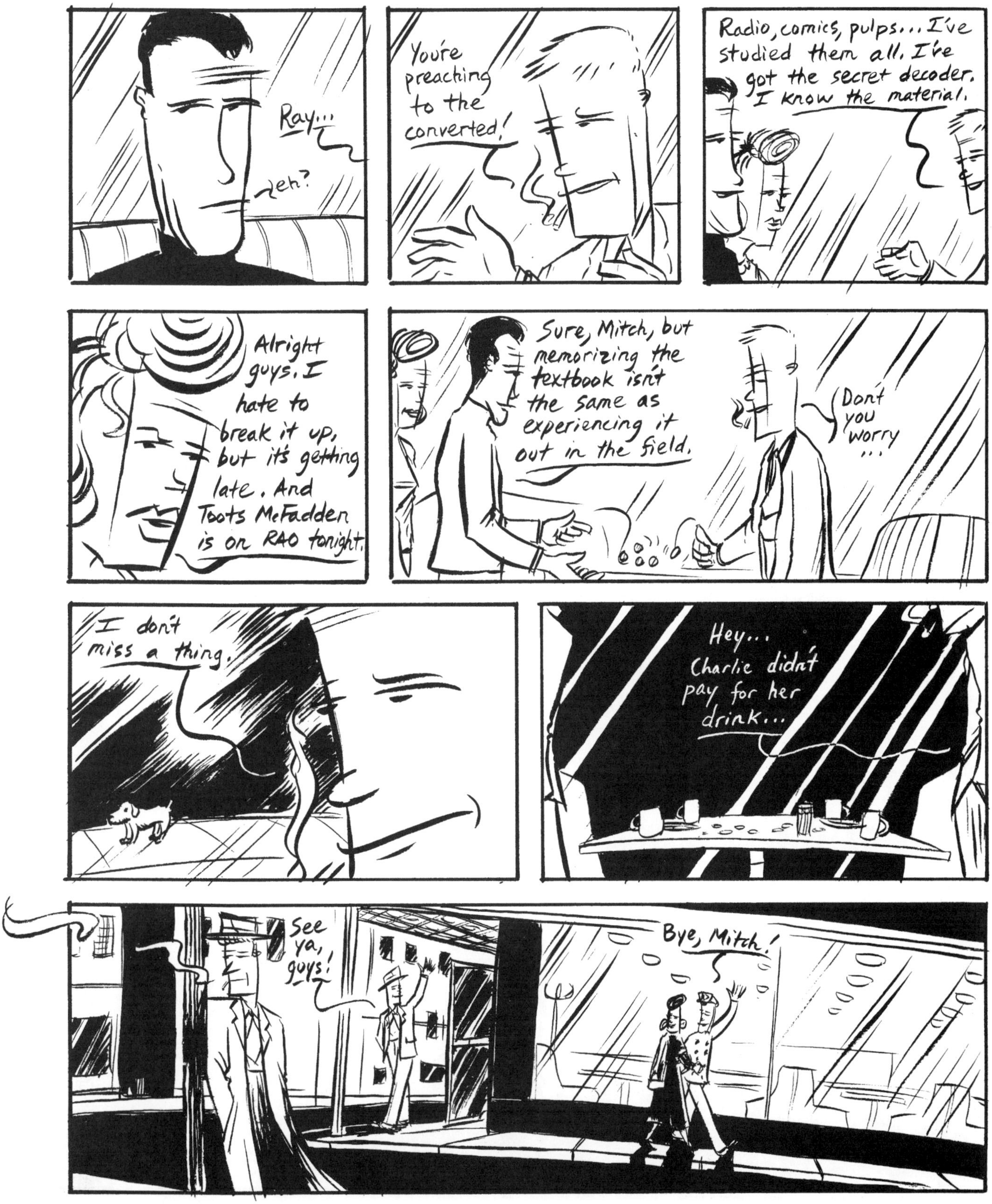
Ray...
eh?
You're preaching to the converted!
Radio, comics, pulps... I've studied them all. I've got the secret decoder. I know the material.
Alright guys. I hate to break it up, but it's getting late. And Toots McFadden is on RAO tonight.
Sure, Mitch, but memorizing the textbook isn't the same as experiencing it out in the field.
Don't you worry...
I don't miss a thing.
Hey... Charlie didn't pay for her drink...
See ya, guys!
Bye, Mitch!

Rosebud, you should take it easy on Mitch. Jack Peril's his hero.

That man is no hero. He's selfish. Putting himself and everyone else in grave danger.

Yeah... well, I'll see you tomorrow...

But if you really believe that, then why are you helping out?

Maybe because I'm just as guilty of it as he is...

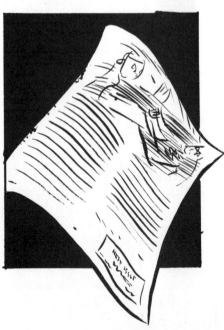

102

He had prayed he would wake up from the fiendish
nightmare his existence had become, but never for
a moment thought that it was literally possible.

had prayed he would wake up from the fiendish
nightmare his existence had become, but never
for a moment thought that it was literally possible. However, when Jack Peril opened his
eyes, the infernal veil had been lifted. There
before him, like an angel, stood Kid Peril—alive
and well. "Kid, you're alive!" he cried.

"Of course, Jack!" she smiled. "You'd kill me
if I wasn't around to save your bacon!" She put
her small hand in Jack's. "It was Madame
Cauchemar. She knocked you silly with that
drug she was going to poison the reservoir with.
But the Chief and I arrived in the nick of time
to stop her!"

"She's safely behind bars, Jack," Bannon
chimed in. "Case closed."

"So, what did you dream about?" Kid Peril
asked.

Jack squeezed her hand, taking comfort that
she could squeeze back. "The end of everything
that mattered, Kid." But Jack couldn't help wonder if his opiate-induced nightmare was some-
how a foretelling of things to come—the unlike-
ly return of his nemesis...The Yellow Menace.

The End.

NEXT ISSUE —

The Gilded Hand

Twice Monthly   **10 cents**

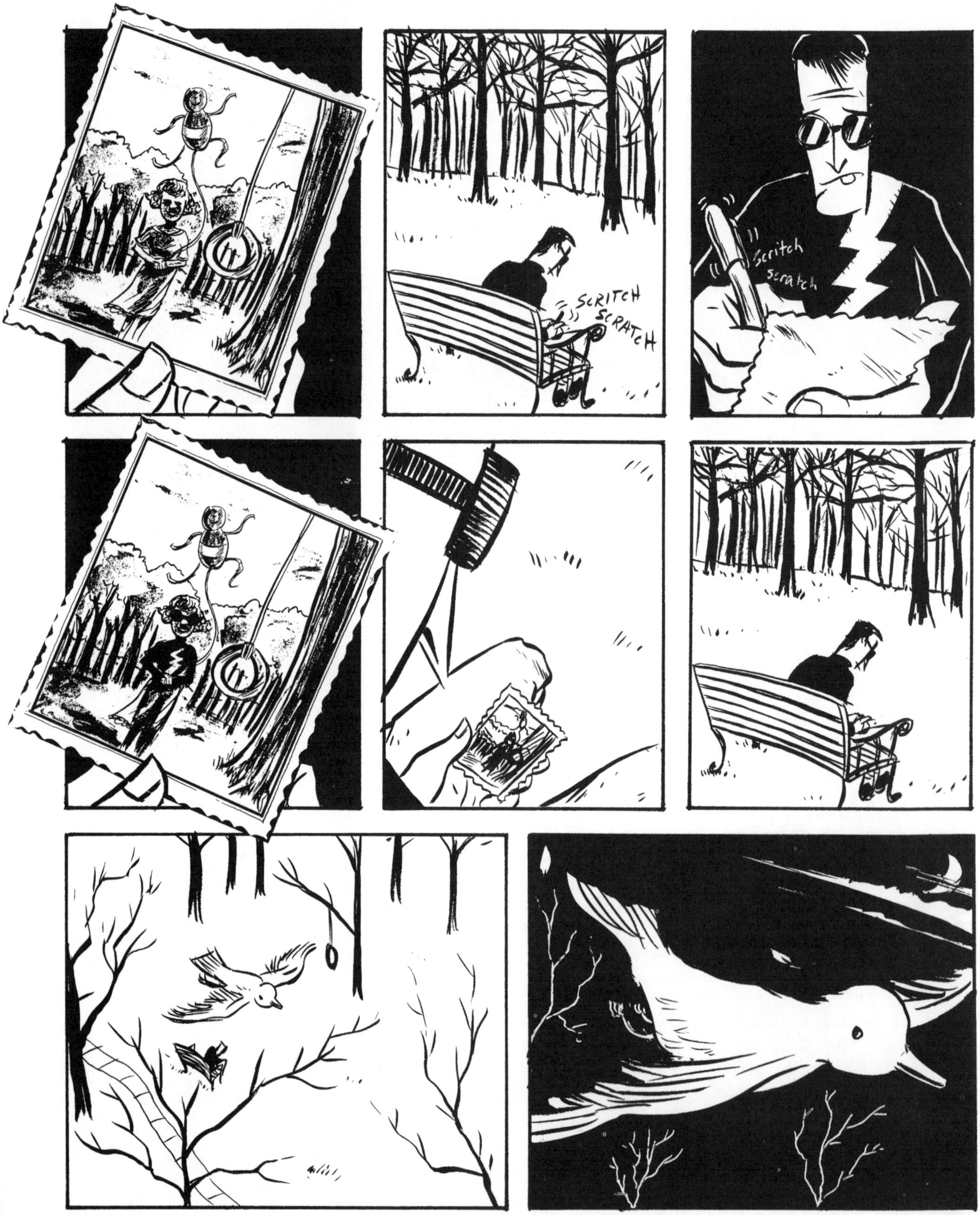
SCRITCH
SCRATCH
Scritch
scratch

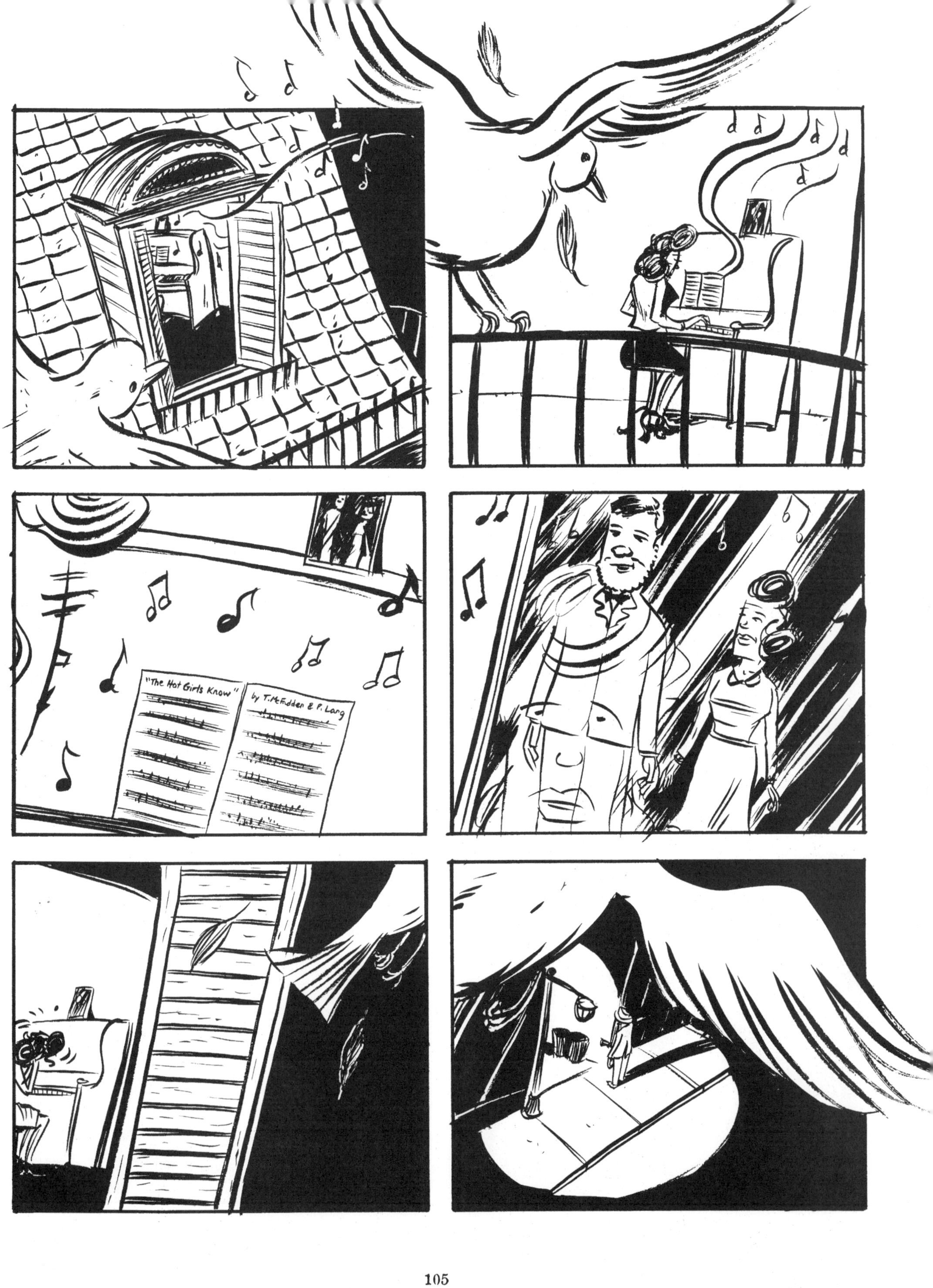
"The Hot Girls Know"
by T. McFadden & P. Lang

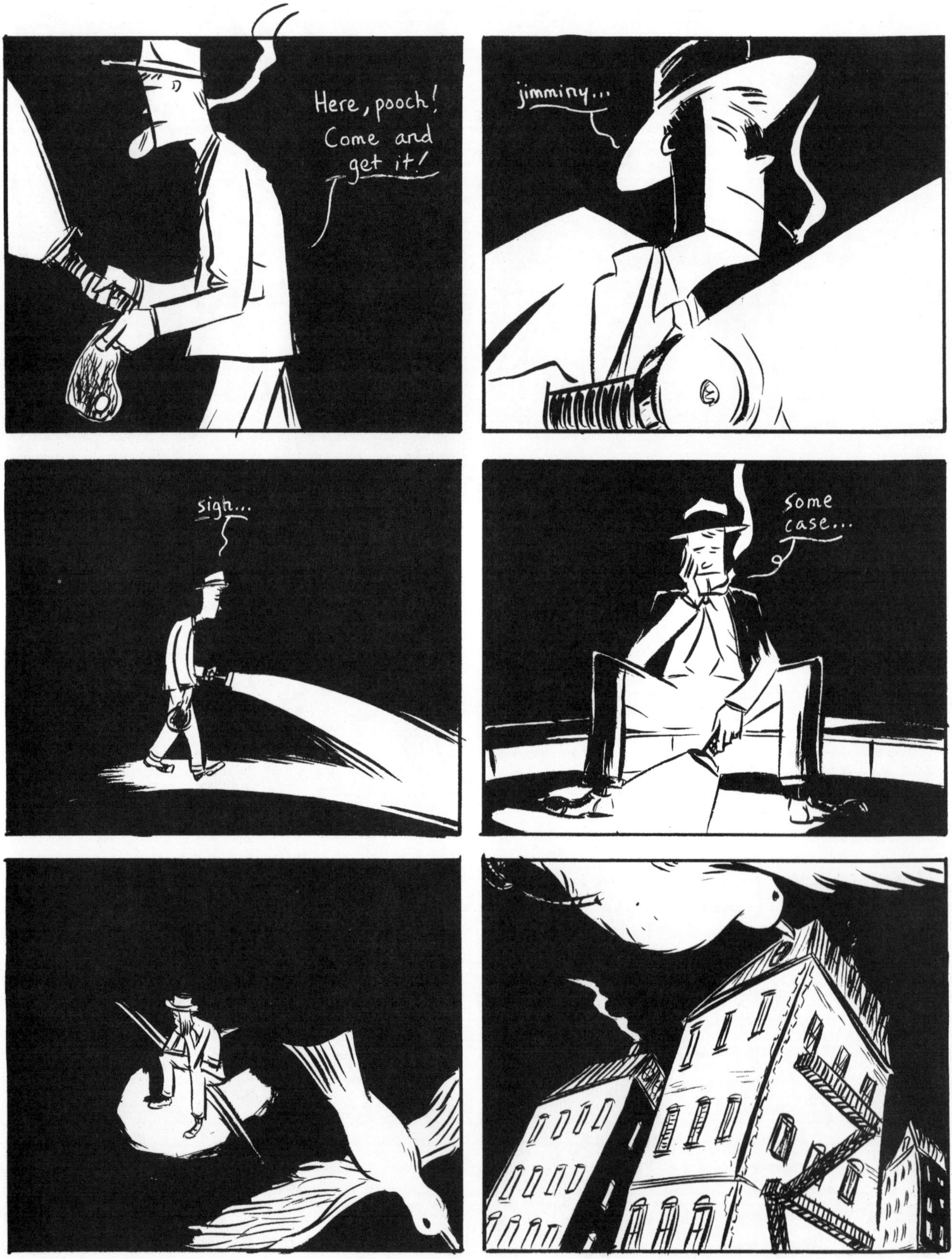
Here, pooch! Come and get it!
jimminy...
sigh...
Some case...

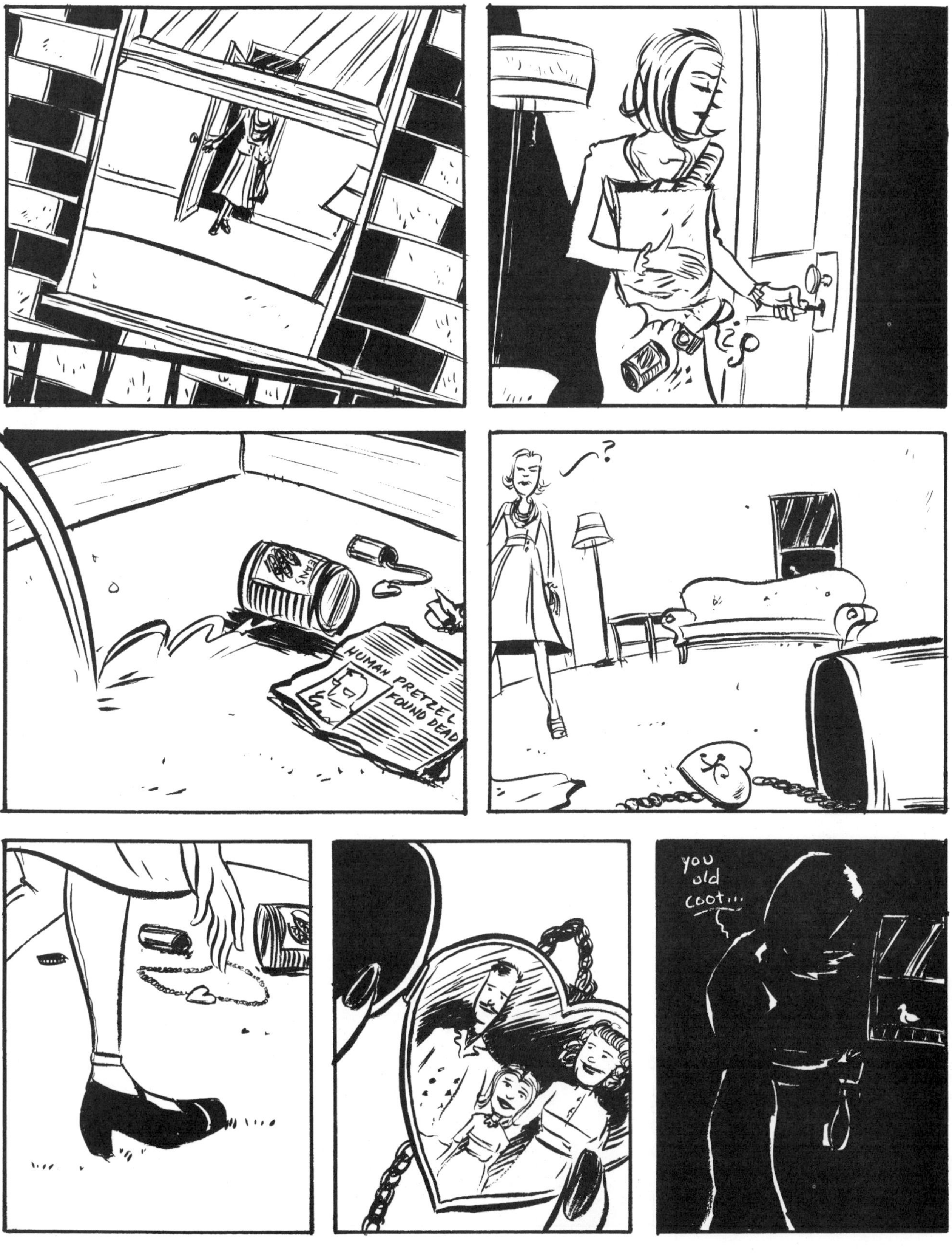

RIP
?
BEANS
HUMAN PRETZEL FOUND DEAD
you old coot...

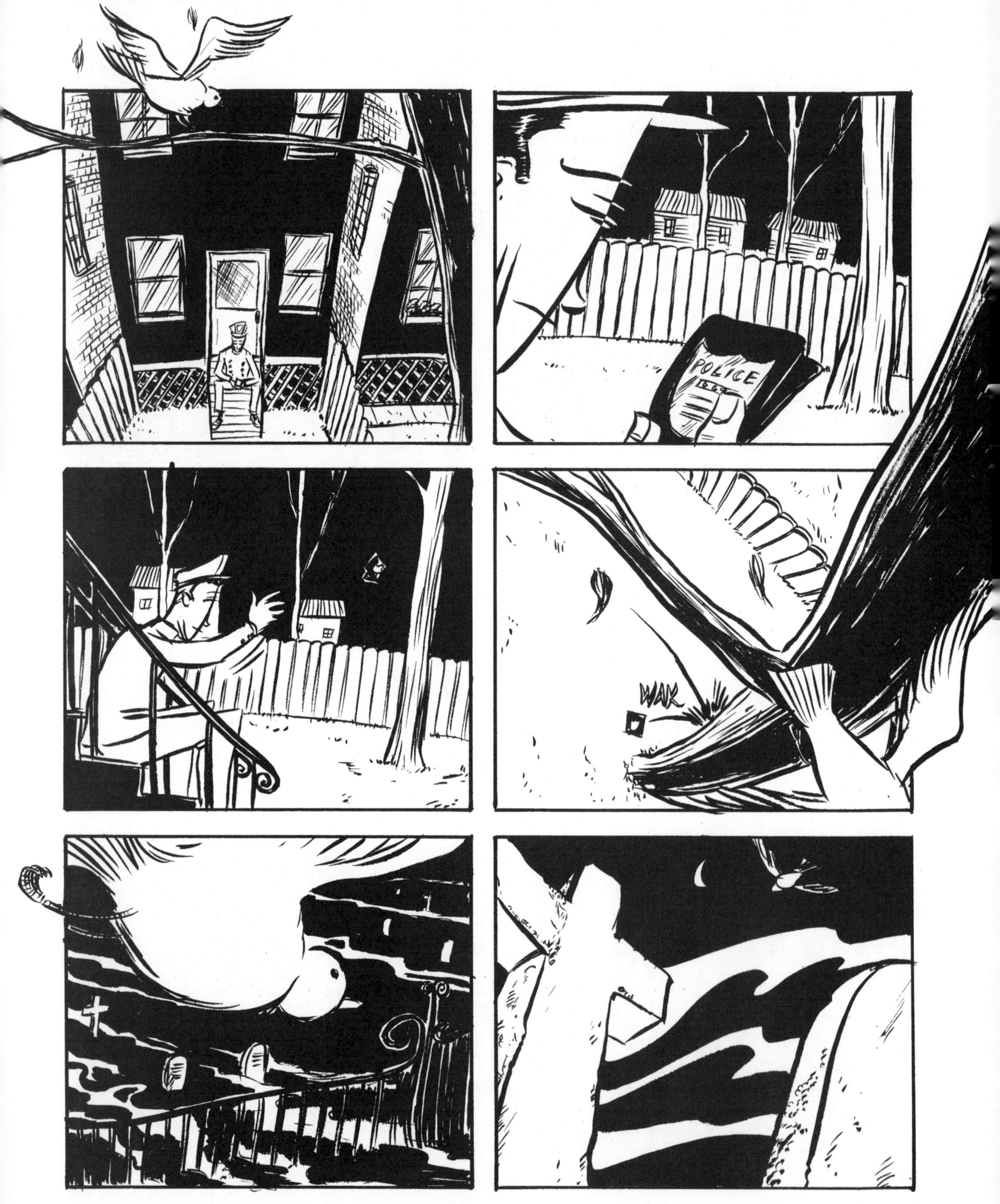
POLICE
WAK

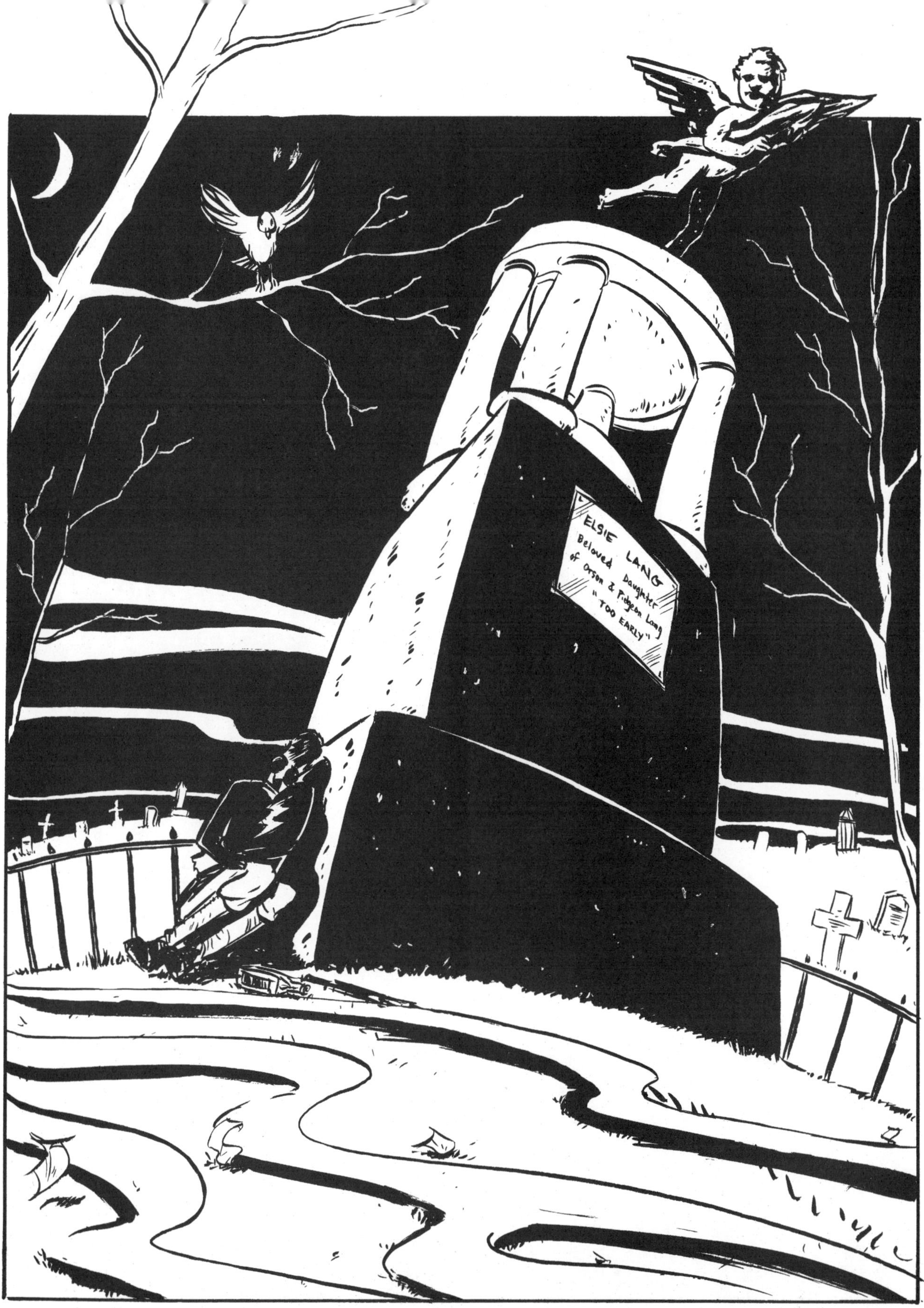
ELSIE LANG
Beloved Daughter
of Orson & Pidgeon Lang
"TOO EARLY"

ENTICEMENT
of the
NAIVE

*Roderick
Loom*

Chapter Five

木訥を誘引する

Enticement of the Naive

HOTEL CHASE
Extra! Extra!
Where will The Yellow Menace strike next!
TAXI
Follow that car!
郵便局
Ohayo, Isla-san!
JACK PERIL

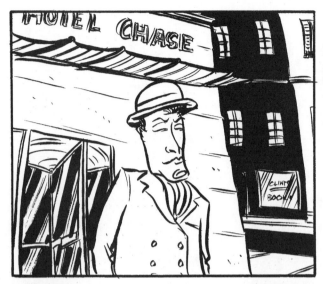

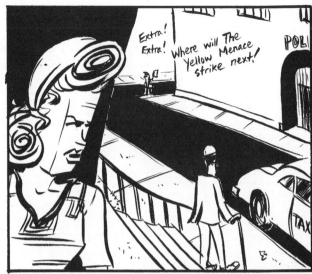

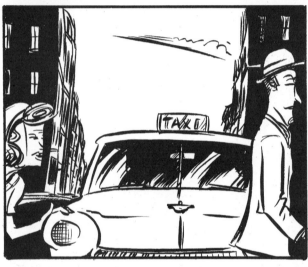

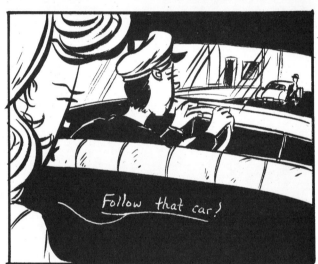

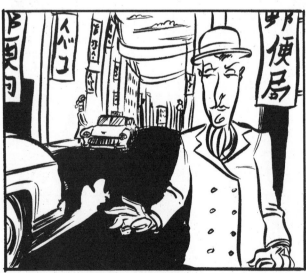

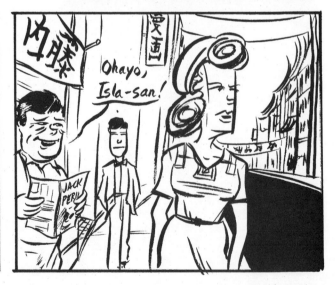

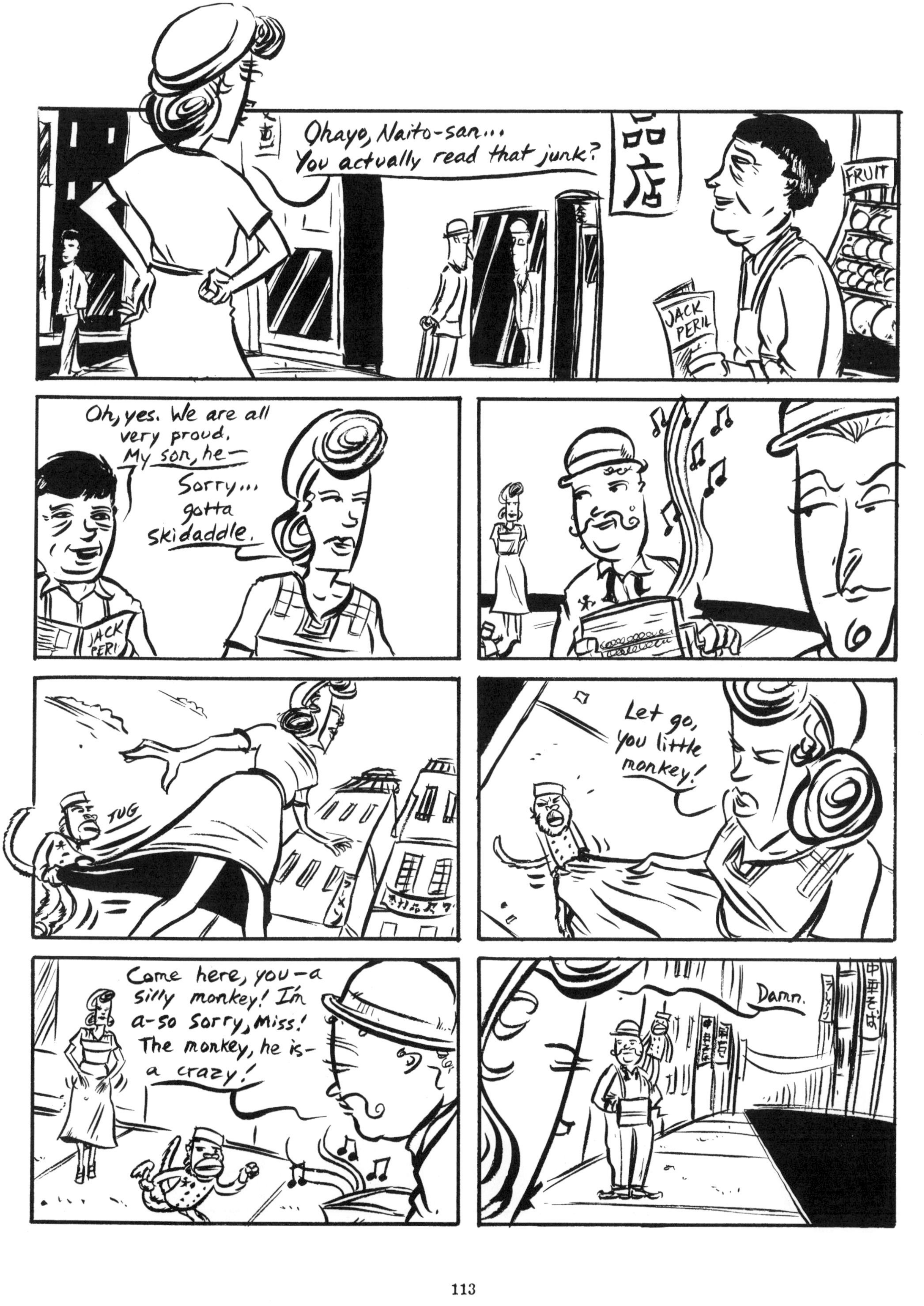

Ohayo, Naito-san... You actually read that junk?
FRUIT
JACK PERIL
Oh, yes. We are all very proud. My son, he—
Sorry... gotta skidaddle.
JACK PERIL
TUG
Let go, you little monkey!
Come here, you-a silly monkey! I'm a-so sorry, Miss! The monkey, he is-a crazy!
Damn.

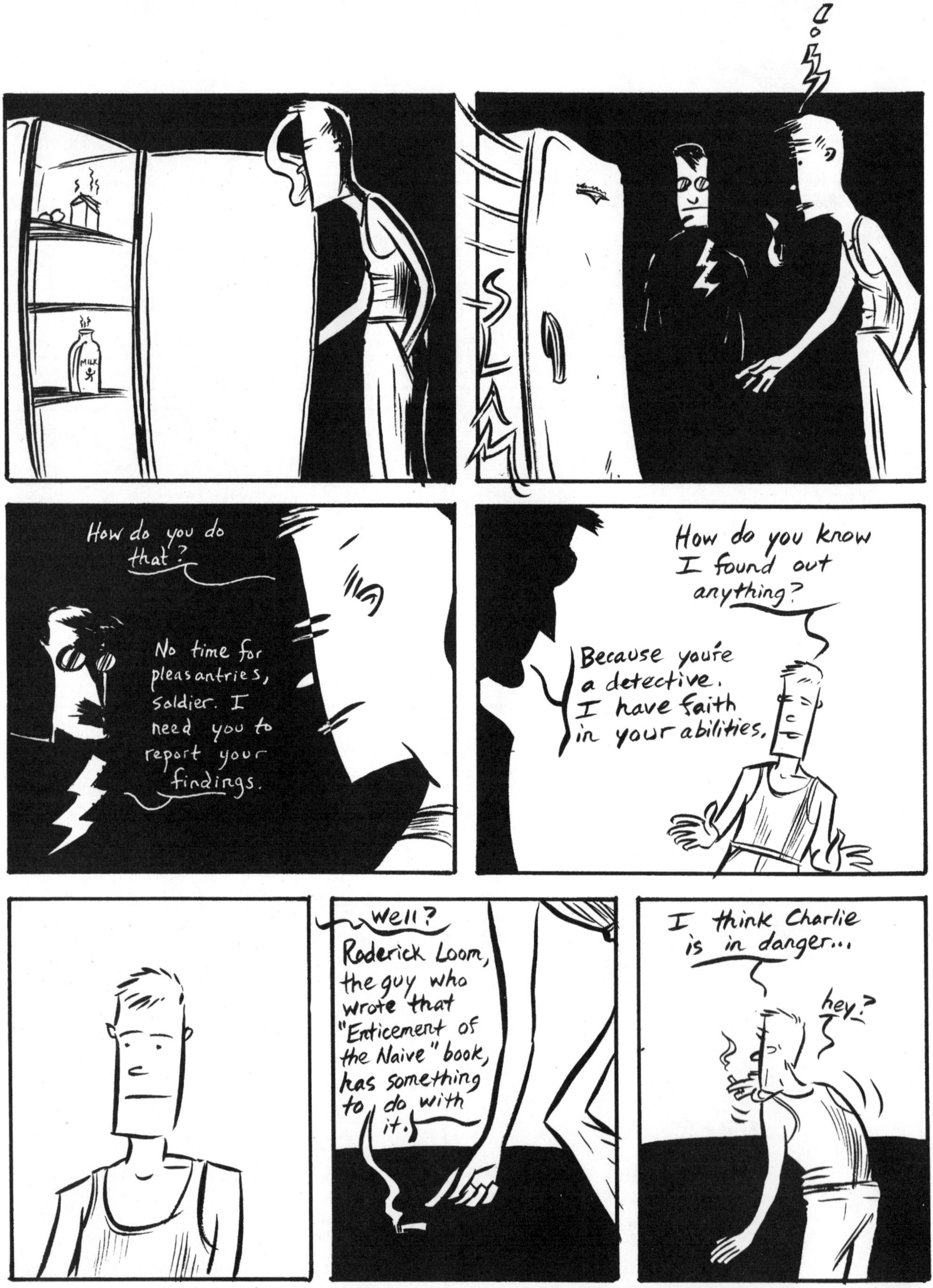

?
SLAM
How do you do that?
No time for pleasantries, soldier. I need you to report your findings.
How do you know I found out anything?
Because you're a detective. I have faith in your abilities.
Well?
Roderick Loom, the guy who wrote that "Enticement of the Naive" book, has something to do with it.
I think Charlie is in danger...
hey?

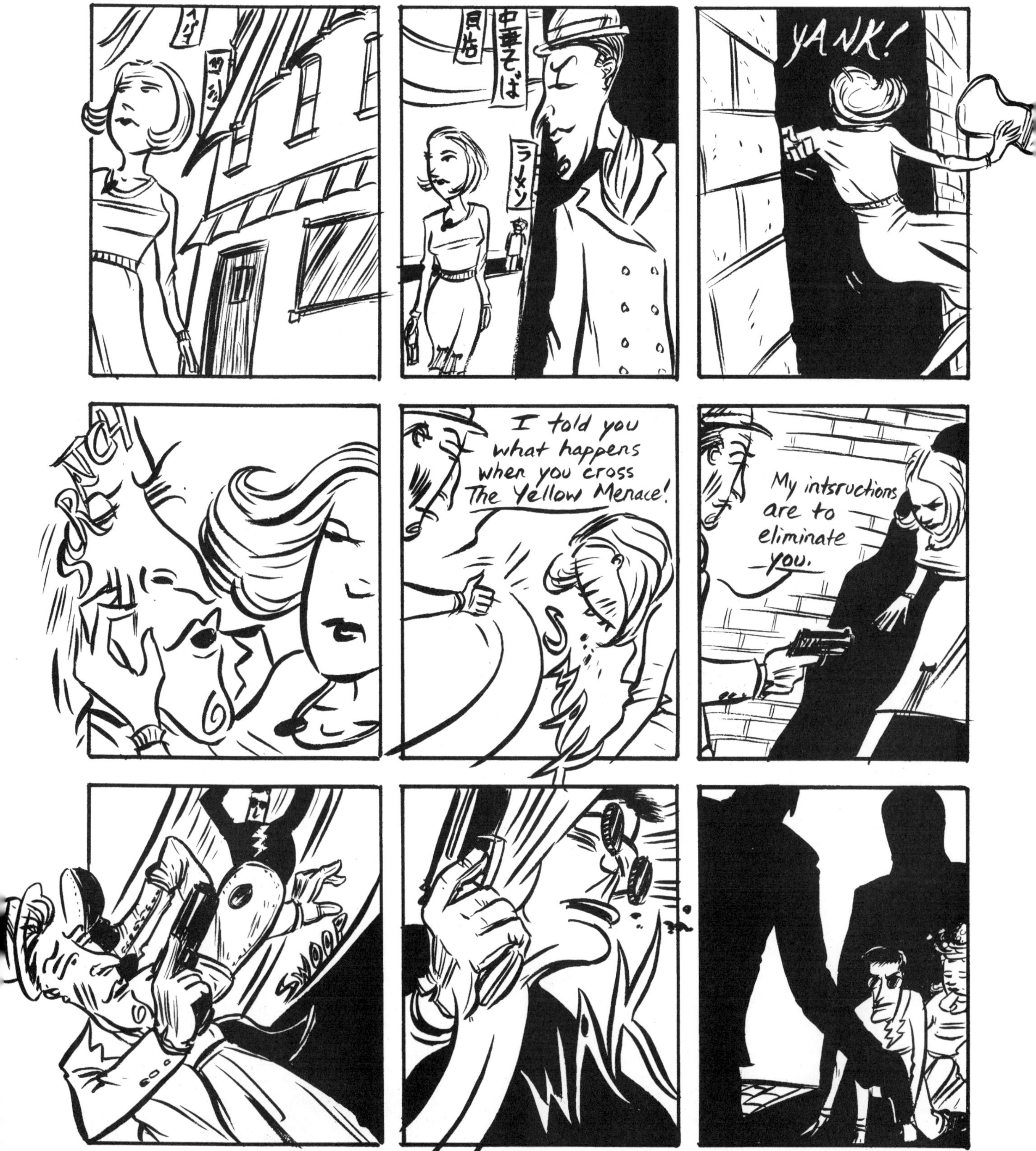

中華そば
ラーメン
YANK!
I told you what happens when you cross The Yellow Menace!
My intsructions are to eliminate you.
SWOOP
WAK

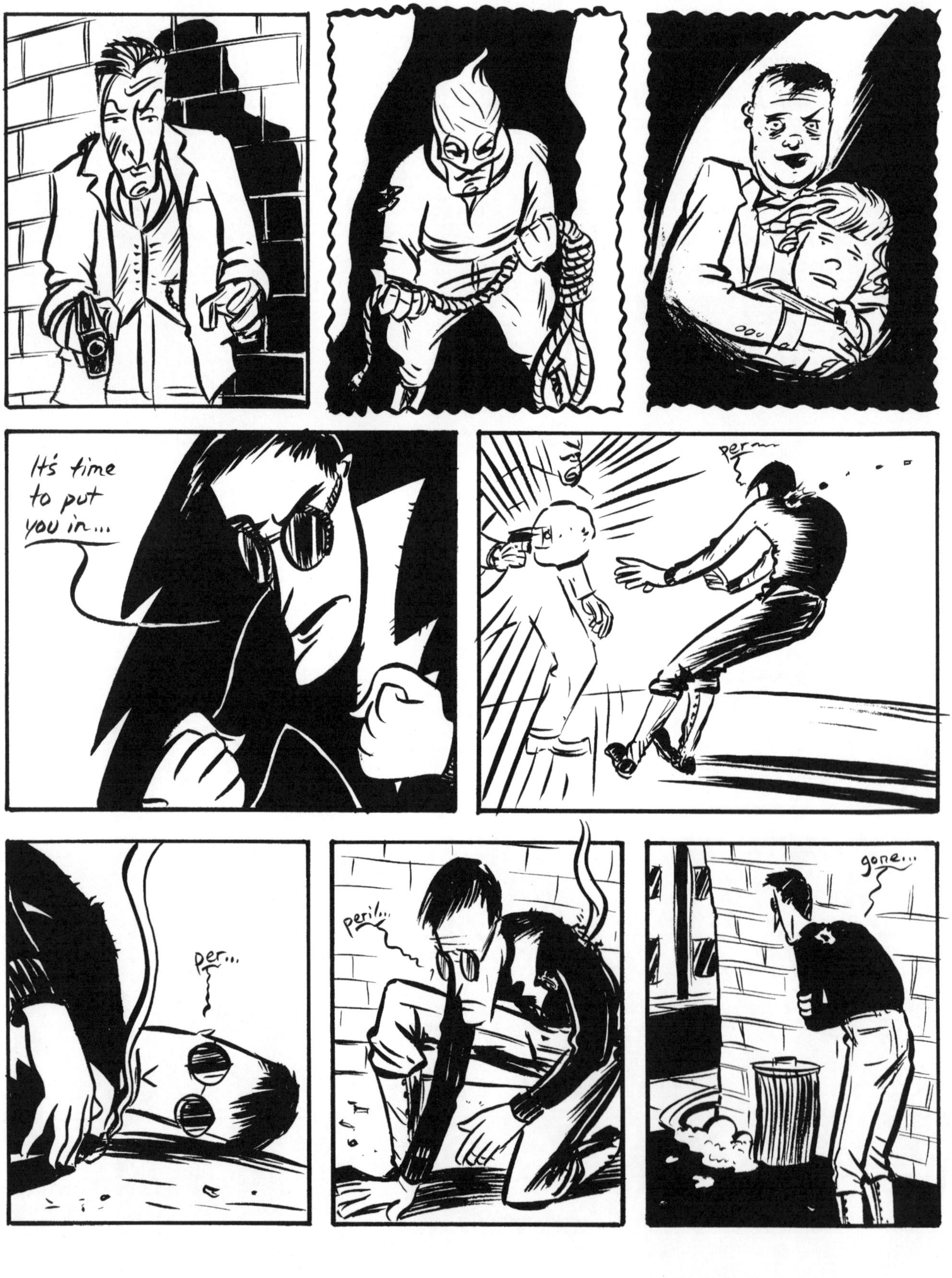
It's time to put you in...
per...
per...
peril...
gone...

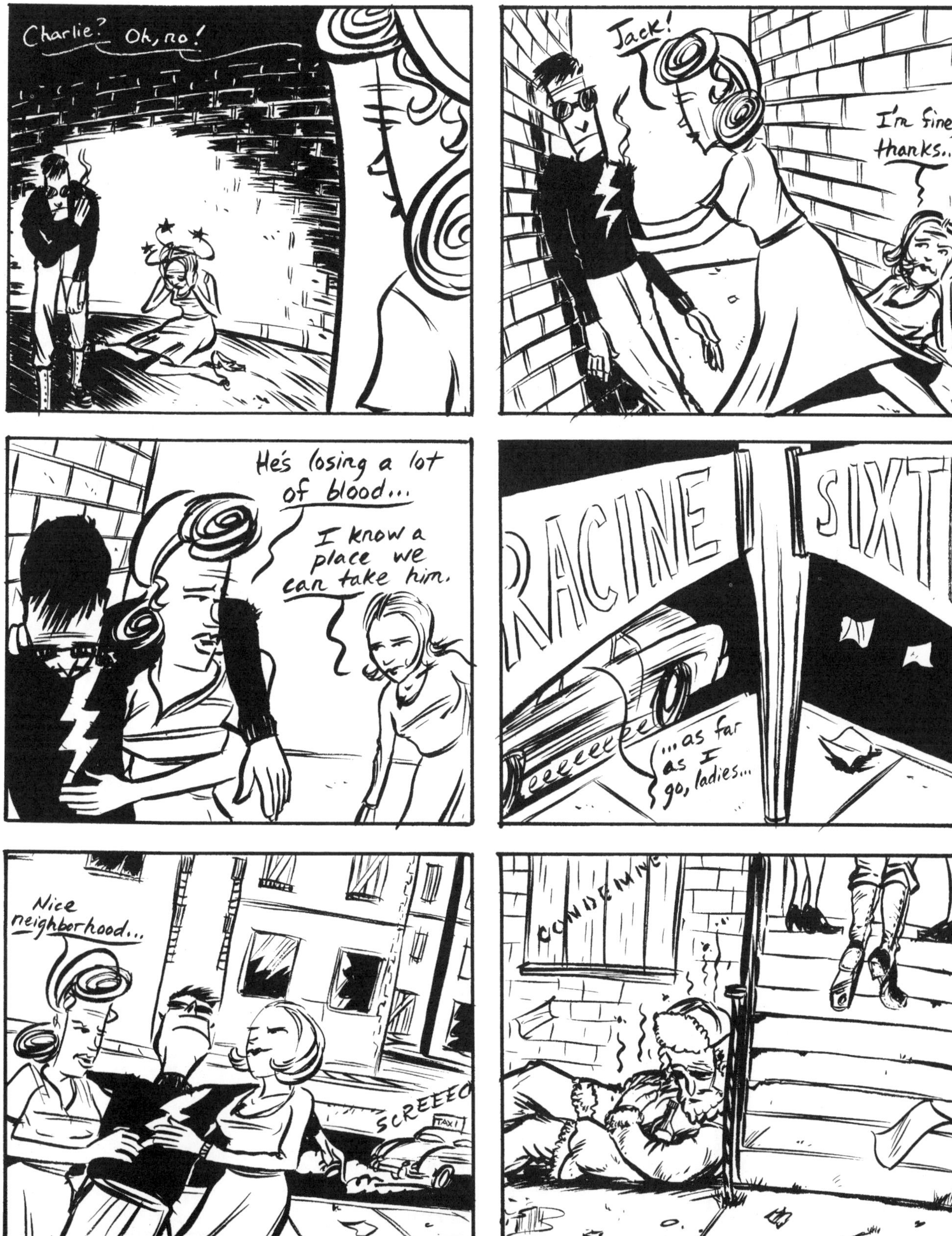
Charlie? Oh, no!
Jack!
I'm fine, thanks...
He's losing a lot of blood...
I know a place we can take him.
RACINE
SIXT
eeeeeeeee
...as far as I go, ladies...
Nice neighborhood...
SCREEEC
TAXI
CONDEMNE

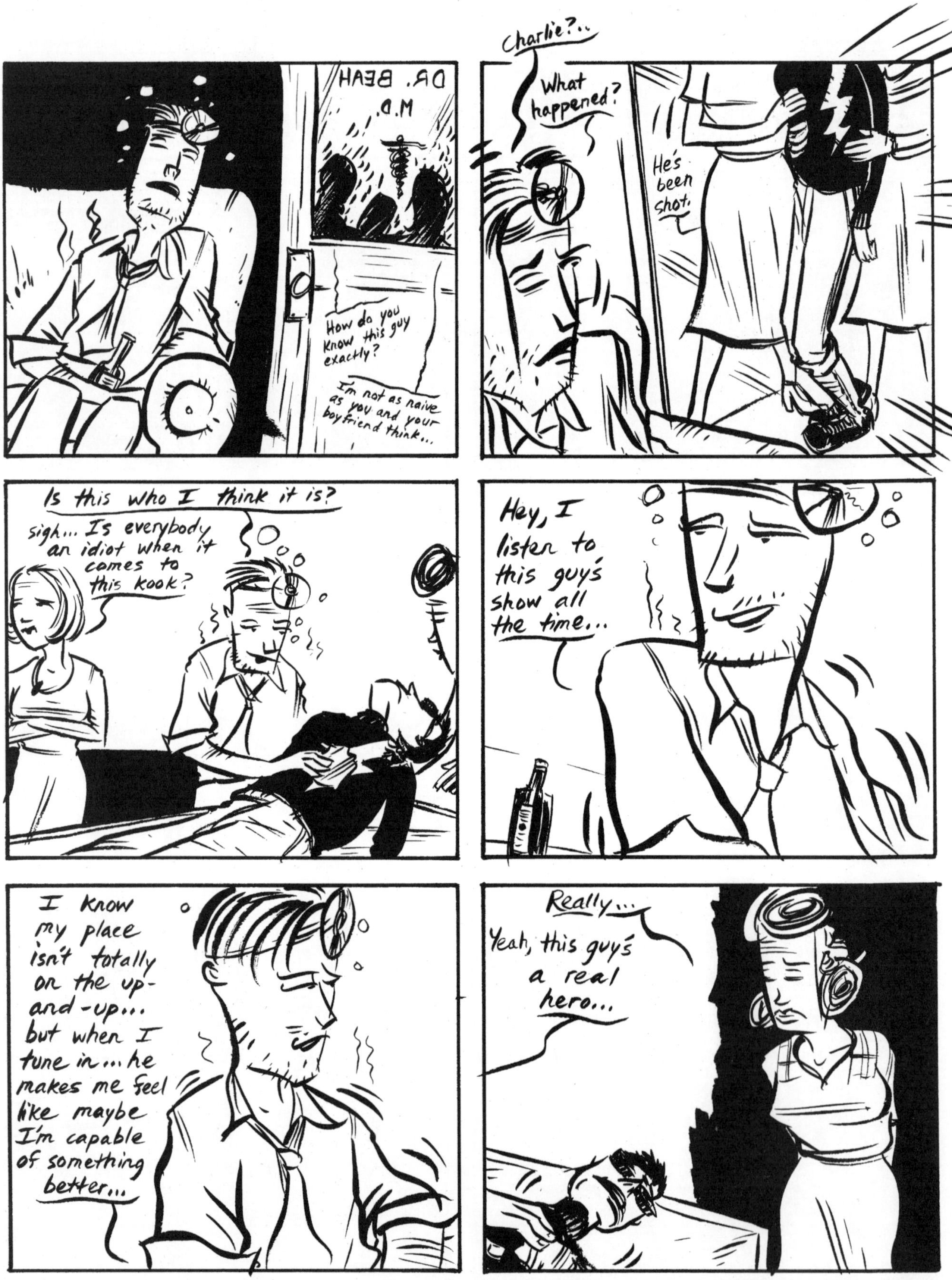
DR. BEAH M.D.
How do you know this guy exactly?
I'm not as naive as you and your boyfriend think...
Charlie?..
What happened?
He's been shot.
Is this who I think it is?
sigh... Is everybody an idiot when it comes to this kook?
Hey, I listen to this guy's show all the time...
I know my place isn't totally on the up-and-up... but when I tune in... he makes me feel like maybe I'm capable of something better...
Really...
Yeah, this guy's a real hero...

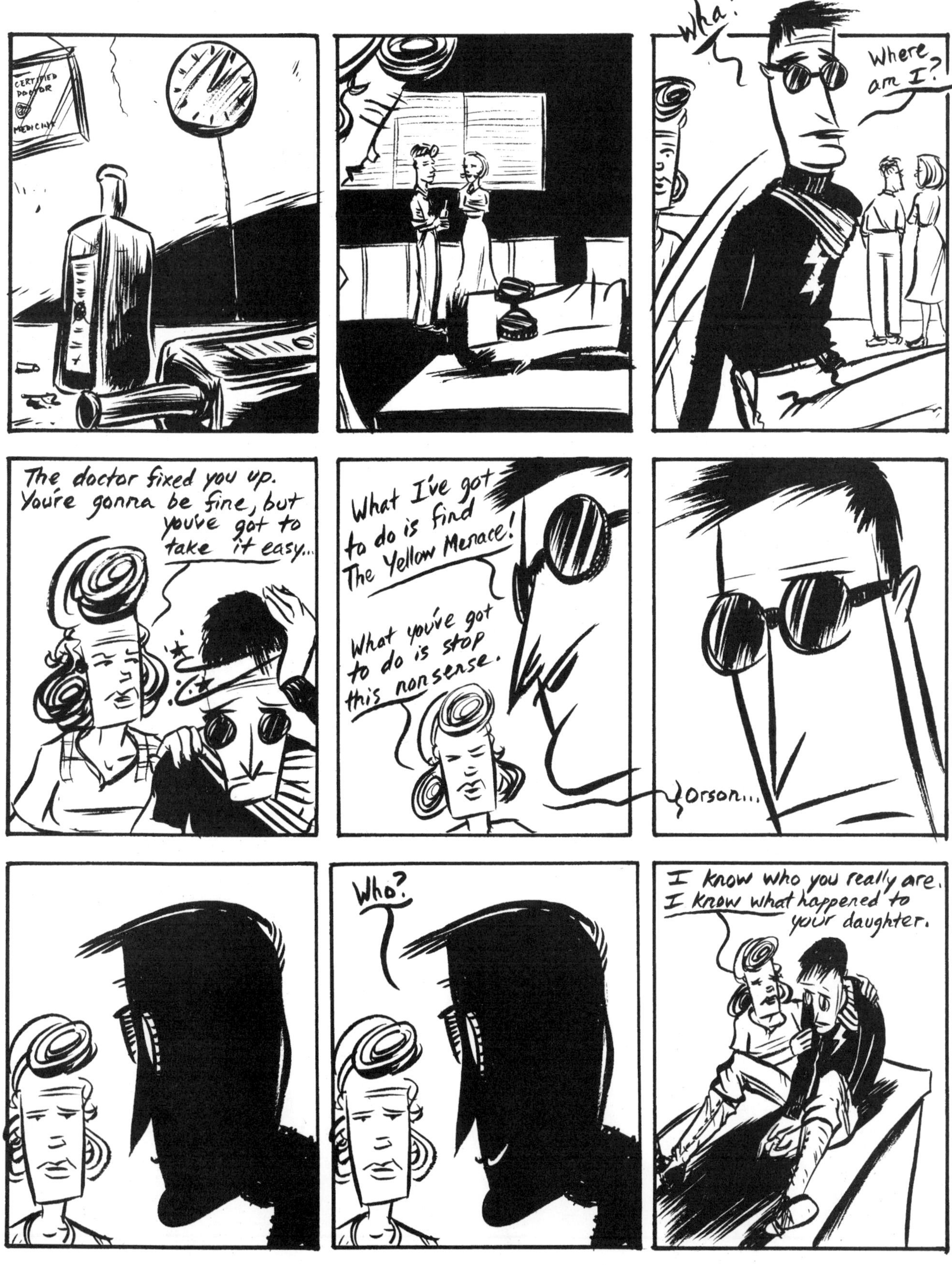

CERTIFIED DOCTOR
MEDICINE
wha?
Where am I?
The doctor fixed you up. You're gonna be fine, but you've got to take it easy...
What I've got to do is find The Yellow Menace!
What you've got to do is stop this nonsense.
Orson...
Who?
I know who you really are. I know what happened to your daughter.

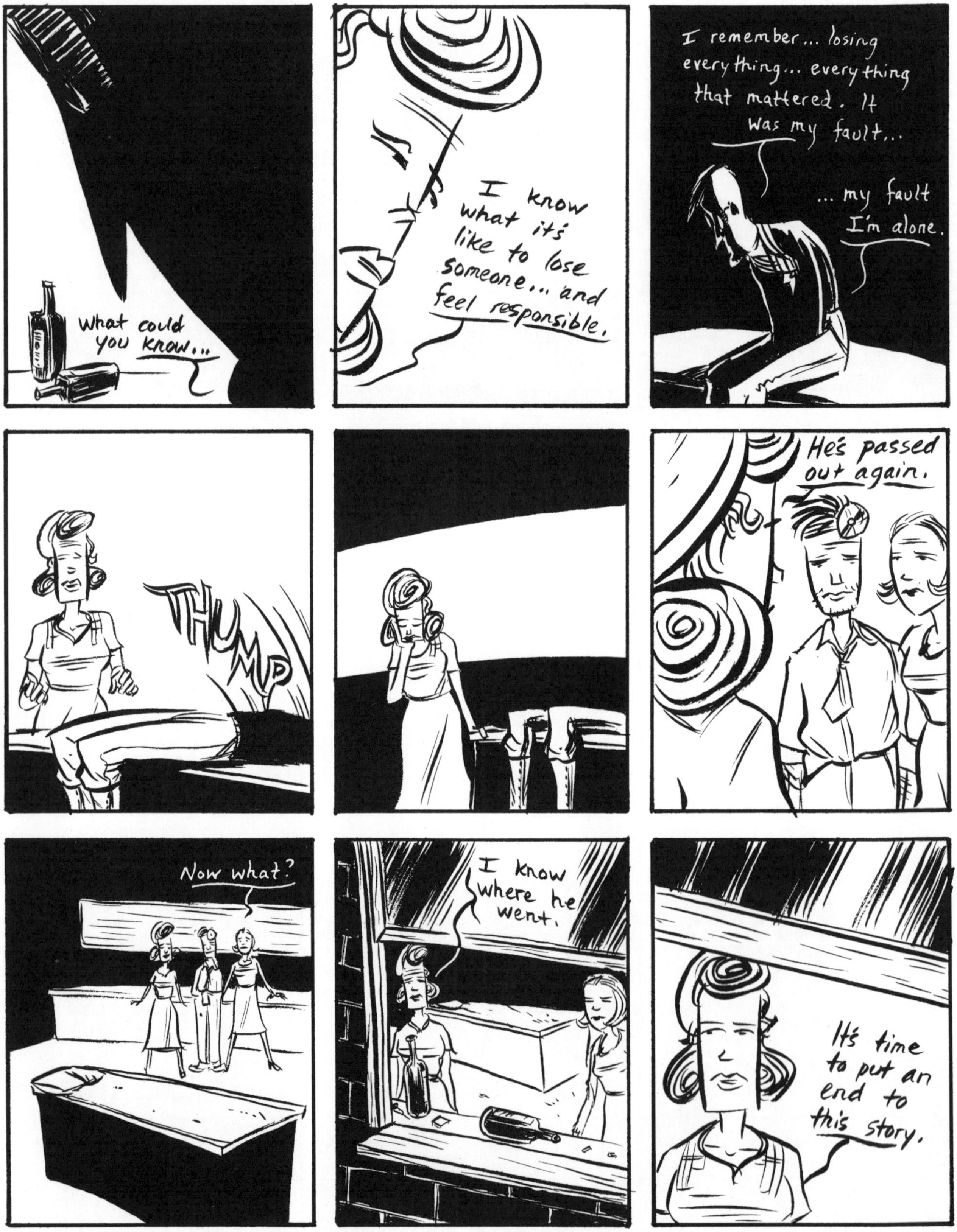
What could you know...
I know what it's like to lose someone... and feel responsible.
I remember... losing everything... everything that mattered. It was my fault...
... my fault I'm alone.
THUMP
He's passed out again.
Now what?
I know where he went.
It's time to put an end to this story.

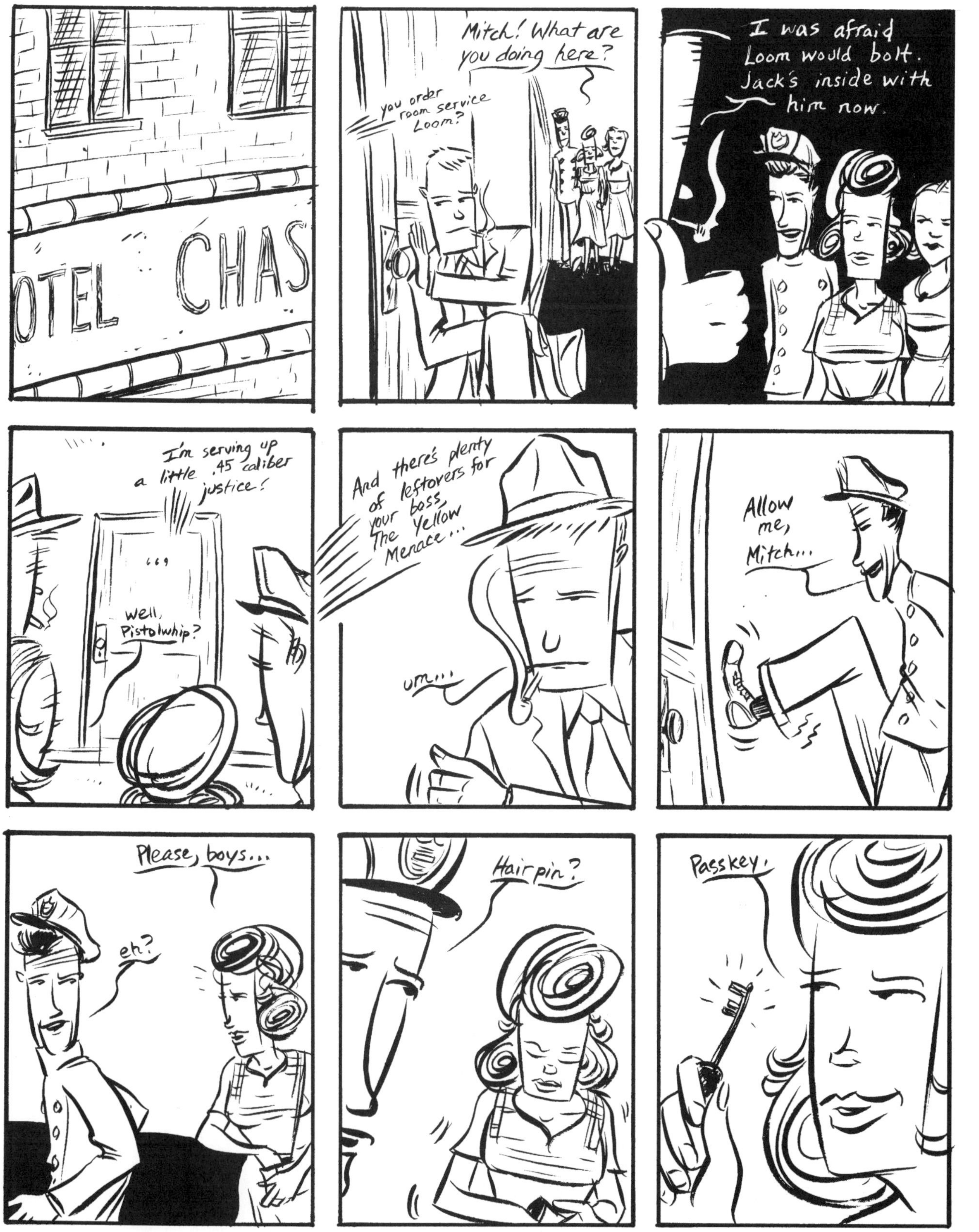
OTEL CHAS
Mitch! What are you doing here?
you order room service Loom?
I was afraid Loom would bolt. Jack's inside with him now.
I'm serving up a little .45 caliber justice!
Well, Pistolwhip?
And there's plenty of leftovers for your boss, The Yellow Menace...
um...
Allow me, Mitch...
Please, boys...
eh?
Hairpin?
Passkey.

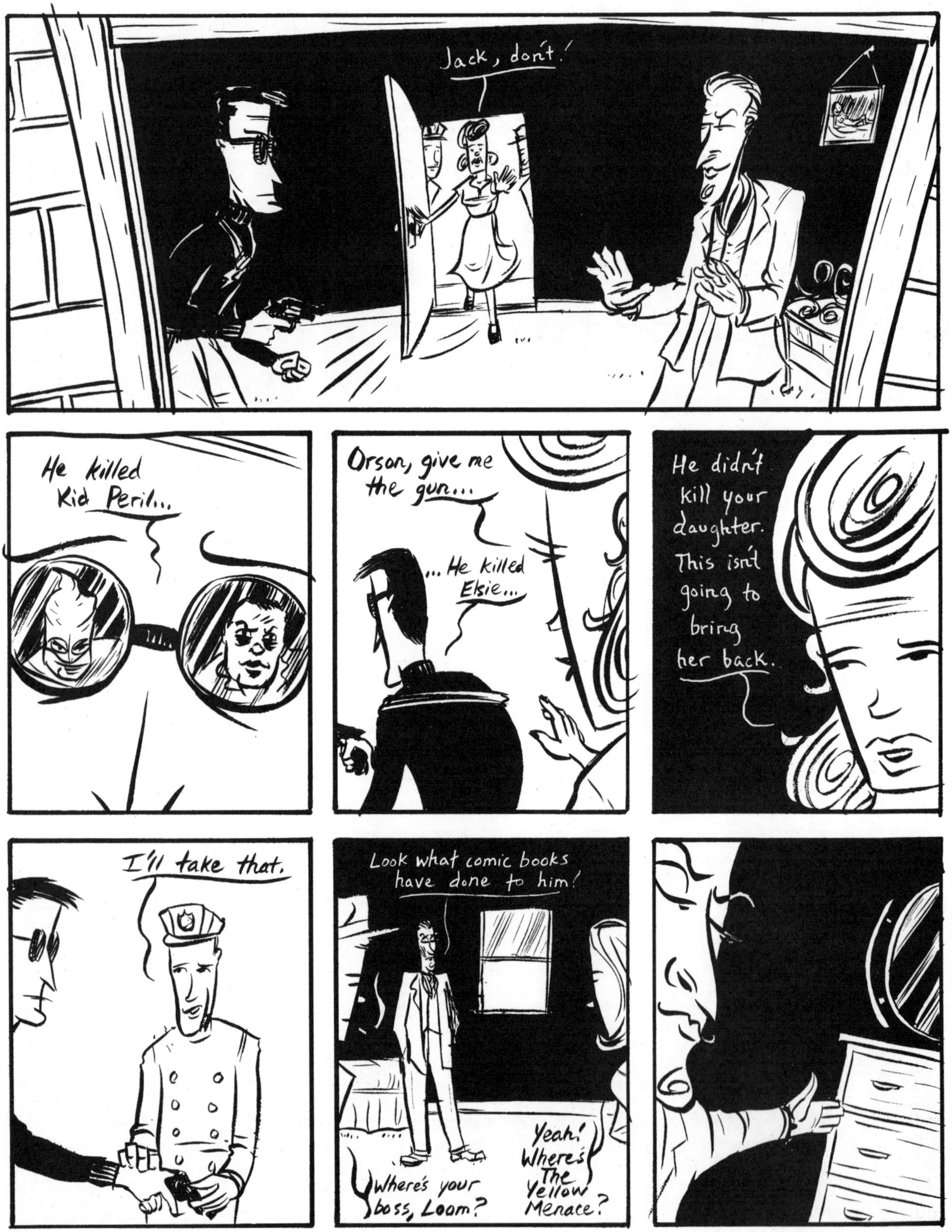
Jack, don't!
He killed Kid Peril...
Orson, give me the gun...
...He killed Elsie...
He didn't kill your daughter. This isn't going to bring her back.
I'll take that.
Look what comic books have done to him!
Where's your boss, Loom?
Yeah! Where's The Yellow Menace?

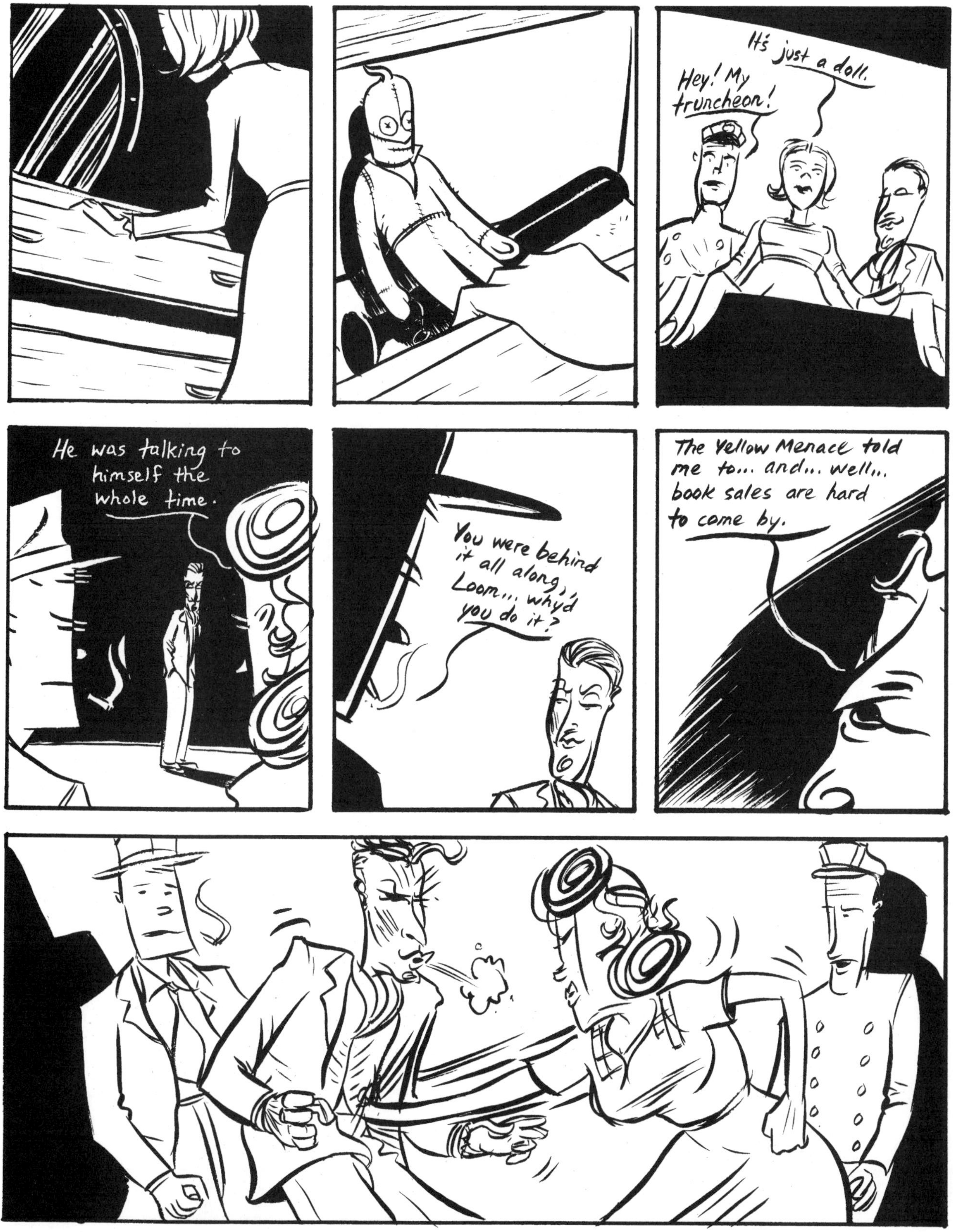
Hey! My truncheon!
It's just a doll.
He was talking to himself the whole time.
You were behind it all along, Loom... why'd you do it?
The Yellow Menace told me to... and... well... book sales are hard to come by.

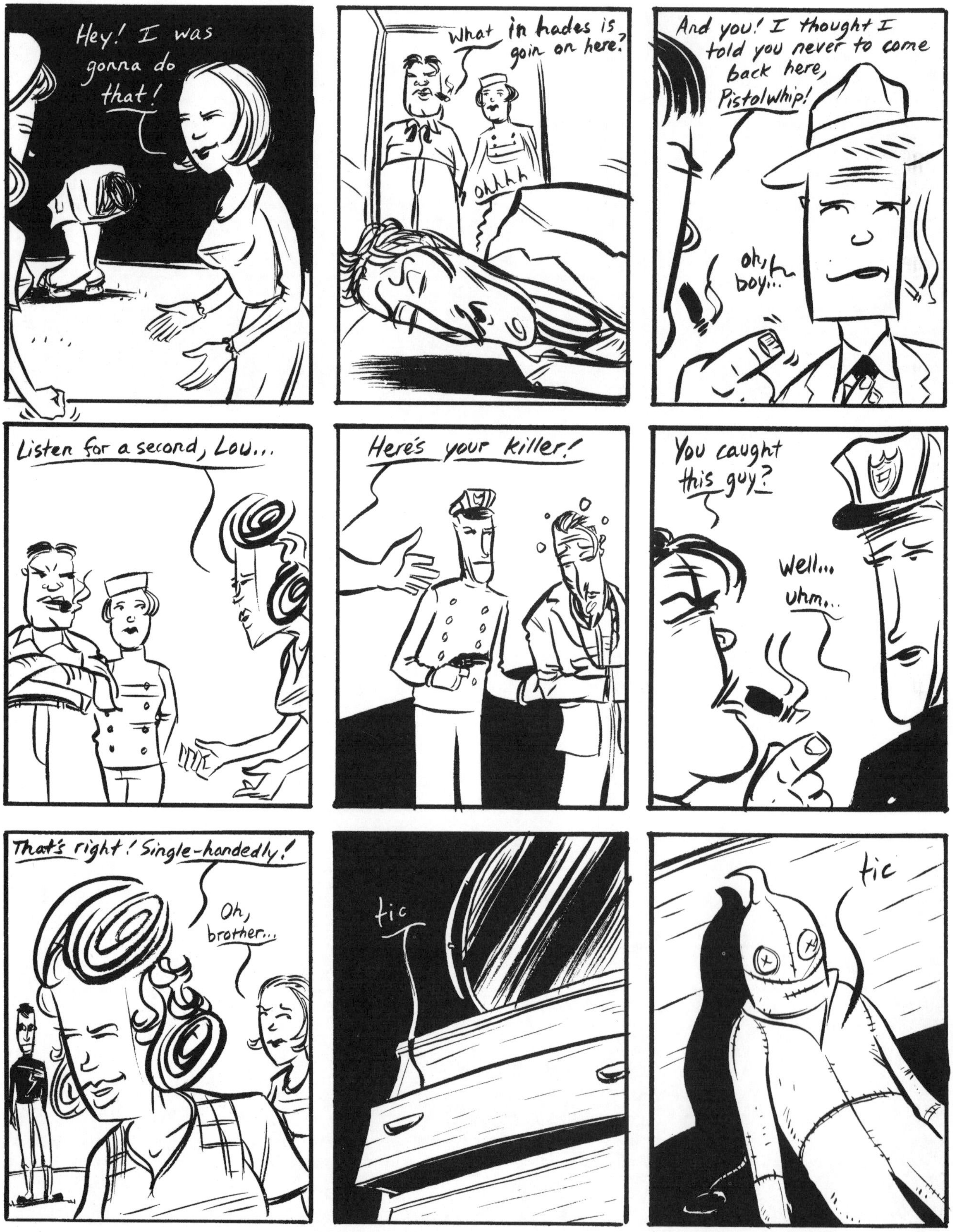
Hey! I was gonna do that!
What in hades is goin on here?
Ohhhh
And you! I thought I told you never to come back here, Pistolwhip!
Oh, boy...
Listen for a second, Lou...
Here's your killer!
You caught this guy?
Well... uhm...
That's right! Single-handedly!
Oh, brother...
tic
tic

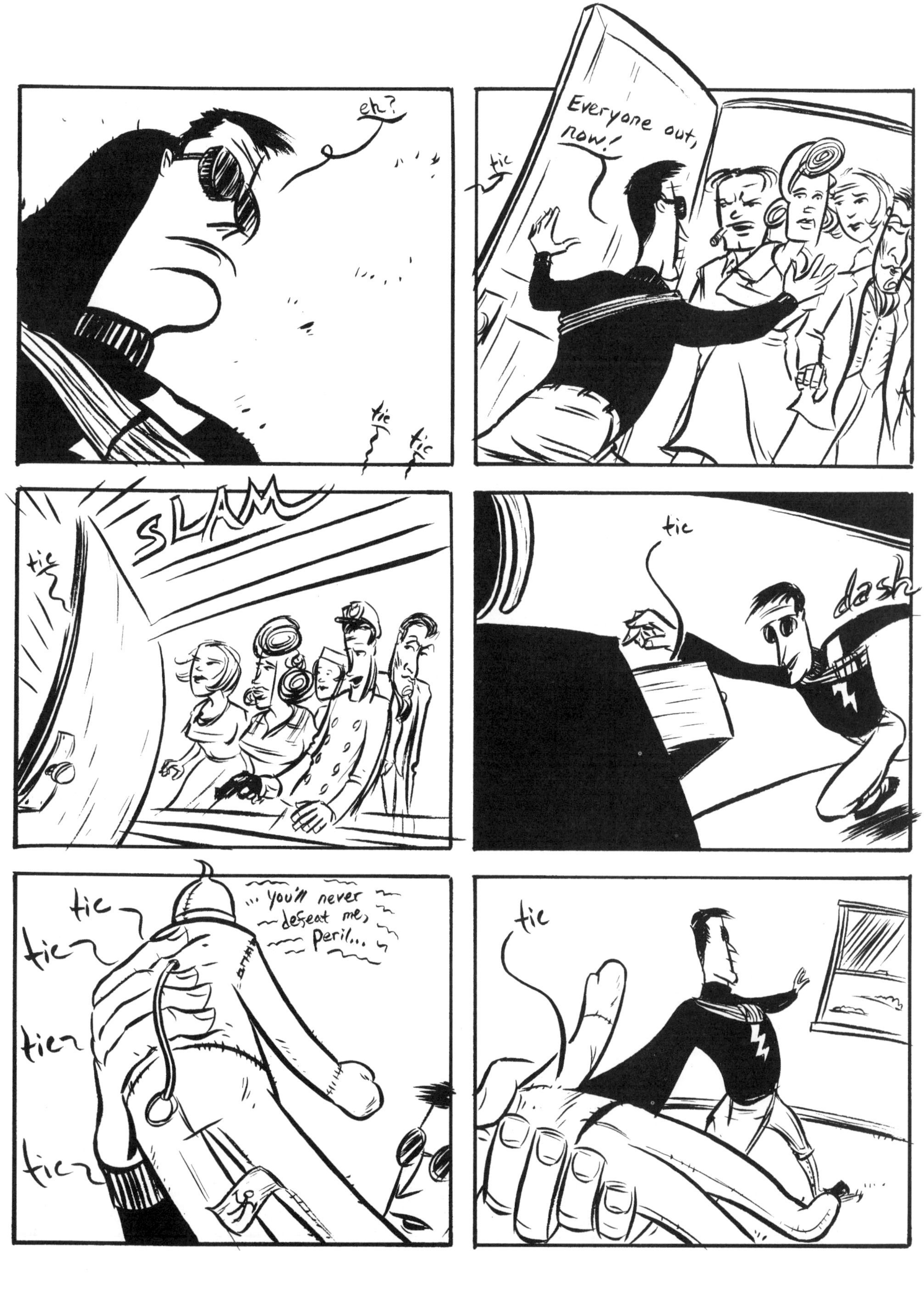
eh?
tic
tic
tic
Everyone out, now!
tic
SLAM
tic
tic
dash
tic
tic
tic
tic
... you'll never defeat me, Peril...
tic

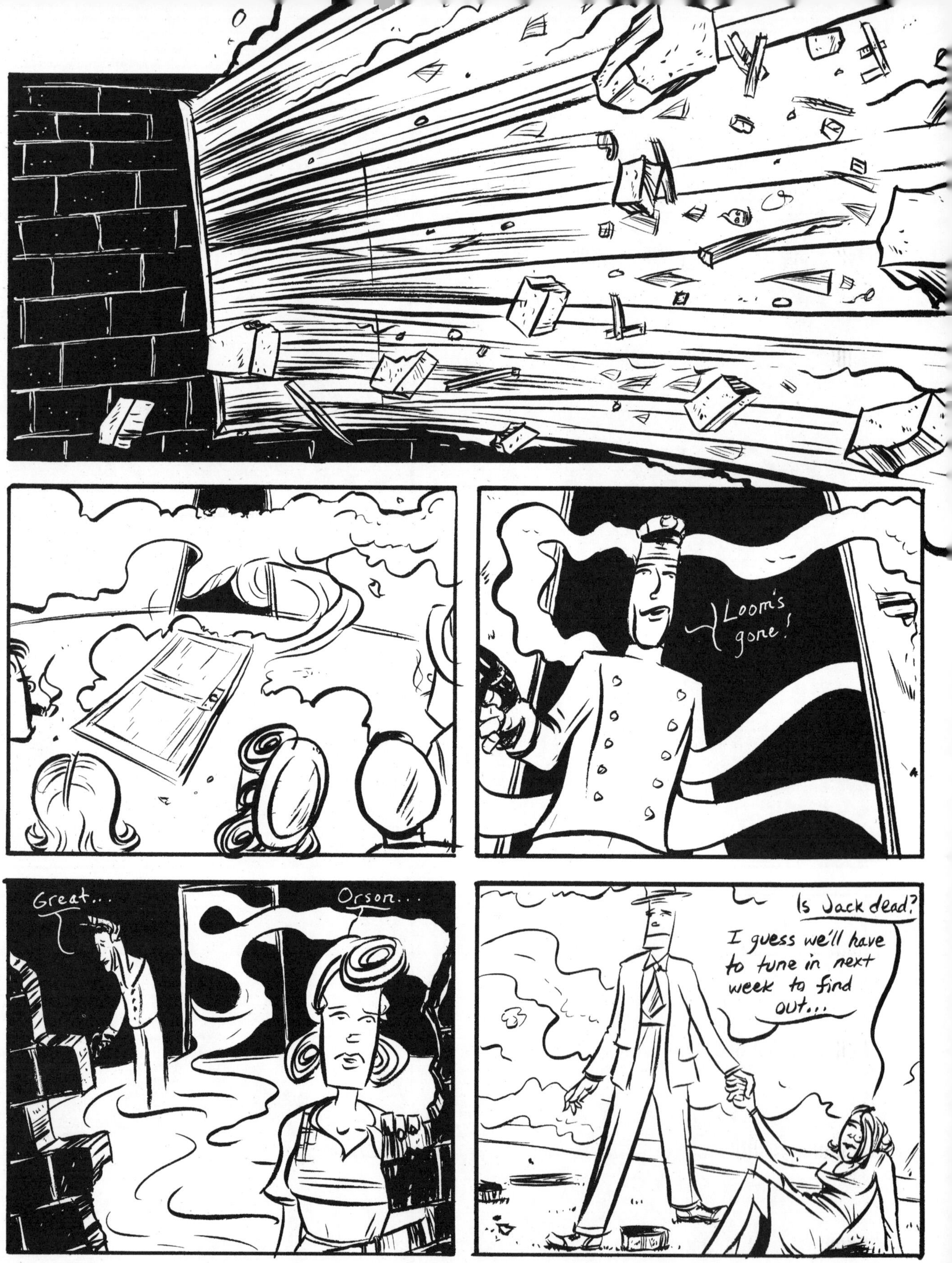
Loom's gone!
Great...
Orson...
Is Jack dead?
I guess we'll have to tune in next week to find out...

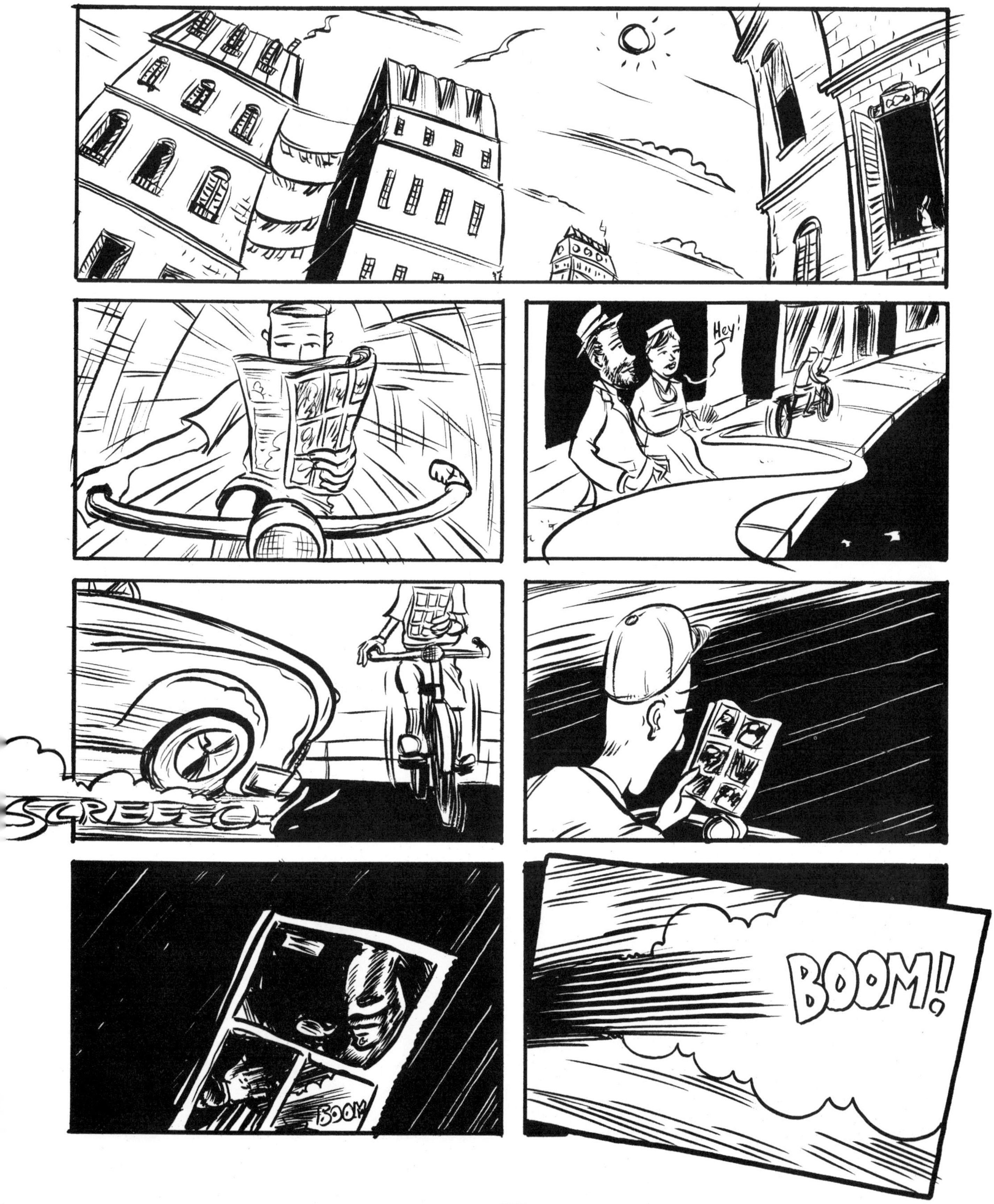
Hey!
SCREEECH
BOOM
BOOM!

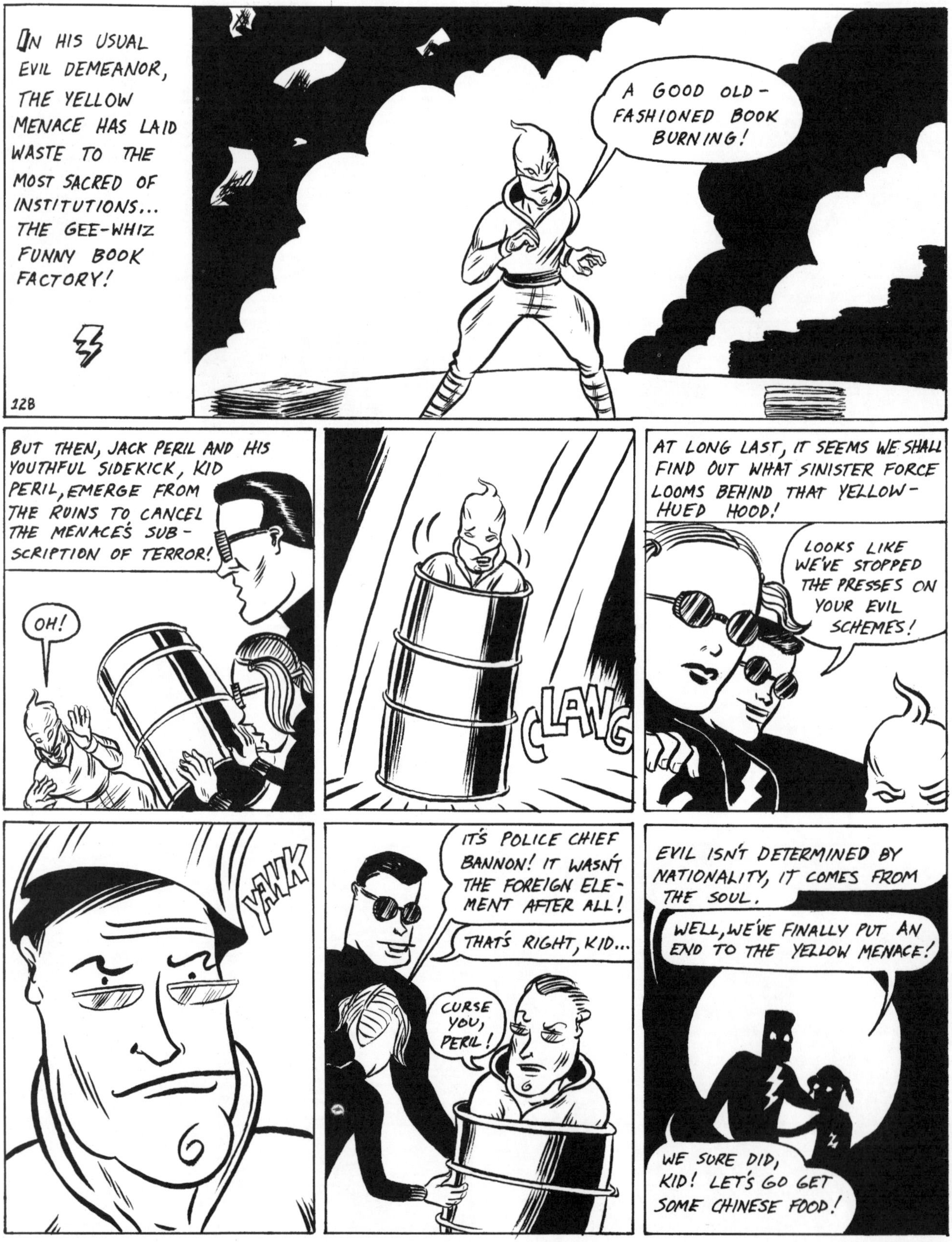
IN HIS USUAL EVIL DEMEANOR, THE YELLOW MENACE HAS LAID WASTE TO THE MOST SACRED OF INSTITUTIONS... THE GEE-WHIZ FUNNY BOOK FACTORY!
128
A GOOD OLD-FASHIONED BOOK BURNING!
BUT THEN, JACK PERIL AND HIS YOUTHFUL SIDEKICK, KID PERIL, EMERGE FROM THE RUINS TO CANCEL THE MENACE'S SUB-SCRIPTION OF TERROR!
OH!
CLANG
AT LONG LAST, IT SEEMS WE SHALL FIND OUT WHAT SINISTER FORCE LOOMS BEHIND THAT YELLOW-HUED HOOD!
LOOKS LIKE WE'VE STOPPED THE PRESSES ON YOUR EVIL SCHEMES!
YANK
IT'S POLICE CHIEF BANNON! IT WASN'T THE FOREIGN ELE-MENT AFTER ALL!
THAT'S RIGHT, KID...
CURSE YOU, PERIL!
EVIL ISN'T DETERMINED BY NATIONALITY, IT COMES FROM THE SOUL.
WELL, WE'VE FINALLY PUT AN END TO THE YELLOW MENACE!
WE SURE DID, KID! LET'S GO GET SOME CHINESE FOOD!

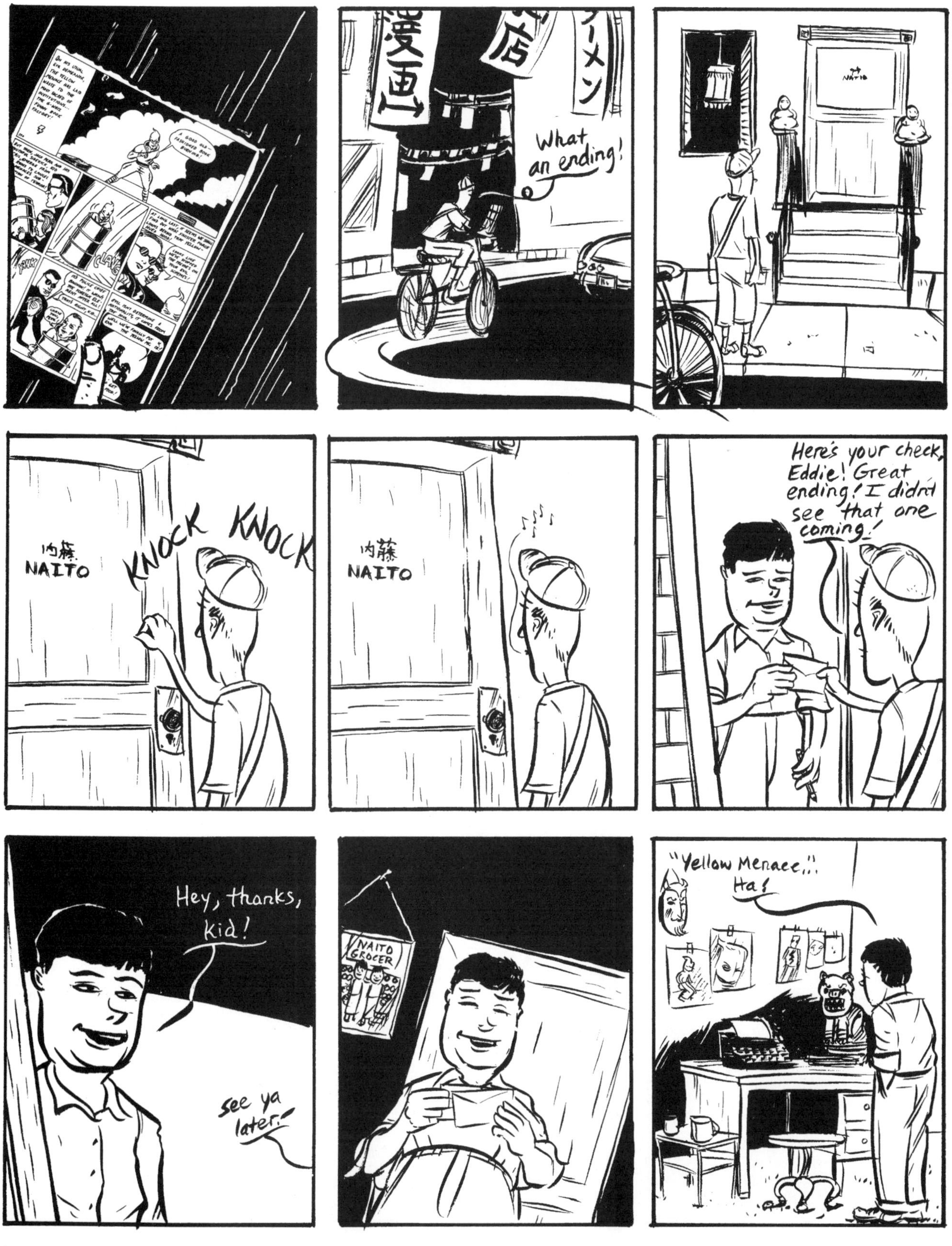
漫画
店
What an ending!
内藤
NAITO
KNOCK KNOCK
内藤
NAITO
Here's your check, Eddie! Great ending! I didn't see that one coming!
Hey, thanks, kid!
See ya later.
NAITO GROCER
"Yellow Menace." Ha!

HOTEL DETECTIVE
Hey, Ray!
You hear your cop pals caught Loom near Mr. Naito's Market?
Read all about it.
A bit misleading, ain't it...?
POLICE CAPTURE YELLOW MENACE IN CHINATOWN!
It's no wonder those chinamen always get a bad rap.
Actually, they're Japanese...
Say... wanna grab some lunch later?
Would I ever!
You look awfully swell in that get-up, Mr. Hotel Detective.
Thanks, Rosebud! I'm on the job!
ZZZZZ
NEW COMICS CODE PUT INTO EFFE

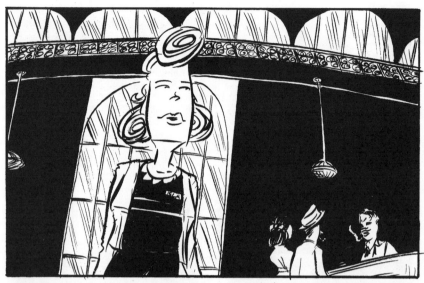

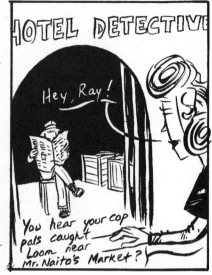

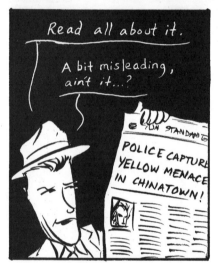

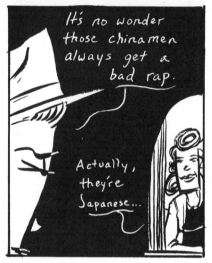

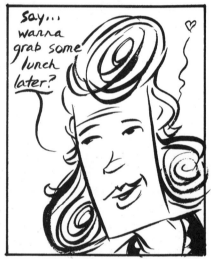

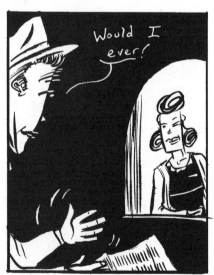

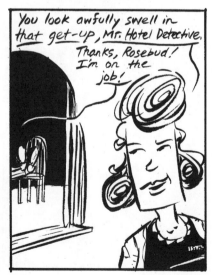

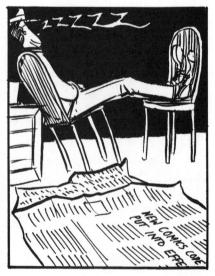

tap tap tap

tap tap

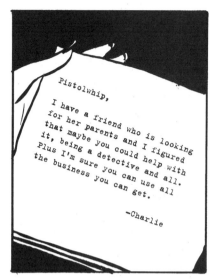

Pistolwhip,

I have a friend who is looking for her parents and I figured that maybe you could help with it, being a detective and all. Plus I'm sure you can use all the business you can get.

—Charlie

ESTLES BOAT REPAIR

Whadaya know?!

I've been looking for you!

How about some flapjacks, girl?

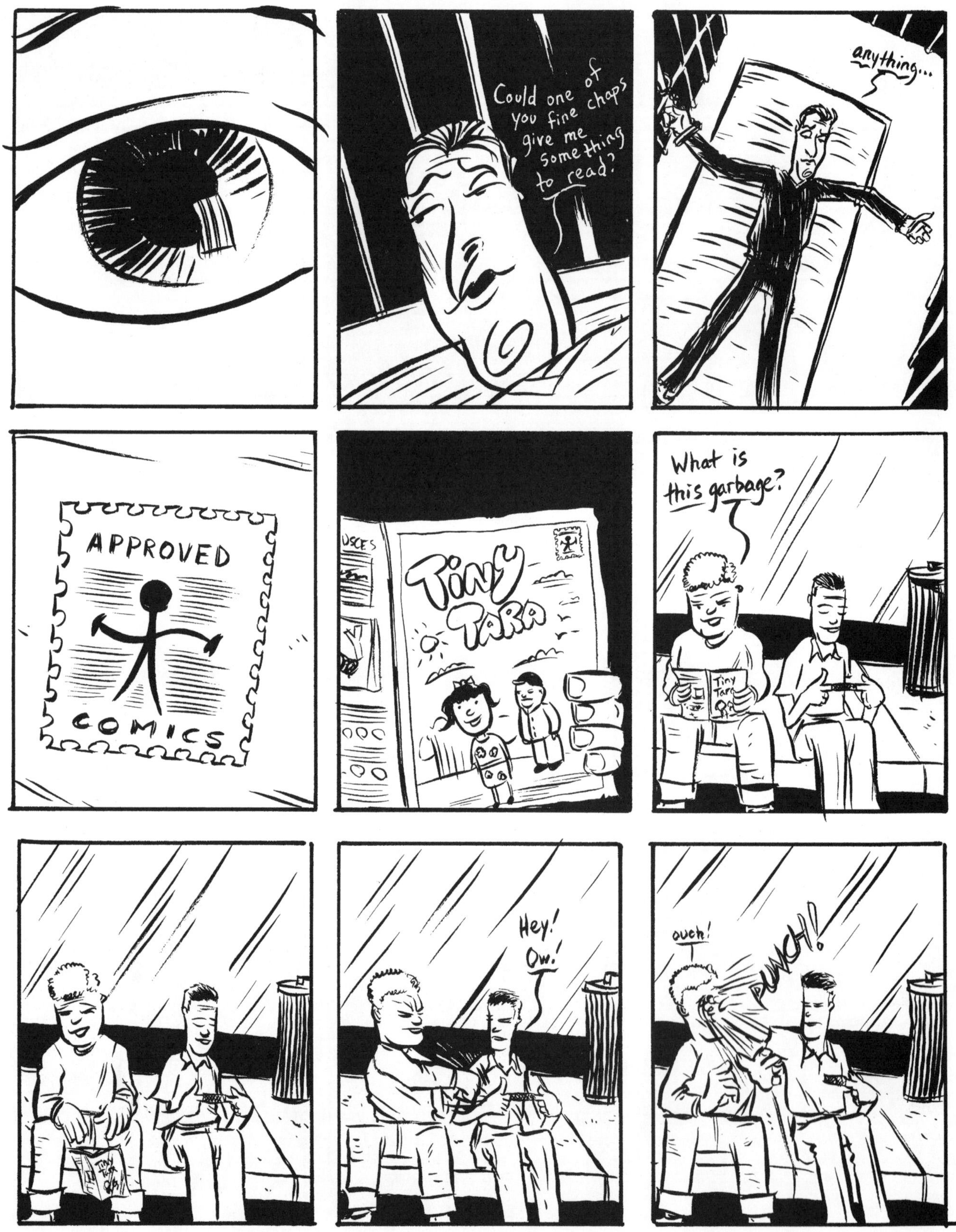
Could one of you fine chaps give me something to read?
anything...
APPROVED
COMICS
Tiny Tara
What is this garbage?
Hey! Ow!
ouch!
PUNCH!

When the cat wants to pet...
but the kitten cries...
the hot girls...
know it's cold outside...
When sugar daddy knows
you done lied...
BAD PENNIES
featuring
Pidgeon Lang
the hot girls know it's cold... outside.

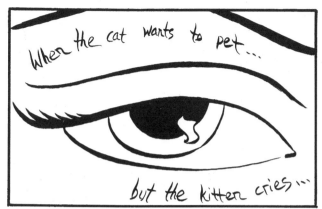

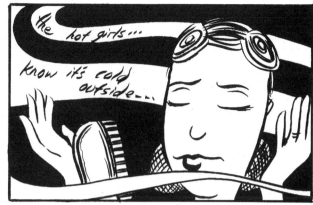

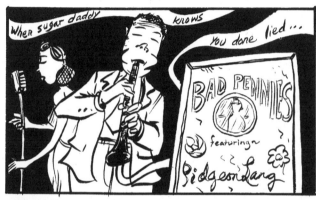

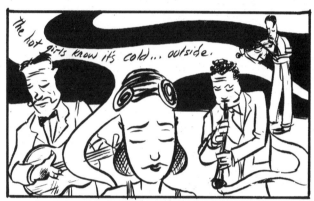

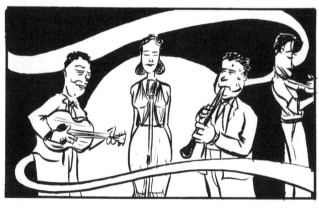

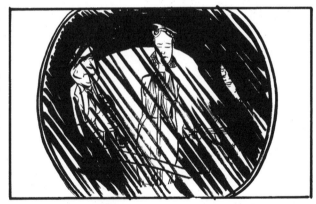

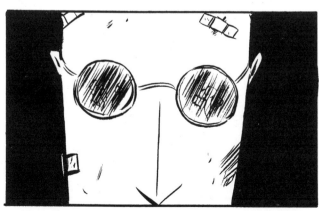

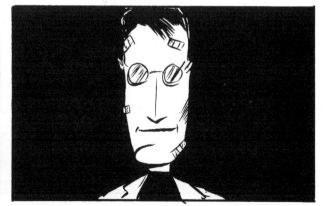

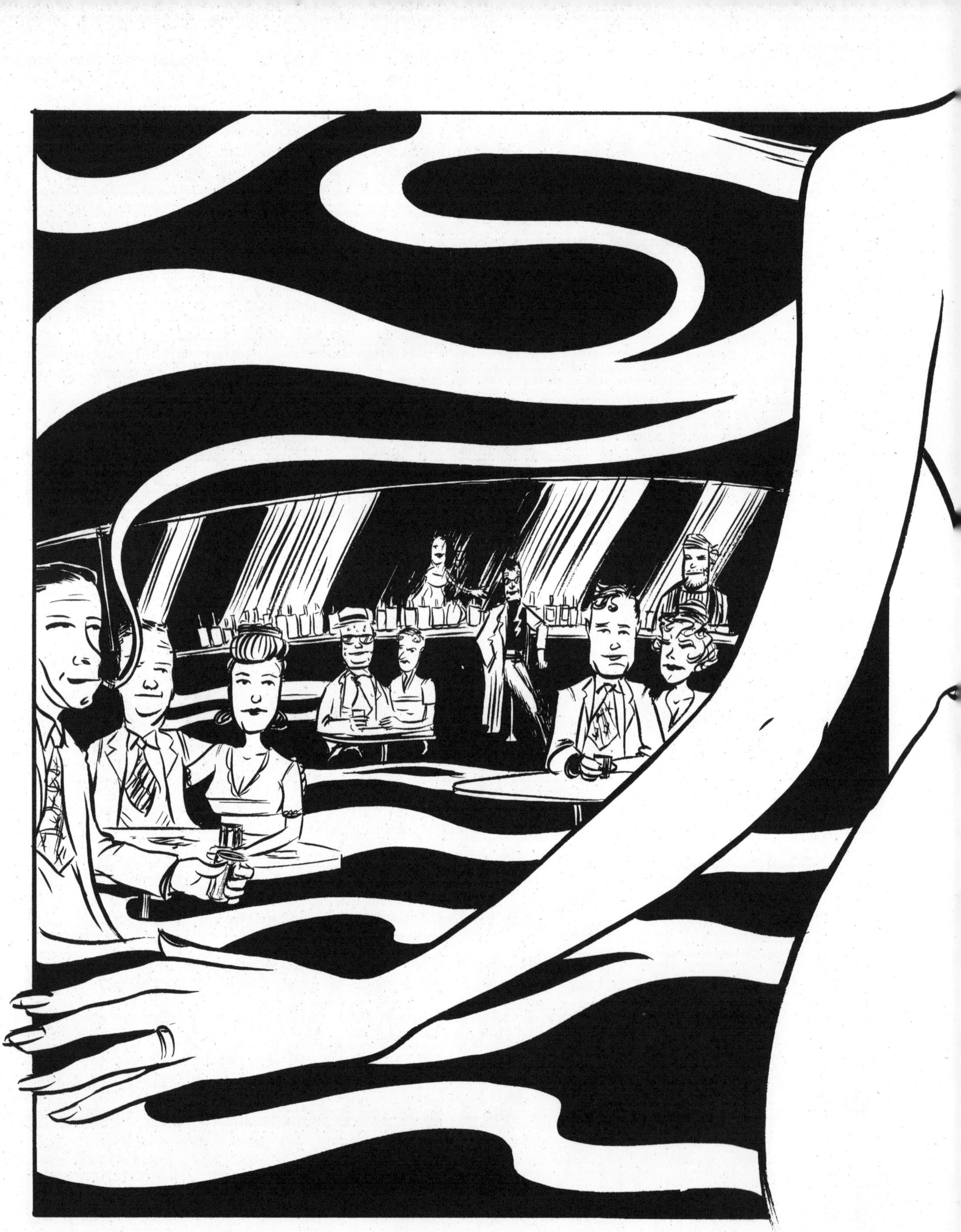

表題

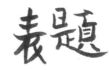

Index

Index (cont.)

Bibliography

The Adventures of Jack Peril
(Lester Poindexter; RAO Radio -- *Radio drama*)

Death Knocks Twice
(Alfonse MacGuffin; M&S Studios -- *Film*)

El Tea U Wanna
(Juan Carlos Sanchez; Cajones Publishing --
Foreign comic book)

Enticement of the Naive
(Roderick Loom; Society Press -- *Criticism/commentary*)

Gill-Man, Criminal Detective
(Frank Clayman & Sheldon Young;
All-National Comics -- *Comic book*)

The Hot Girls Know
(Pidgeon Lang & Toots McFadden; RAO Records --
Musical recording)

Jack Peril
(Eddie Naito & Jack King; Gee-Whiz Comics --
Comic Book)

Jack Peril vs. The Yellow Menace
(B. Fink; RAO Pictures -- *Movie serial*)

Jack Peril Records
(Sal Bufont; RAO Records -- *78rpm record*)

Le Chat People
(Luc Renoir; Cinema du Paris -- *Foreign film*)

Perilous Adventures
(Eddie Naito & Jack King; Gee-Whiz Comics --
Comic book)

Police Report -- October 31st
(Detective Robert Copper -- *City Police*)

Real Detective
(Maxwell Gibson; Penny Ante Publishing --
Pulp magazine)

Sister Suzie
(Ivana Sala; RAO Pictures -- *Film*)

The Standard
(Kane Publishing -- *Newspaper*)

Stories of Peril
(Walter Grant; Gee-Whiz Publications -- *Pulp magazine*)

The 3 Racketeers
(Leland Stanley; RAO Publishing -- *Little-Big book*)

Tiny Tara
(J. Hall & M. Kindt; Gee-Whiz Comics -- *Comic book*)

Jason:
To Grandma and Grandpa Carmello,
and Grandma and Grandpa Ford

Matt:
To Grandma and Grandpa Brunworth,
Grandma and Grandpa Funke,
Grandpa Kindt,
Grandma and Grandpa Prescott

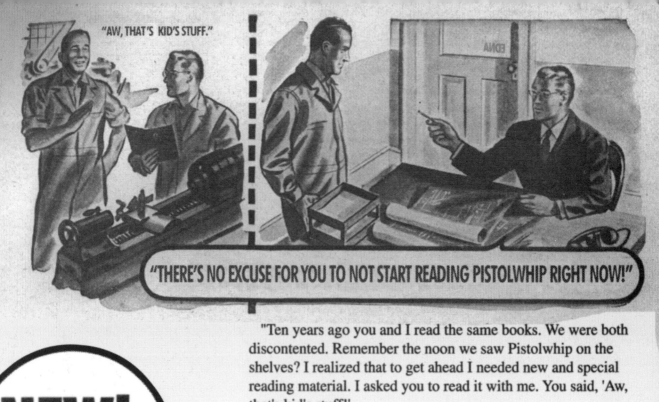

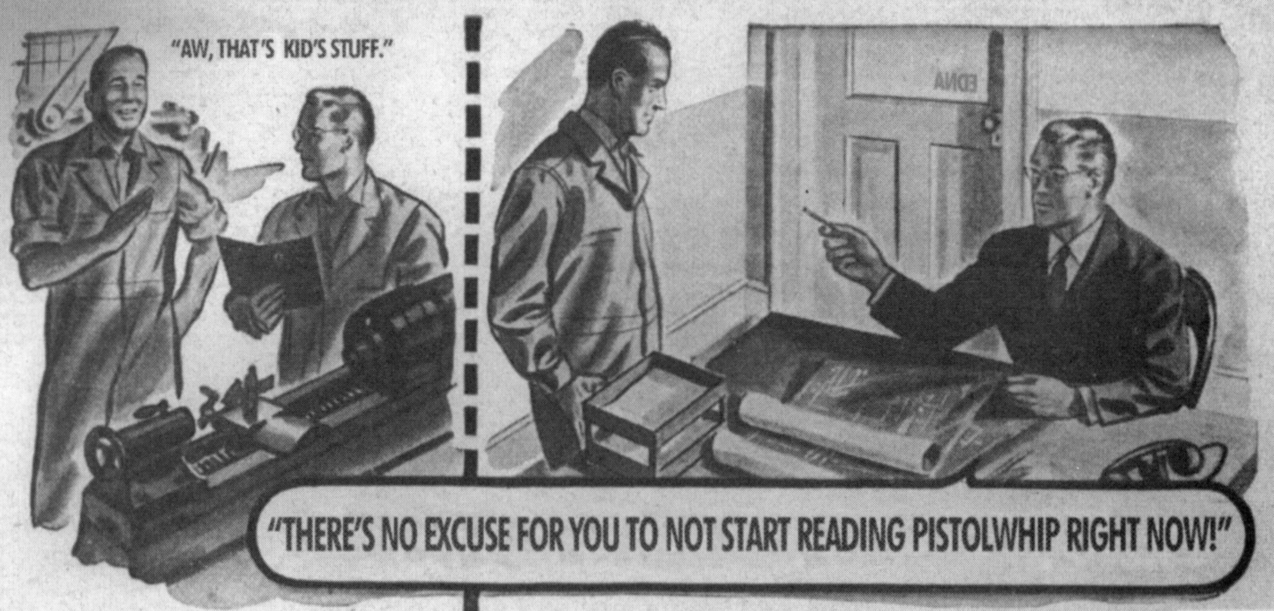
"AW, THAT'S KID'S STUFF."
EDNA
"THERE'S NO EXCUSE FOR YOU TO NOT START READING PISTOLWHIP RIGHT NOW!"

"Ten years ago you and I read the same books. We were both discontented. Remember the noon we saw Pistolwhip on the shelves? I realized that to get ahead I needed new and special reading material. I asked you to read it with me. You said, 'Aw, that's kid's stuff!'

"I made the most of my opportunity and have been climbing ever since. You had the same chance I had, but you turned it down. No, Jim, you can't expect a promotion until you've trained yourself to read better material"

There are lots of "Jims"— in your office, at school, everywhere. Are you one of them? Wake up! Your chance is staring you in the face. Don't turn it down.

NEW!

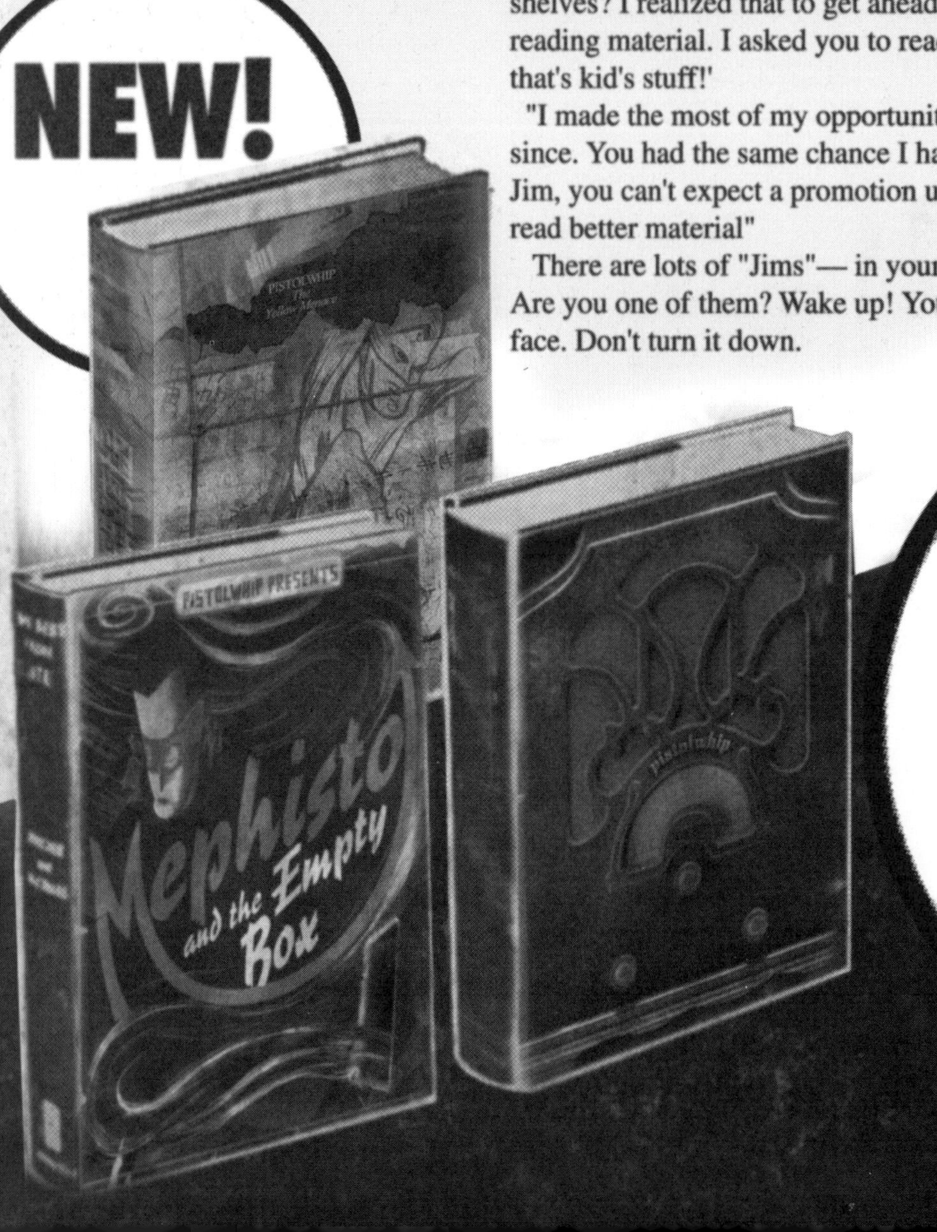
PISTOLWHIP
PISTOLWHIP PRESENTS
Mephisto and the Empty Box
pistolwhip

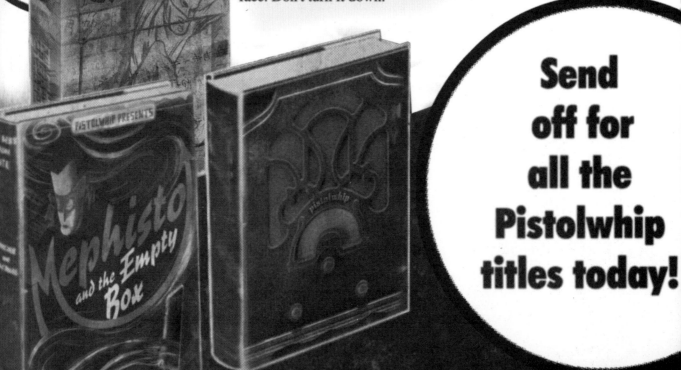

Send off for all the Pistolwhip titles today!